Advance Praise for *Quiet Counsel*

"Larry Thompson has come a long way from his beloved Hannibal, MO. He's served his country with distinction as a United States Attorney and as my Deputy Attorney General. Larry was my go-to person for many difficult assignments. His deep experience makes *Quiet Counsel* worthwhile for anyone wanting to know more about the U.S. legal system."

—**John D. Ashcroft,** former United States Attorney General

"Larry Thompson, with his deep experience and superb judgment, served as my trusted advisor. Larry's quiet counsel helped us successfully navigate a host of difficult legal, corporate governance, and public policy issues. Every CEO should have a Larry Thompson!"

—**Indra Nooyi,** former CEO of PepsiCo, Inc.

"Larry is a man of remarkable faith, integrity, and compassion—a courageous and brilliant leader with an unwavering commitment to fighting injustice. He's attributed the righting of grave injustices his pro bono counsel has achieved to an act of G-d. *Quiet Counsel* should be studied by generations to come as a textbook on faith, moral clarity, and the relentless and altruistic pursuit for justice."

—**Rabbi Zvi Boyarsky,** Director of National Policy, The Aleph Institute

"During my tenure as PepsiCo's Corporate Treasurer, Larry was a crucial business partner and invaluable ally. His knowledge of corporate law was impeccable and instilled in me an unwavering sense of confidence, reliance, and trust. Larry's captivating discussion of Milton Friedman's ideologies and the intricate dynamics of smart capitalism is an absolute must read for all business leaders seeking profound insights and strategic excellence."

—**Lionel L. Nowell III,** former Senior Vice President and Treasurer, PepsiCo, Inc.; Lead Independent Director, Bank of America

"I worked with Larry in 2001. Larry's poignant description of the events leading up to 9/11 and how they affected him is a testament to the challenges of public service. Larry has demonstrated humility and candor about the hardest decisions, before and after they are made, and the larger excitement and anguish of serving in positions of responsibility, in government and the private sector, particularly in times of division and uncertainty."

—**David S. Kris,** former Assistant Attorney General, National Security Division, United States Department of Justice, and Founder of Culper Partners LLC

"Larry Thompson embodies the unique qualities of all great lawyers: unwavering integrity, great judgment and compassion, a willingness to listen to others, and an uncanny ability to come up with creative and practical solutions to difficult problems. I worked closely with Larry both in private practice and at the Department of Justice. His discussion of the challenges that he and other government officials faced in the aftermath of 9/11 offers an important lesson on what our country should keep in mind as we strive to protect ourselves against future terroristic acts on U.S. soil."

—**Paul B. Murphy,** former Chief of Staff, Federal Bureau of Investigation, and Partner, King & Spalding, Special Matters and Government Investigations

QUIET
COUNSEL

QUIET
COUNSEL

Looking Back on a Life of Service to the Law

LARRY D. THOMPSON

DISRUPTION
BOOKS

New York | Washington, DC

Published by Disruption Books
Washington, DC
www.disruptionbooks.com

Distributed by Disruption Books

For information about special discounts for bulk purchases, please contact Disruption Books at info@disruptionbooks.com.

Cover and book design by Sheila Parr
Library of Congress Cataloging-in-Publication Data is available
Printed in the United States of America

Print ISBN: 978-1-63331-096-4
eBook ISBN: 978-1-63331-097-1

First Edition

CONTENTS

I reported to Indra Nooyi, CEO of PepsiCo, Inc., for some seven years. In her compelling book My Life in Full: Work, Family, and Our Future, *Indra describes our relationship. She noted that I was one of her closest advisors, but that I was "pretty quiet" during PepsiCo executive team meetings. Indra also noted that in one-on-one sessions with her I was candid and forthright.*

This quiet counsel is, I think, how I've always tried to conduct my professional life.

I would like to acknowledge and thank Marc Dunkelman and Cara Musciano for their considerable assistance in bringing this book to fruition. Marc provided expert professional editorial planning and writing assistance in the completion of this work. Cara provided the steady and brilliant legal research that went into completing this project. Finally, I want to recognize and thank my very capable Executive Assistant, Alison Dealy, whose attention to detail has been invaluable.

Finally, this book is dedicated to my parents, Ezra and Ruth Thompson. I appreciate their love and sacrifices. My siblings and I were raised to believe there were no limits on what we could accomplish. I'm lucky. I picked the right parents.

.

CHAPTER ONE

LEVER OF THE LAW

I've spent my life in service to the law. Although I've enjoyed representing the underdog or powerless in low-fee or pro bono cases, for most of my career I've practiced law at the highest levels of our nation's government and inside some the world's most influential corporations. It's been a heck of a ride for a boy from Hannibal, Missouri, the son of a railroad laborer and a cook. I've applied the law in pursuit of a more secure country, a more just justice system, and a more responsible private sector. All of this has been enormously satisfying. I've helped individuals with seemingly intractable legal problems. I've helped institutions become better and more responsible.

I've been practicing law for over 49 years. A substantial number of those years have been dedicated to the federal criminal justice system, where I served as a prosecutor, first as the U.S. Attorney for the Northern District of Georgia. From 2001 to 2003, I had the honor of serving as Deputy Attorney General of the United States.

The other years of my legal career were spent in the private sector. For 16 years, I was a partner at the Atlanta-based law firm King & Spalding.

From 2004 to 2014, I served two terms as Executive Vice President for Government Affairs, General Counsel, and Corporate Secretary at PepsiCo. And in 2017, the United States Department of Justice (DOJ) appointed me Independent Compliance Monitor and Auditor for Volkswagen, the world's largest automaker at the time, after the company agreed to a multibillion-dollar settlement for cheating on emissions tests and defrauding American consumers and regulators.[1]

Throughout my career, I have had the good fortune to work with and learn from great lawyers. Chief among them is my former law partner and friend, former Attorney General Griffin Bell. As I look back on my career, I believe I have successfully followed Judge Bell's charge that successful lawyers should be, first and foremost, problem solvers.

Of course, while the practice of law requires at times great judgment and relevant experience, it is often guided by precedent. Such is the great irony of our profession: The act of moving forward first requires looking backward. Thus, I'm primarily writing this book for the next generation of legal, government, and business leaders. By sharing lessons from my life in the law and identifying areas in which we need sound judgment in solving difficult legal problems, I hope this book will serve as a guide for those who want to make our country more just and more secure.

In the following pages, I will lay out several areas in which I believe the law, when understood anew and applied with rigor by people of good conscience and judgment, can address some of our nation's greatest challenges. I provide my thoughts on how we can use the lever of the law to improve our nation's security and to encourage and enforce more ethical and responsible behavior in public service and private enterprise.

My path to a life in the law was neither obvious nor expected.

Growing up in Hannibal, Missouri, I didn't imagine becoming a lawyer. Nobody had ever told me that law was something I might be good at—or should even consider. Neither of my parents had high school degrees.

Hannibal was, in many ways, a typical Midwestern town on the Mississippi River. Typical, at the time, also meant segregated. The restaurants in Hannibal would not serve Black people, or they would serve Black people but only through the back door. I went to an all-Black school, segregated first by law and then by practice, for eight years of my life. From a young age, I had a clear-eyed view of how the law and precedent shaped my family's way of life.

I grew up in a neighborhood somewhere between poor and working class. My father worked for the railroad as a switchman and a laborer, and my mother was a part-time cook. When I was 15, my father died in a train accident. I was getting dressed for a basketball game when a neighbor told me after I had been pulled from the locker room. In the aftermath, my first reaction was to try to take my father's place. But as an adolescent, I couldn't fill that role. I'm lucky that I had a terrific mother who wouldn't let me try—and a tight-knit community that never let me feel alone.

If Hannibal was a typical town, I demonstrated an atypical curiosity about what could lie beyond our little corner of Northeast Missouri. I remember thinking one day that I might want to go to optometry school. So the next morning, I walked straight into Dr. Hunt's office, the local eye doctor, and asked, "What does it take to become an optometrist?" The next week, I strolled into our dentist's office, and the week after that, the county coroner's office. And several times a week, I walked to the public library and read *The Wall Street Journal* and other national newspapers. I turned pages for hours, reviewing the stock tables and anything else that caught my eye. Almost everything did.

That curiosity was nurtured by dedicated teachers at Douglass School, Hannibal's Black school, who told me that I was just as good as anyone else and that with hard work I could not only match the achievements of others but actually surpass them. Nothing felt outside the realm of possibility, including being President of the United States. And while I never became President, I often sat in the same room as one on many mornings for over two years—not bad for a kid from Hannibal.

When it was time to consider college, I chose Culver-Stockton College, a small liberal arts college in Canton, Missouri. I didn't know anyone there. And I didn't look like many people there. It was 1963, and I was the only African American student on campus. I don't remember exactly why I chose Culver-Stockton. I wanted to play football in college, and I was certain I could play football at a small college. But looking back, I think I was more comfortable at a small college. I thought about attending the University of Missouri but was afraid of being overwhelmed by the indifference of a large college campus.

Until my junior year, I was planning to become a social worker.

That changed when I met Professor John Sperry.

Professor Sperry showed up to his classroom with nothing but a briefcase and a pipe. I seldom saw him lecture from notes. Sometimes, he gave entire lessons with his eyes seemingly closed, and he taught everything, from archaeology to astronomy, hieroglyphics to history. Age of Revolution, a wonderful survey course, really opened my eyes to Western civilization. He was part of a lost erudite tradition.

After history class one day, Professor Sperry pulled me aside, unprompted, and said, "Larry, I understand you want to be a social worker. There's nothing wrong with being a social worker—but have you considered law?"

Truthfully, I hadn't. I didn't know any lawyers. There were very few lawyers in Hannibal, and my family never had to deal with one.

I didn't know that was an option for me until Professor Sperry asked that question.

It's ironic that toward the end of my legal career, I served as General Counsel of a global company that did business in over 200 countries and territories, but when I applied to law school, I only applied to schools located in the Midwest. My vision and comfort level were very much restrained. I graduated from the University of Michigan Law School in 1974 and passed the Missouri bar the same year.

And now, 49 years later, I'm sharing these thoughts with you because I still believe in the power of the law. I believe in the power of our legal system to hold wrongdoers accountable and to make corporations more responsible. I believe in the power of our legal system to protect us from international threats. Yes, I believe in the power of our legal system to help remedy almost everything that's wrong with America and help preserve almost everything that's right. Using the legal system as a tool to solve problems and as an instrument to benefit the larger society as I see it has not been easy. I have been bitterly criticized, even attacked. And I have at times failed. Yet my career has been satisfying. To paraphrase President Teddy Roosevelt, I have enjoyed being in the "arena." I am satisfied that my life has been one of purpose and grateful that I'm not one of "those cold and timid souls who neither know victory nor defeat."[2]

One of my favorite quotes is from former Secretary of State Elihu Root: "About half the practice of a decent lawyer consists in telling would-be clients that they are damned fools and should stop."[3] Over the following pages, I will share with you what I believe we need to do to become a safer, fairer, and better nation. I hope you will listen, take me seriously, and not automatically dismiss what I've learned. While I doubt that anyone who reads this book is a "damned fool," we all should heed the lessons I've learned and what I continue to believe: The law, properly applied, is a powerful force for good in our society.

·

CHAPTER TWO

MAKING OUR COUNTRY MORE SECURE

A Scary Hypothetical

Imagine for a moment that you had been appointed the nation's second-ranking federal law enforcement official just a few months before 9/11. Now imagine that one Sunday morning two years later, while still serving as Deputy Attorney General, you get a call on your secure phone while seated in the pews of a church just a few blocks north of the White House. Quietly, but urgently, you make your way outside, where the intelligence official who placed the call informs you that overseas intelligence officials believe that a bomb may have been planted beneath an NFL stadium set to host a football game later that day. Spectators, the intelligence official explains, will begin gathering in a matter of hours, and there are only two people who can shed light on the credibility of the underlying threat. One is in custody at a detention facility in Afghanistan—he provided the limited information analysts already have. The other is a young man having breakfast at that very moment at his home in Alexandria, Virginia.

As a former federal prosecutor, you would understand immediately that there is no way to follow the procedures that typically guide law enforcement officials ahead of making an arrest. There simply isn't time. For that matter, it's unlikely that the existing intelligence derived from the source in Afghanistan would meet the standard required by federal law before issuing a warrant. But that just makes the need to talk to this singular figure across the Potomac River in Virginia that much more pressing—his firsthand knowledge is integral to determining the veracity of what interrogators gleaned from the source in Afghanistan. Two years after nearly 3,000 people were killed on American soil, Congress and the public are still questioning on a daily basis why officials failed to "connect the dots" ahead of 9/11. Is the same thing now poised to happen again?

Ultimately, it's up to you to decide what to do—and you quickly realize, standing there in the chill of an early autumn morning in Washington, that all the options have significant drawbacks. The first is to cancel the game entirely. But you know that would amount to a kind of cowardly surrender—you'd be the American official giving terrorists the implicit victory of disrupting an American tradition on the basis of what might be a spurious rumor. You could do nothing, simply let the game go on and leave the public unprotected. A third option, and the one fraught with the most peril for you personally, is to authorize the FBI to pull the young man in Virginia off the street for what might be termed a "chat" at a local Holiday Inn. The downside to that option is obvious: Law enforcement in the United States isn't authorized to whisk people out of their homes willy-nilly even in moments fraught with peril.

This is hardly the most difficult sort of decision Deputy Attorneys General are required to make. But this hypothetical puts in stark relief the underlying challenge of the job. If you choose to do what seems most expeditious—if you green-light what amounts to an unauthorized interrogation, short-circuiting standard judicial proceedings—you will open yourself up to accusations that you violated this young man's constitutional rights, subjecting him to false imprisonment. As a lawyer, you may well face sanctions. As a political appointee, you may well be subject to intense scrutiny. But if you fail to authorize the interrogation, you may be guilty of willfully refusing to "connect the dots," thereby sending thousands of people to their graves.

I want to stop here to acknowledge that well-intentioned people who revere the freedoms bestowed by the American Constitution will not be of one mind on how to handle this hypothetical; various experts would provide a whole range of recommendations. Some will vehemently reject any suggestion that the government should ever compromise what they see as a core civil liberty, namely the protection against unlawful search and seizure. Better that the game be canceled, or even that people die, before granting government officials the power carte blanche to sweep individuals off the streets absent approval from an independent member of the judiciary.

Others will take an entirely opposite view. The Constitution, to paraphrase Justice Robert Jackson's famous dissent in *Terminiello v. Chicago*, is not a suicide pact.[4] In the face of potentially catastrophic consequences at a time when terrorists are looking to kill American citizens, Washington's national security apparatus must be given the leash required to do its job effectively. Whatever the threat of executive branch overreach, the threat to democracy from a potentially endless string of attacks on the homeland is even more severe. This morning in 2003, you, as the nation's second-ranking federal law enforcement officer, are being forced to make a choice balancing the twin American ideals of liberty and security. You are keenly aware that there is no "right" decision, but in the end, you have to make the call and live with it. What would you do?

Ticking time bomb scenarios are, in the normal rhythms of law enforcement, quite rare. But the one laid out above is not unlike a few I faced while serving as Deputy Attorney General. Despite being few and far between, they nevertheless frame one of the most important tensions in the world of law enforcement: namely, the laden balance between prevention and prosecution or, to put it another way, between intelligence and law enforcement. This is a topic that's too frequently obscured by the public's expectation that government protect them from "bad guys" *writ large*. But among those charged with carrying out the sacred duty to keep society safe and secure, the two distinct responsibilities can quickly become nothing short of blurry when it comes to fighting terrorism.

Take, as a first example, what may seem an entirely rudimentary law enforcement responsibility: namely, protecting the public from would-be bank robbers. How do government officials in the United States prevent people from walking into bank branches and demanding money? Banks, of course, employ a range of tools: locks, cameras, bulletproof glass, etc. But ultimately the element that works most directly to prevent bank robbery is the threat of prosecution. If you rob a teller and walk out of a branch office with money to which you are not entitled, you're liable to get caught. When you get caught, you're likely to be charged with a crime. And when you're convicted, you're most likely going to spend time in prison.

Note that, for the most part, the government's efforts to deter bank crime are what we might call *post hoc*. The promise of what might happen *after* you commit the crime serves to prevent criminal behavior. The FBI, of course, is always interested in tips that might help them disrupt individuals conspiring to commit crimes—better to catch a bank robber before she makes her move. But in the realm of traditional law enforcement, the primary focus is to respond to crimes after they've occurred so that the perpetrators can be brought to justice. In most realms of traditional law enforcement, prosecution is prevention. But that's not true with terrorism—and that distinction makes all the difference.

Most Americans do not want—and the protections established in our Constitution do not permit—the government to go too far in gathering intelligence so as to be able to *anticipate* the next bank heist. Innocent

Americans would likely have to be surveilled if law enforcement were going to cast a net wide enough to prevent every would-be bank robber from making an attempt. But when it comes to terrorism—when we're faced with threats to kill thousands of Americans from one attack to the next—the equation changes. Prosecuting an offender *post hoc* isn't a sufficient deterrent when you're up against a would-be suicide bomber. As a result, in America's efforts to battle terrorism, *prosecution* does not suffice—the government needs to *prevent* the attack. And that's a whole different ball game.

For lawyers, herein lies the real complication. For more than two centuries, members of the American Bar have worked to hone and refine the machinations of a criminal justice system poised to hold wrongdoers accountable while protecting the innocent. And while the system we have today is not perfect, that mission has in large part been held distinct from what is traditionally considered national security, a role assigned instead to the federal government's national security apparatus. In other words, for the better part of our history, America's law enforcement and intelligence functions have largely operated independently of one another.

There have been exceptions. During one particularly bloody railway strike in the late nineteenth century, the President called out the military, and Congress was so outraged that it passed the Posse Comitatus Act, which limits the executive branch's ability to use the military in service of domestic policy concerns.[5] And, of course, through the twentieth century, the lines were blurred on several occasions. For example, the Red Scare that followed the First World War prompted the Palmer Raids,[6] and during the upheavals of the 1960s, intelligence officials too frequently spied on American citizens.[7] But really in the years prior to 9/11, the primary mandate for many in government wasn't how to blend the twin goals of prevention and prosecution; in the pursuit of preserving the nation's civil liberties, it was to keep them separate and distinct.

This may come as a surprise to some who may have preconceived views about me because I served in a senior role in the Bush Administration, but

I'll say it anyway: There was, and is, good reason to keep the government's law enforcement and intelligence capabilities separate—so far as doing so still gives government the ability to keep the nation safe. The civil liberties that put guardrails around our criminal justice system—the protections from unreasonable search and seizure, the expectation that law enforcement has "probable cause" before tapping your phone or reading your email, the presumption that information law enforcement collects outside proper channels may not be used against you in court—are hallmarks of our civil liberties.

The challenge is to keep those liberties intact when they might be used to hide a plan to kill thousands of people. In *that* circumstance, government has to strike a slightly different balance. Lean too heavily in favor of intelligence and prevention, and you pierce notions of individual liberty. Lean too heavily toward civil liberties, and the nation is left vulnerable to attack. We can't afford to be puritanical from either perspective. And finding a balance requires trade-offs.

The Wall

During the 1970s, congressional investigations led in large part by Senator Frank Church (D-ID) revealed what can happen when government leans too heavily toward prevention.[8] Previously, in various bids to disrupt purported national security threats—perceived threats sometimes conjured in bad faith—the nation's intelligence community applied the more lenient hurdles permitted in intelligence operations against American citizens. Rather than honor the rules that would generally have enjoined an investigator from monitoring American citizens, government authorities simply undertook their spying through intelligence-gathering techniques. And information gleaned inappropriately by intelligence agents was then sometimes used to prosecute individuals through the courts, essentially short-circuiting the protections enshrined in our Constitution.

During the 1960s, for example, Dr. Martin Luther King (MLK) was subject to wire-tapping that did not meet the protections he *should* have been afforded.[9] By conjuring MLK erroneously as the agent of a foreign conspiracy to undermine American government, federal officials justified efforts to keep tabs on the Civil Rights movement well beyond what they would have been permitted to do had they pursued warrants through the courts. They did much worse as well, but the core principle remains: By misusing the tools available to those tasked with preventing an attack against America's national security, the balance between intelligence and law enforcement came undone. And that bred abuse.

In response, Congress passed, and President Carter signed, the Foreign Intelligence Surveillance Act of 1978, a bill that more explicitly mandated a separation between intelligence operations against foreign threats and law enforcement operations aimed at bringing criminals to justice.[10] FISA, as it's generally known, established a court explicitly designed to help federal authorities divine when and if they could place wiretaps on foreigners in the United States despite, in some cases, not having the probable cause that's required to get approval in a criminal investigation. FISA, in short, was an attempt to rebalance the government's twin missions.

Over the course of the next two decades, however, what had been fashioned as a well-warranted adjustment became, in my view, a misguided overcorrection. In 1995, those preeminently concerned with potential civil liberties violations succeeded in convincing a Deputy Attorney General appointed by President Clinton, Jamie Gorelick, to issue a memorandum establishing what became understood by some as a "wall" between the government's law enforcement and intelligence communities.[11] To that end, if the FBI was conducting a counterintelligence operation, the FBI's criminal investigator might not know anything about it. And if a defendant revealed something the intelligence community might find important in the course of a confidential grand jury investigation, prosecutors were prohibited from passing the testimony along to the CIA.

Gorelick had a clearly defensible reason for issuing her memorandum. She was fearful, given the FISA law, that criminal indictments brought using evidence collected from intelligence operations would be imperiled by judicial concerns about civil liberties—that a murderer might escape prosecution by claiming that smoking gun evidence could not be presented in court. But her memo had the effect of siloing government more broadly. I know Jamie Gorelick and believe she is an excellent lawyer and was a dedicated prosecutor. This siloing effect was clearly unintentional on her part. Suddenly, bureaucracies that shared responsibility for keeping the nation safe became strangers to one another. Intelligence agents and criminal investigators interpreted the policy as an impenetrable barrier. And it was through the fog of that dysfunction that the federal government failed to "connect the dots" when, at the turn of the millennium, members of a terrorist group called al-Qaeda plotted to attack the United States.

My service as the nation's Deputy Attorney General had begun only a handful of months before evil struck on the cool, crisp morning of 9/11. No single event has had a more profound impact on how I think about the government's need to balance power and individual liberty. I spent the chaotic hours following the attack at an undisclosed location, worried about my two sons. At the time, one worked in downtown Manhattan for a health care company at Hanover Square, not far from the World Trade Center. The second, a law student at NYU, had called me days earlier to discuss an interview he had scheduled at a law firm in the Twin Towers. It turned out to be on September 12, but on that frightening morning, I could not for the life of me remember precisely for which day the interview had been scheduled. Eventually, my wife was able to get ahold of each of our sons and relayed to me that they were both unharmed. Like millions of others, I immediately felt relieved. But as a senior law enforcement official, my mind immediately turned to those who were not so fortunate.

Over the next several months, the focus of my work inside the Justice Department centered on what amounted to an all-hands-on-deck program to put the federal government more broadly on a better footing to address the terrorist threat. In the years since, I've spent an inordinate amount of time defending decisions we made about how to protect the nation's homeland. My thinking is still informed by the work we did in those first few months, and that's one of the reasons I remain worried today. But before I explain my present-day concerns, you have to understand the roots of my experience, many of which are searing.

Three things were clearly relevant in this realm when I was sworn into the job I held on 9/11. First, the "wall," as established by the 1995 memo, was fully operational, meaning that the nation's law enforcement and intelligence communities were largely estranged from one another. Second, there was, as had been said, significant "noise in the system," meaning that it was clear to the intelligence community that radical Islamists were planning to attack the United States, though the specifics—when and where—remained largely a mystery. I'm not aware of any prediction that an attack would fall on the homeland. Third, aware that various bureaucracies were *not* sharing information, some inside the government were agitating for reforms to bridge the existing divide.

In the months and years that followed 9/11, independent commissions worked assiduously to uncover how the nation had been left so vulnerable. In the course of delving into the evidence, various narratives took shape, some of which were unfortunate and appear to have been driven by political motives. Some would come to claim that Attorney General John Ashcroft had dismissed concerns that a terrorist attack was imminent, laying blame for the attack at his feet. That notion was laughable on its face. Others would claim that I had reviewed the specifics of Gorelick's 1995 memo and essentially re-endorsed it—in other words, that I had done nothing to chip away at the wall. That simply wasn't true either.[12] But while no one was singularly culpable, save for those who planned and carried out the attacks, there was clearly a breakdown in the system. And I know everyone who served in government ahead of the attacks wishes he or she had done more to reform the system when there was time—including me.

Here's the reality from my perspective. Over the first three months of my tenure, I examined in great detail how the wall was impacting information sharing even as reports of burgeoning terrorist banter circulated through the intelligence community. Mike Chertoff, a friend who had taken the helm of the Justice Department's Criminal Division soon after George W. Bush's election, and David Kris, an expert in national security law retained by me at the Justice Department from my Clinton-era predecessor, Eric Holder, had flagged for me their concerns about the government's inability to synthesize information. So even as I worried about the very dynamic that had spurred Gorelick to write her memo, I grew so concerned about how siloed information had become that I resolved to make a change.

On August 6, 2001, I issued new guidance through an internal Justice Department memorandum designed to supersede Gorelick's six-year-old memo.[13] Instead of maintaining the "wall," my new guidance required the FBI to notify the Criminal Division when "facts or circumstances are developed" in a foreign intelligence or counterintelligence investigation "that reasonably indicate that a significant federal crime has been, is being, or may be committed," per the requirements of the Attorney General's Procedures for Contacts Between the FBI and the Criminal Division Concerning Foreign Intelligence and Foreign Counterintelligence Investigations. I further instructed the FBI to notify the Criminal Division of this kind of important information without delay.[14] Little more than a month later, after the Twin Towers had fallen, the Pentagon had been attacked, and a plane had crashed in Shanksville, Pennsylvania, Attorney General Ashcroft and I took the wall down in its entirety. And the more cooperative arrangement that prevailed from that point on—a constellation of norms that for the most part still exists today—was subsequently codified in the Patriot Act.[15]

This so-called wall was especially a source of controversy during the 9/11 Commission hearings. Many, including Attorney General John

Ashcroft, blamed the wall for impeding promising investigations of al-Qaeda operatives. Some on the commission noted that I had reaffirmed the wall procedures in my August 2001 memo.

A part of this commission controversy also included my denial of ever hearing John Ashcroft say that he didn't want to hear about al-Qaeda during a briefing by Acting FBI Director Tom Pickard. Quite frankly, this put me in an uncomfortable situation. During my time in government, I worked very hard to do my job in a professional way that protected Americans. Even after I left government, I tried to avoid the political fray and pursue what I believed to be objective reviews of the 9/11 horrors and how they might be prevented from happening again.

Kurt Eichenwald, in his book *500 Days: Secrets and Lies in the Terror Wars*, recognized my efforts by noting that I had a reputation in Washington of being an honest broker.[16] I was deeply honored by what he wrote.

Balancing Security and Civil Liberties

Today many still debate the nuances of the balance established after 9/11, a framework that, with mild adjustments, is still in effect as of 2024. But to my point of view, the cooperative framework that presently ties together the nation's intelligence and law enforcement agencies largely preserves the citizenry's constitutional protections while allowing government to remain effective in combating terrorist threats. Section 203 of the Patriot Act, for example, expressly empowers law enforcement officials to share criminal investigative information that contains foreign intelligence or counterintelligence, including grand jury and wiretap information, with intelligence, protective, immigration, national defense, and national security personnel.[17] And that sort of change has worked to real and positive effect.

For example, enhanced information sharing led directly to the indictment of Sami Al-Arian and other alleged members of the Palestinian Islamic Jihad, a group with members in Tampa that is alleged to be responsible for murdering over 100 innocent people, including Alisa

Flatow, a young American killed in a bus bombing near the Israeli settlement of Kfar Darom.[18] To the same end, absent having deconstructed the "wall," authorities might not have been able to catch New Jersey's Hemant Lakhani, an arms dealer charged with attempting to sell shoulder-fired anti-aircraft missiles to terrorists for use against American targets.[19]

In the years since I left government service, I've replayed in my own mind the bureaucratic wrangling that preceded my issuing that August 2001 memo thousands of times, often in the middle of the night while staring up at the ceiling. What if I'd chosen to go a step further, allowing agents to talk to one another locally rather than requiring them to use the Criminal Division in Washington as a pass-through? Would that have given analysts working in silos enough time to "connect the dots" before the terrorists boarded those planes early on the morning of 9/11? Did I give too much credence to those worried about the sorts of abuses uncovered in the Church Committee investigations? Am I partially culpable for the government's failure? Did I take the easy way out by tweaking the Gorelick memo and even stating in mine that the general guidance of the Gorelick memo remained in place?

Two decades later, I can only acknowledge that I have never been able to answer those questions to my complete satisfaction. I'm far from convinced that, even had the wall been deconstructed entirely a month earlier, authorities would have headed off the attack. Nor am I sure I would have been able to pull off a more drastic change in the guidance before the horrors that befell the nation—resistance from many in the civil liberties community would have been fierce. As it was, Judge Royce Lamberth, sitting at that time as the Chief Judge of the FISA Court, properly called me to inquire about the nature of the memo. But that does not mean that I'm not still heartsick and profoundly troubled by the outcome. There may be nothing more I feasibly could have done, but I still wish I'd done more. And I'll admit that, in the years that immediately followed the attacks, my anguish spurred me to seek professional help for the one and only time in my decades-long career. I'm not ashamed to talk about this fact. Making this public has, in fact, been cathartic for me.

That's in large part why this topic remains so difficult even now. In this realm of the law, where applying the norms established in the world of criminal justice can leave the nation vulnerable to attack, and where applying the standards that frame intelligence operations can undermine cherished civil liberties, the question is ultimately about balance. People of good will can argue the trade-offs. Likely there is no perfect solution. But today, a full 20 years after the worst terrorist act ever committed on American soil—in fact, an act of mass murder—I believe our government needs, once again, to review the incumbent regime. While I hope nothing will ever rise to the level of angst that defines my view of those critical months before 9/11, this issue, too, keeps me up at night.

A Personal Crisis

To understand the roots of my present-day concern, consider a small but serious crisis I faced roughly a year after 9/11. In September 2002, a young Canadian-Syrian citizen named Maher Arar purchased tickets to fly to Montreal. He first boarded a flight from Tunis to Zurich.[20] In Switzerland, he transferred to a flight bound for New York's John F. Kennedy Airport. Because foreign intelligence officials were monitoring his movements, as he boarded that second flight to the United States, these intelligence officials shared with their American counterparts evidence indicating that Arar was likely a member of al-Qaeda. So after Arar landed at JFK, American intelligence officials sought clarity from me on how they should handle the situation. If Arar was permitted to travel on to Montreal, some argued, he might well disappear into the wild and perhaps then slip back into the United States. Was there something Washington could do to deal with the potential threat presented by this individual based upon the information known about him at the time?

I need to be clear here that the American government had not at this point designated Arar an "enemy combatant," which would have given authorities license to seize and send him to the military detention facility at Guantanamo Bay in Cuba. The intelligence in the government's possession simply suggested he was affiliated with al-Qaeda. By the same token, because Arar was not American, he was not entitled to all the civil protections due an American citizen. Once he arrived in Canada, the Canadian authorities would likely have had to grant him all the accommodations due any other Canadian citizen—and the nature of the intelligence might not have permitted Canadian authorities to do anything whatsoever. Which left to me the burden of signing off on recommendations as to what to do. What, if anything, was the American government inclined to do?

The first decision was easy: We would not immediately allow Arar to transfer onto his connecting flight. Were he, in fact, a danger, I had no intention of letting him slip through our fingers in the name of expediency. Immigration law permits the government to detain those who come into the country (for a limited amount of time) in advance of charging them with a crime, expelling them, or admitting them. And so, in order to give the intelligence community more time to gather additional information, federal officials at the airport detained Arar. He spent his first night at the airport and was then transported to the Metropolitan Detention Facility in Brooklyn.

But that provided for only a temporary resolution. The intelligence we had on Arar would likely have been inadmissible in court—and intelligence officials were loath to reveal the scope of what they knew for fear of tipping off the bad guys as to their intelligence methods and sources. Under questioning, Arar merely admitted to knowing members of al-Qaeda—he repeatedly denied maintaining any personal allegiance. In meetings with law enforcement and intelligence counterparts from Canada and elsewhere, a fairly harrowing picture of Arar began to emerge in clearer definition: He did not appear, from what we understood at the time, to be someone with entirely benign intentions. But the burden of responsibility fell to me. Given the limited intelligence we had and the even more limited intelligence we could share publicly or in court, what was I going to do?

The first option—and certainly the most expeditious—was to let him travel on to Canada as he had originally intended. Canadian authorities would almost surely have been compelled at that point to let Arar go. I'm prohibited from revealing the nature of high-level cross-border conversations in detail, but you have to ask yourself whether someone in my position would have chosen to preclude a Canadian citizen from traveling to Canada without discussing the circumstances with the Canadian government ahead of time. The risk here, of course, was that Arar would go on to engage in activities in Canada or in the United States that would have been unacceptable. Ahead of 9/11, of course, American officials had infamously failed to "connect the dots." So I was keenly sensitive to the possibility we might make the same mistake again.

The next option was to arrest and prosecute him in the United States. But as a former U.S. Attorney, I was acutely aware that we did not have evidence sufficient to charge him, let alone win a conviction. The last option was to "render" Arar to a foreign country better equipped to determine whether he was, in fact, a terrorist. American law precluded me from bequeathing him to a country that would torture him. But if another nation's intelligence service had reason to believe Arar was a threat, I had the option of relinquishing him to their control. Al-Qaeda, of course, was not singularly focused on attacking the United States—Osama bin Laden was considered a threat to regimes across the Middle East. So in much the same way the United States might expect the Jordanian government to hand over someone suspected of plotting to blow up a courthouse in Atlanta, the Jordanians had good reason to want to speak to potential members of al-Qaeda.

I want to be very clear here: Each option had serious drawbacks. The Department of Justice is not generally in the business of releasing suspected bad guys in American custody. But if Arar was entirely innocent—if he had committed no crime and, as he claimed, was simply acquainted with someone who belonged to al-Qaeda—the American government had no interest in curtailing a Canadian citizen's freedom. But rendering Arar to

Jordan came with its own complications. If Arar were, despite guarantees, to be tortured after being rendered, I could be subject to prosecution under American law. And so, the factors involved in my decision spanned beyond the nation's best interest. Even if handing him to Jordanian officials was liable to best serve the nation's calculations, I couldn't help but have countervailing personal considerations.

I did what due diligence I could under the circumstances. I asked plenty of questions and had several briefings. Grave national security concerns remained. I even checked with other government officials outside of the Department of Justice, including Deputy Secretary of State Richard Armitage.

In the end, I decided to set those self-interested concerns aside. After the Immigration and Naturalization Service Regional Director made a determination that Arar was a member of al-Qaeda, I signed a "final notice of inadmissibility" to the United States and noted that Arar's removal to Jordan and Syria was consistent with the United Nations Convention against Torture. It's what happened next that's instructive: Jordanian officials handed Arar off to Syrian officials who allegedly tortured him at a prison inside Syria. When he was eventually released, he did, in fact, make his way to Canada, where he sued the Canadian government for complicity and won an $8 million judgment. And then he sued me personally under a Bivens claim,[21] alleging that I was culpable for the torture he endured at the hands of Syrian authorities. In the months that followed, House Judiciary Committee Chairman John Conyers (D-MI) recommended that a special counsel investigate me for criminal liability. The Homeland Security Inspector General began to look more thoroughly at the case and my conduct in office.

I suffered in turn. Typically when an officer of the law is charged with wrongdoing in his or her official capacity, he or she is defended by the agency for which he or she worked. Over the course of the grueling several years in which Arar's lawsuit against me wound its way through the courts, eventually leading to a final decision in my favor before the Second Circuit

Court of Appeals in New York, the Department of Justice provided me counsel. But while the Department's lawyers represented me in court, they did not represent me when I was questioned by the FBI, by the Inspector General, by congressional investigators, or in other realms. I hired my own lawyers to represent me in those circumstances and in the larger case itself. It became clear to me that I was the focus, and the late John J. Cassidy, Jeff Larkin, Jamie Kilberg, Paul Nathanson, and Stephen Braga, of the law firm Baker Botts, all very ably represented me in the case. Department of Justice lawyers represented all the other named defendants in their official capacities as government officials. And so not only did I put my career at risk by making my decision, I also faced economic consequences as well. Doing what I thought was in the nation's best interest as a public servant ended up making it necessary for me to retain private counsel.

I mention this not out of personal pique, though I'll admit to resenting the out-of-pocket costs and, most important, my personal time spent on the case. Rather, I highlight this issue because I fear that, down the line, another public official might face a similar crisis and, rather than doing what's best for the country, choose instead to protect herself from the ordeal I went through by not acting affirmatively or simply not doing anything. Americans should want their Deputy Attorney General—or, for that matter, every officer of the law—to make decisions on the basis of the evidence at hand and sound judgment. Personal peril should never come into play. And while we should hope that anyone appointed to such a high position would never veer in putting country first, we would do well not to be so naive.

A National Security Court

Efforts to balance security and liberty can't be done in a vacuum—context is crucial. So in 2023, after four years during which the specter of authoritarianism from within hovered so ominously across America, I've no intention of arguing for giving future Justice Department officials blanket immunity for decisions in their official capacity. Many of us who served in the Bush Administration argued, in the 2000s, most often correctly, that the executive branch needed more latitude if it was going to delivery safety and security in an age of terror. But that prerogative should not be left without limits. As a government official, I spoke many times on the government's efforts to deal with terrorism and always said the government's authority in dealing with terrorism should not be unchecked and should be subject to the rule of law. In other words, the government should not be given a blank check to deal with terrorism.[22]

The riot at the Capitol on January 6 of 2021 illustrates how, if those sitting atop a presidential administration don't have the nation's best interests at the top of their agenda, the damage can be incalculable. To paraphrase a famous aphorism written into a Supreme Court decision, the government should be able to strike "hard" blows against terrorism, not "foul" ones.[23]

For that reason, debates that we had about civil liberties and national security in the wake of 9/11 feel dated now—or at least oversimplified. The question today isn't merely whether government is an evil monolith undermining the promise of our constitutional democracy. Even those of us who sought more executive authority in the aftermath of 9/11 see now in starker terms that checks and limits are absolutely essential. By the same token, however, those who worry about executive overreach don't do themselves or the public any favors by simply seeking to make it harder for government officials to do their jobs and protect us from the prospect of mass murder. Those of us who care about both need to create a system that balances liberty and security in the right way. I believe that to do that we need to focus on *process*.

Here's the crucial question: How should our government expeditiously weigh conflicting prerogatives in a clear time-based emergency? In the ticking time bomb case described in the opening of this chapter, and again in the Arar case, I was compelled as Deputy Attorney General to make a quick decision at my own peril. Responsible officials should, of course, be expected to carry out their duties in a way that both serves the public and adheres to limits imposed by the Constitution. But culpability can work both ways—it might well make future public officials too reluctant to do what a dangerous situation requires.

For that reason, I believe that Congress should establish and the President should sign legislation establishing a reformed process for overseeing, weighing, and ultimately ratifying requests to detain, interrogate, and render potential international threats in real time. In a phrase, Washington should stand up what some have called a "National Security Court."

This idea is not entirely *sui generis*. In the course of many ordinary law enforcement investigations, detectives are compelled to seek warrants from judges in advance of collecting evidence or making an arrest—and that process requires a disinterested judicial arbiter to determine whether authorities have sufficient probable cause for seeking that warrant. That process guarantees individual citizens protection against unreasonable search and seizure and prevents authorities from going on what some call "fishing expeditions." But the process is often slow. And the standards change when you're dealing with, say, an investment fraud case that might take years to resolve and a terrorist threat that could claim casualties merely hours in the future.

As previously noted, decades ago, in the wake of the Church Committee investigations, Congress established a Foreign Intelligence Surveillance Court to determine when and if the executive branch could, for example, tap a phone line that might lead analysts to overhear a U.S. citizen discussing something with a foreign person without the typical process of establishing probable cause. FISA warrants are tools used largely to aid in gathering intelligence. But no such entity exists to provide that sort of blessing or cover for executive branch officials who want to quickly pull someone off the street to talk to them about a would-be bomb planted in an NFL stadium as outlined in my opening hypothetical. The ability to interrogate someone who may have valuable information is critical in what I've called the ticking bomb scenario. There's no process designed to protect a Deputy Attorney General who decides it's in the nation's best interest to render a suspected terrorist to a foreign country.

While certain details would need to be worked out—which active federal judges, for example, would staff the court, and who might present the case *against* a proposed executive action such that those sitting in judgment hear arguments on both sides—those on both the right and left have endorsed the core idea. Neal Katyal, who often represented the Obama Administration before the Supreme Court as Acting Solicitor General, has embraced at least some aspects of this proposal. Despite being representatives of different political traditions, both he and I know that executive branch officials need to make tough calls free of the dangerous fear that they might be held personally liable for making a bad decision down the line. A National Security Court could provide that answer. And while the court should not be called into service very often, its ability to render judgment quickly and seamlessly would be an indelible benefit to the executive branch, those under suspicion, and the nation as a whole.

As Deputy Attorney General, I became convinced that if the government's antiterrorism efforts were to be successful, they would need to have the support of a clear majority of Americans. American citizens must believe that the efforts, while strong, are also fair and impartial.

This is why a National Security Court is so important in the ticking bomb scenario. A National Security Court would subject executive branch emergency decisions to judicial review. Judicial review is an essential element of a free democracy, which is what the United States is.

Notwithstanding the increasing threat of domestic terrorism, potential acts of terrorism by foreign nationals represent threats that can be uniquely addressed by a National Security Court. We need to be continually more vigilant in dealing with domestic terrorists, but the processes of a National Security Court could obviously not extend to U.S. citizens who, however, would remain subject to constitutionally permissible aggressive law enforcement actions.

Shortly after 9/11, I met with retired Justice Bach of the Supreme Court of Israel. It was a profound experience. He left me with a copy of a decision of his court. As the Supreme Court of Israel stated when confronted with the question of the propriety of so-called "moderate physical pressure" in interrogating terrorism suspects, "A democratic peace-loving society does not accept that investigators use any means for the purpose of uncovering the truth . . . . At times, the price of truth is so high that a democratic society is not prepared to pay for it."

The Israeli court's conclusion applies equally to our country: "This is the destiny of democracy, as not all means are acceptable to it, and not all practices employed by its enemies are open before it. Although a democracy must often fight with one hand tied behind its back, it nonetheless has the upper hand. Preserving the rule of law and recognition of an individual's liberty constitutes an important component of its understanding of security. At the end of the day, they strengthen its spirit and [add to] its strength and allow it to overcome its difficulties."[24]

In the months that followed 9/11, as lawyers at the Justice Department thought creatively about how the executive branch could work more effectively to thwart the next attack, a young lawyer proposed an expansive new program to Attorney General Ashcroft in a staff meeting. As he finished, many of us averted our eyes, knowing that the young man had proposed something that would never pass constitutional muster. Ashcroft listened patiently and then responded in such a way as to make clear his position on the idea without humiliating the young aide in front of his colleagues. "I told you to think outside the box," the Attorney General said, "not outside the Constitution."

In a phrase, that remains my view of the subject more broadly. American government has a fundamental and almost sacred responsibility to keep its citizens safe and secure and to protect the homeland. But overzealous efforts to hold threats in abeyance threaten the fabric of our democratic society. The challenge is not to choose prevention to the exclusion of prosecution *writ large* or to abandon security for liberty entirely.

The question is how to strike the proper balance in nearly every realm. And while I believe the federal government has done a yeoman's job in some circumstances over the last two decades, there is yet room for substantial improvement.

We cannot go back to an age where government officials fail to connect the dots out of fealty to artificial strictures. The world is simply too dangerous to embrace that sort of naivete. But neither can we presume that giving the executive branch a blank check will produce the security and stability that allows for a free and democratic society. Those who make the personal sacrifice of public service—many of whom sacrifice lucrative private sector opportunities and precious time with their families—deserve the nation's support as they make what are often gut-wrenching decisions. The federal government should establish and nurture a system poised to shape the best outcomes and protect those working in the public interest.

Serving as the nation's Deputy Attorney General was one of the greatest honors of my career. And I hope those who follow in my shoes come away feeling as fulfilled, if less anguished, by the legacy of their service.

CHAPTER THREE

SMART CAPITALISM

Ignoring Stakeholders Imperils Shareholders

When you lead a corporation of PepsiCo's size and breadth, you're bound to face a litany of tough decisions. But when Indra Nooyi became CEO in 2006, she was almost immediately forced to confront a nearly impossible dilemma. At the time, the company's business was running strong—the market for PepsiCo's broad array of products, a catalog steeped with all kinds of (generally what we called fun-for-you) sodas and salty snacks, was robust. But Indra properly worried about how the consumer market would evolve over the long term. Would demand for the company's products continue to deliver for shareholders? Or, by staying the course, were shareholders likely to see their equity erode down the road?

Among business executives, that is, of course, the perennial question. Corporate success hinges largely on a company's appeal to an ever-evolving consumer marketplace, and CEOs are hired to understand what's around the corner. But when Indra assumed the top post at PepsiCo, the question wasn't simply whether the company could evolve with global tastes. It was whether the company was well-advised to lean into what it was already doing very well or, alternatively, whether shareholders would be better served if the company focused on governmental and policy trends favoring product bans, warning labels, and even taxes on the company's fun-for-you products and invested in making and selling products that were more nutritionally balanced and acceptable. The right move from a business perspective wasn't entirely clear.

The easy answer in this type of situation is to stay the course—and staying the course almost surely offered shareholders the best immediate return. But as Indra understood, the *short term* can't be the only consideration for an executive charged with looking out for the shareholders' best interests. Those who invest in a corporation like PepsiCo, those who put their faith in any given management team to steer that massive investment, also expect the company to grow more valuable over the *long term.* And so those of us on the company's executive team had to grapple with the question of strategic direction in a very tactical way. How much of our revenue should be invested driving up sales for the immediate future? And how much should be invested in preparing the company to compete in the consumer and regulatory market of the future?

In addition to her overarching concern for shareholders, Indra focused on PepsiCo's sustainability. She had absolutely no intention of putting philanthropic or altruistic concerns above the interests of the company's shareholders. But she knew that, over time, if consumers came to associate our products with harmful health outcomes (as had happened with the tobacco industry, for example), PepsiCo's profitability could be severely imperiled. If the production methods used to manufacture our products came to be perceived as bad for the environment, we would eventually face a backlash from government regulators. And if our corporate culture failed to adhere to employee-centered standards, we risked losing some of our best talent. None of these concerns were imminent, we all acknowledged. Nevertheless, in Indra's view, they needed to be weighed against the company's near-term business strategy.

After a thorough internal vetting with management and the Board of Directors, Indra decided to steer the company toward long-term success. She unveiled what she termed "Performance with Purpose." PepsiCo, she determined, would begin investing much more of its revenue in developing better-for-you products.[25] We would invest substantially in ensuring the viability of our supply chain—most importantly fresh, clean water in places that were at risk for depletion, including Indra's home country of India. We would embrace employee-centered work policies to ensure that talented employees were incentivized to stay with the company over the long haul. And we would make those investments even if the company had to endure some short-term opportunity costs.

Soon after its unveiling, Performance with Purpose was attacked by a small, vocal minority of the company's shareholders. Nelson Peltz, an "activist investor" who had purchased more than a billion dollars' worth of PepsiCo stock, not only took Indra to task for embracing a strategy that threatened short-term profitability—he announced in response plans to split the company up, arguing that the beverage business would be more profitable if it were to be set apart from the snack business. That spin-off, in his view, should be merged with the snack businesses he'd recently spun off from Kraft's grocery business. Of note, merger talk often drives up share prices, and when Peltz's plan reached the public, shares of PepsiCo rose 2.3 percent—augmenting his investment by roughly $30 million.[26]

Peltz may have been Indra's most vocal critic, but he was hardly alone. In another instance, one of the company's big investors asked whether her plan to defer profits in favor of investment was lawful from a corporate governance standpoint, insinuating that she had a legal obligation to champion quarterly returns, always maximizing shareholder profits. Faced with what was sure to be a battle for the company's future, Indra turned to me with a simple question. What, she wanted to know, was a corporate executive's obligation? "Larry," she said to me, "I simply want PepsiCo to be a responsible corporation." As the company's General Counsel, it was my job to define exactly what that entailed from a legal standpoint. Here's what I and my team uncovered, especially when we went deep and examined how and why corporations came into being from a historical perspective.

The Business Judgment Rule

If most ordinary Americans were asked today, few would likely be able to explain exactly how "corporations" differ from "businesses" or "companies." But corporations are, in fact, a very specific type of private organization, each one established legally through a government licensure that imbues it with a specific set of rights and responsibilities. Through their governments, citizens give corporations various privileges that they would not otherwise have as private companies. In return, corporations and those to whom they are responsible assume obligations they might not have absent their corporate license.[27] The specifics of those arrangements—and the way experts have interpreted them—have evolved over time. And the prevailing view on Wall Street today, or at least the prevailing view since the 1970s, is now clearly due some reconsideration.

I am an undergraduate history minor, and history is important here. When the corporate form first came into being, government tended not to hand out corporate charters or licenses as of right. Instead, charters were reserved for organizations offering to take up projects designed explicitly to benefit the public-at-large. Absent a promise to build a new road or dig a new canal, state legislators were often disinclined to give any given enterprise the protections that a charter would grant. In 1809, for example, the Supreme Court of Virginia denied an application explicitly because a sufficient public purpose was important for obtaining a corporate charter.[28] But when a government *did* provide the charter, three invaluable assets came in hand.

First, and perhaps most widely understood still today, those investing in any company granted corporate status enjoyed the benefits of "limited liability," meaning more explicitly that if the company's business went awry, creditors would not be able to go after each investor's *personal* assets.

So, for example, if a millionaire invested $10,000 in a corporation that subsequently declared bankruptcy, any personal assets beyond the millionaire's $10,000 would, in most instances, remain beyond a creditor's reach.

Second, corporations were given the right to perpetual existence, meaning that when the company's ownership transitioned, the business did not perish as well—it would be passed on to successors.

Third, the American corporation has long been permitted, within certain parameters, to operate under bylaws of its own choosing. Once a company was given a charter to build a canal, the government could not micromanage its affairs.

Over time, as corporations have become larger, more prevalent, and more powerful, the balance of rights and responsibilities has evolved. By 1900, the rights had become more sacrosanct—those investing in various ventures saw limited liability as a prerequisite to most major investments. At the same time, the responsibilities have ebbed. States eager to encourage entrepreneurialism (and in many cases to collect the tax revenue that came with it) began at a certain point to permit businesses to incorporate even when they served no purpose beyond making a profit. And that's when broader debates began to emerge over what, if anything, corporations owe the communities they serve—a debate that is alive again today.

Less than two decades into the twentieth century, none other than Henry Ford, who had a controlling interest in the behemoth Ford Motor Company, proposed to cut the corporation's dividend in order to raise the wages of the company's employees because, in his view, the corporation had "too much money." Objectively, the bonuses would have provided the employees with compensation well beyond a market rate. The Dodge brothers, who at the time were among Ford Motor's other investors, complained that Ford's proposal was illegal, that the corporation's executive team was prohibited from giving away investors' assets as some sort of personal charity. Ford Motor Company, they argued, was not a philanthropic enterprise. It existed to make money for its owners, and Ford himself should be proscribed from breaching that obligation.

The Michigan Supreme Court agreed with the Dodge brothers, ruling that Ford's executives were generally prohibited from giving corporate assets away. But the justices ruled at the same time that executives *could* invest a corporation's profits in capital expenses that would return value only in the out years—Ford himself at the time had proposed to build what would become the massive River Rouge manufacturing plant in Dearborn, Michigan. This standard came to be known in legal circles as the "Business Judgment Rule." Much as executives were prohibited from giving a corporation's assets away as a large-scale charity, they were empowered to balance short-term profits against long-term gains.[29]

Adolf Berle vs. Merrick Dodd

In the roaring decade that followed the Michigan Supreme Court's ruling in the Dodge brothers case, business flourished in America, and the spirit of *laissez-faire* largely left corporations to govern and market themselves. So when the stock market crashed in 1929, the legal academy began to reconsider the basic values surrounding the corporation as a legal entity. Wall Street had, in large part, been responsible for exposing the broader economy to disaster, even while enriching some who had sold various securities to now-befuddled investors. And that prompted scholars to begin reexamining the founding principles of corporate law. At root was a simple question: How could the relationship between a corporation's investors and managers be reformed such that managers did not squander the investors' assets as had happened with such abandon during the 1920s?

In 1931 and 1932, two prominent legal scholars, Adolf Berle of Columbia Law School and Merrick Dodd of Harvard Law School, debated the issue in the pages of *Harvard Law Review*. Berle, who would go on to become a member of President Franklin Roosevelt's "Brain Trust," offered what appeared to be a clear and simple solution: make it clear that a management team's sole responsibility was to the company's shareholders. Managers were "trustees" for the shareholders. If, in Berle's view, executives understood themselves to be agents solely of shareholder interest, they would not be distracted by the range of other potential priorities—community philanthropy, employee conditions, community reputation—that might otherwise steer them in the wrong direction. These ulterior concerns too often papered over failures wrought by managers who simply weren't doing a good job maintaining a business venture's broader purpose: maximizing profits for the shareholders. But in Berle's view, that was not a death knell for the broader public interest. Because shareholders were members of the community—and in many cases also customers and employees—it would follow that a management team pursuing shareholder interests would serve society's broader interests best as well.[30]

Dodd took a different view. He argued that a corporation's executives should strive to balance between profit-making and social benefits—that shareholder interests weren't the only pertinent indicator of a corporation's success.[31] But his argument wasn't born of altruism. Rather, Dodd feared that if executives failed to pay close attention to community interests, government would end up having to compel businesses to reform, and regulators would end up prescribing otherwise avoidable solutions that cut against the corporation's interests.

Accounting for "social" concerns, in Dodd's view, was something akin to a regulatory prophylactic. If a company harmed its consumers, abused its employees, or sullied the natural environment, government would eventually end up putting external constraints on the corporation's management. And in that circumstance, Dodd argued, investors were liable to be harmed much more than had the company's management taken those considerations into account in the first place. To that end, better for management to manage community concerns proactively than have "social service" thrust upon it from the outside.

Over the course of the decades that followed this legal debate, and even in spite of Berle's subsequent disavowal of his own argument, the shareholder primacy advocated by Berle prevailed, eventually becoming something akin to Wall Street gospel.[32] Decades later, a Nobel laureate, Milton Friedman, would publish a famous (but frequently misunderstood) essay in the *New York Times Magazine* arguing that "there is one and only one social responsibility of business—to use its resources and engage in activities designed to increase its profits."[33] This has been interpreted in certain corners of the business community to mean that management's mandate is, in all circumstances, to accumulate as much money for a corporation's shareholders in as fast and furious a way as feasible.

Over the same time period, when businesses have caused harm— when miners were injured in mines or sickened from exposure, or when chemical companies released harmful substances into the environment— society has often sought to rectify the situations by identifying bad actors within the companies themselves. In other cases, government has sought to put new restrictions on business. But rarely have critics returned to the first principle of asking whether a corporation, even if *permitted* to abuse various stakeholders in search of profit, should do so. Is it in the corporate shareholder's interest to have managers seek profits at all costs, or does that ensuing myopia end up doing shareholders more harm than good?

I believe this is at the crux of present concerns. Ask yourself: If a corporation would benefit financially from overworking its employees or selling its consumers dangerous goods or sullying the broader environment, is the corporation's management obligated, as Berle's 1931 argument seems to suggest, to pursue that approach? Or, as Dodd argued, is there an alternative view that should prevail? Beyond being bad for the community at large, is the broader impact of no-holds-barred, short-term profit maximization actually bad for the shareholder? That, in essence, was what Indra Nooyi was asking me when she unveiled Performance with Purpose. And it's that core question that unfortunately, in much of the corporate world today, remains broadly unanswered or misunderstood.

The PepsiCo Challenge

Shortly after Performance with Purpose was unveiled, Nelson Peltz and a few other investors and observers responded with skepticism and even outright disdain. Indra explained the new effort forcefully and convincingly. Few doubted—and she explicitly acknowledged—that the company would be less profitable in the short term under the terms of her plan. If PepsiCo was going to invest in new, healthier consumer products, in more environmentally sustainable production processes, and in a more employee-centered approach, the company would have to redirect a portion of its sales and marketing budget. That could give competitors a short-term advantage. But that then prompted another question: Was that permissible given the prevailing view of "good" corporate governance?

As some of Indra's critics argued, Performance with Purpose was explicitly distinct from Henry Ford's plan to build a large new factory in Dearborn. To their way of thinking, employee-centered personnel policies were nothing like a down payment on the company's future profits. Her strategy was more akin to corporate altruism. Indra and I took a different view. After I set aside the rather turgid legal memorandum provided to us by a large law firm, my team at PepsiCo, as noted, began to dive more deeply into the history of corporations. And what became clear was that Indra's critics, like others in the corporate world, were too prone to frame the distinction between short-term and long-term profits as something akin to the distinction between profit-making and altruistic sensibilities. In reality, the two notions are entirely different. Today this muddle continues to be a source of ongoing confusion.

Performance with Purpose, described by critics at the time as a cleverly shrouded effort to place stakeholder interests above those of PepsiCo's shareholders, was not designed as any sort of philanthropic enterprise. PepsiCo's management team simply saw how the marketplace was evolving and wanted to put the company in a position to serve consumers not only through the following month or year but several years down the road as well. Indra's thinking was driven exclusively by a worry that, as obesity and other health challenges grew to become more prevalent concerns, consumers would likely refrain from purchasing fun-for-you drinks and snacks in the same volume. Governments might impose unrealistic and unquantified policies, regulations, or even taxes. To that end, Performance with Purpose was management's attempt to prepare PepsiCo to be a market leader down the line, to make the company's success more sustainable.

But Indra's thinking went a step beyond even that. She recognized that if the company came to be viewed as imposing health costs on society at large—if, for example, a company producing what some called junk food came to be viewed like the second coming of Philip Morris— PepsiCo might lose what some call its "social license" to operate. Government might do to potato chips suffused with saturated fat what government today is doing to menthol cigarettes: namely, banning them from the marketplace altogether. If our beverage facilities extracted too much from a regional water table, she worried that our production capacity might be limited by regulation. So to Indra's way of thinking, reducing the company's environmental impact and finding ways to expand its product portfolio wasn't about "doing good." It was PepsiCo's effort to protect its long-term business model.

Indra's insight—and one that pierces the "shareholder first" ethos articulated by Berle and more frequently today ascribed to Milton Friedman—was that short-term profits were liable to cut against a company's ability to make more money. Those looking for quick returns could criticize her efforts as unrealistic, but PepsiCo realized that investing in society's well-being would be as rewarding for a food and beverage company as investing in a new massive production facility in River Rouge outside of Dearborn, Michigan, could be for Ford Motor Company in 1919. Set any environmental, employee-, or consumer-oriented concern aside—sacrificing short-term profits was explicitly in the long-term interests of the company's shareholders.

As it was, Indra's vision was entirely prescient. In the early days of PepsiCo's investment in Performance with Purpose, the company's financial performance ebbed a bit and suffered in relation to its competitors. Brand Pepsi, which had long reigned as America's second-best-selling soft drink after Coca-Cola, fell to third behind Diet Coke. And that shift was reflected in the value of each company's respective equity: PepsiCo's value slipped in 2010, while Coca-Cola's rose by 40 percent.[34]

But during that same period, PepsiCo began investing worldwide in ways to replenish water supplies. The company elevated health-conscious brands, such as Quaker Oats. And the company's research and development teams began developing ready-to-drink teas, new sugar-free soft drinks, Propel, and Life Water. It found healthier ways to apply salt to chips and crafted vegetable-based alternatives to potato chips. And those investments paid off for shareholders: Three years after the fateful encounter with Peltz, PepsiCo's earnings per share grew 10 percent even as its less future-minded competitors' value experienced what they call a "correction."[35]

Performance with Purpose proved to be a success not because of its philanthropic impact but because it served as a foundation for the company's long-term success. Perhaps more important, by steering both the company and industry away from its reliance on products and production methods that threatened the company's stakeholders, Indra helped obviate the most dire threat to PepsiCo's shareholders. And while it's impossible to know what might have happened had Indra not exercised such prescient leadership, it's not hard to imagine how broad-based government regulations might have curtailed the company's ability to operate and sell its products in the manner and quantity investors had come to expect. Performance with Purpose clearly advanced PepsiCo's business interests. I'm proud to have been a part of it.

I clearly remember Indra describing to me the difference between corporate social responsibility and corporate responsibility. Corporate social responsibility, she said, was simply philanthropy, what a company did with its money after it was made. Corporate responsibility was how a company made its money. PepsiCo has made more money over the long term for its shareholders because it was a responsible corporation.

The Hidden Contours of Today's Debate

If PepsiCo's history appears on paper to be a successful rejoinder to the "short-termism" that now seems to be so prevalent on Wall Street, Indra's persistence remains an outlier. That's not simply because corporate leaders have lost sight of Merrick Dodd's argument from over 90 years ago. It's in large part because Milton Friedman's admonition written decades later that a corporation has "one and only one social responsibility—to increase its profits" has largely been misinterpreted on Wall Street in the years since.[36] I believe it's well past time for conventional wisdom to issue a market correction of its own. I strongly believe we need to look at this issue from a legal standpoint (within the wisdom of law) and not solely as some sort of economic maxim.

Here's the reality: Friedman's views, which began to take hold in the 1960s and then became much more widely publicized in the 1970s and after, were born from not just an embrace of unadorned greed. Rather, like Berle before him, Friedman worried that if corporations began to put other concerns above profit—or even to put other factors on an equal footing—the underlying businesses would be more likely to fail, souring broad-based investor confidence, curtailing growth, and undermining the economy as a whole. The Dodd-Berle debate had centered on legal doctrine, and Friedman, by the 1970s, was more focused on economics. But the substance of their inquiries focused on the same core problem: namely, defining the incentives that drive corporate decision-making.

Unfortunately, two core elements of Friedman's thinking have been lost amid Wall Street's zeal to emphasize quarterly returns as the corporate world's preeminent measuring stick. First, Friedman never suggested that corporations should market poisonous foodstuffs or dangerous baby toys in their pursuits of profit. Rather, his view was that the market would naturally disincentivize companies from selling products that did not serve the market well, either through consumer choice or otherwise by statute or regulation. As he put it, business has only one social responsibility, and that is to increase its profits "so long as it stays within the rules of the game [and] engages in open and free competition without deception or fraud."[37]

But there was another element to Friedman's maxim, one that has too often been overlooked: He never specified the time frame over which businesses should focus their quest for returns.

For example, Friedman notes, "[I]t may well be in the long-run interest of a corporation that is a major employer in a small community to devote resources to providing amenities to that community or to improving government." However, Friedman would say that it's disingenuous to call this "social responsibility." It's nothing more than old-fashioned smart capitalism.[38]

In the decades since his famous article was published in the *New York Times Magazine*, many have come to presume that Friedman believed that corporations were obligated to prioritize maximizing profits quarter-by-quarter. But upon closer examination, it's not clear at all that Friedman would have castigated any given executive for choosing a larger return tomorrow over a smaller return today. By the University of Chicago economist's way of thinking, a CEO should not have license to pursue a philanthropic effort in lieu of profit. But she certainly *could* choose to forgo a big shareholder payday in the near-term for an investment likely to bring in more revenue down the line and make the business more sustainable in the future.

Oddly enough, by conveniently forgetting those two elements of Friedman's work, certain voices on Wall Street have managed to hijack his legacy in defense of a philosophy that prizes short-term profit seeking. When the Business Roundtable, a trade organization representing businesses including PepsiCo, released a statement in 2019 arguing that companies need to look beyond short-term interests,[39] the Council of Institutional Investors reacted with ferocity: "Accountability to everyone means accountability to no one," the trade group countered. "If 'stakeholder governance' and 'sustainability' become hiding places for poor management, or for stalling needed change, the economy more generally will lose out."[40]

Today's debate over *timing* should not be obscured by confusion over *purpose*. The Business Roundtable's point is entirely in line with Friedman's broader perspective. In much the same way that long-term interests should not be sacrificed for short-term returns, corporations cannot ignore the interests of customers, employees, and broader communities. That's not because, as the Council of Institutional Investors would seem to suggest, the CEOs who comprise the Roundtable are abandoning the doctrine of shareholder primacy. It's that the men and women responsible for serving shareholders have become increasingly aware that if they ignore their other stakeholders, other factors—most notably possible onerous government regulation—will curtail their ability to perform for shareholders down the line.

The question then is how to maintain shareholder primacy while ridding C-suites of their obsession with short-term results. In other words, we need to create a mechanism that allows those who prioritize long-term thinking a way to ensure that they are not inadvertently incentivized to mismanage a growing enterprise. That is, potentially, a difficult needle to thread. But it's not the first time that the broader business environment had to correct for misplaced incentives. When considering how best to dial back Wall Street's obsession with quarterly numbers while performing for shareholders, we need to look back at how similar shifts have been accomplished in the past. And to that end, there's no better place to start than with the market crash of 1929.

The Path Forward

The bull market of the 1920s had unquestionably been rife with perverse incentives. To drive up stock prices, corporate executives had sometimes obscured news that might dampen investor enthusiasm. When selling securities to their clients, stockbrokers had frequently withheld crucial information. So when, in 1929, investors suddenly lost faith in the value of their securities, panic ensued, with a dramatic sell-off that presaged the Great Depression of the 1930s. To reestablish confidence in the broader marketplace, Franklin Delano Roosevelt's (FDR) Administration, elected in 1932, championed legislation imposing new standards in 1933 and establishing the Securities and Exchange Commission (SEC) in 1934.

FDR subsequently appointed Joseph P. Kennedy, a maven of the 1920s stock market, to be the SEC's chairman. And while Kennedy remains a controversial historical figure today, the Roosevelt Administration's reform approach has emerged as a model: To restore public confidence, regulators needed to ensure that the information that investors receive about individual companies is, in fact, accurate. But rather than issue complex regulation, they relied on a simple approach: Washington began requiring companies to undergo independent audits on a quarterly basis using generally accepted accounting principles, or GAAP. Moreover, the commission required publicly-traded companies to make those audits widely available.[41]

Sunshine almost immediately proved to be an ample disinfectant, and this approach has largely withstood the test of time. Ironically, however, the quarterly audits that became standard during the New Deal are now the bane of those who want corporations to take a longer view. The precedent remains: Simply setting reasonable standards can vastly change the incentives driving corporate behavior. Today that wisdom should prompt those who support the Business Roundtable's position to develop objective standards beyond the quarterly financial results. We need to help investors understand a corporation's viability in the long term.

This can be done though any number of distinct strategies. Some argue that we should upend the core arrangement between business and society—that we should shift the purpose of what are now profit-seeking enterprises to be more publicly minded. On the fringes, that could well prove successful. Some corporations today are being chartered as B Corporations, which unlike their more traditional counterparts are designed to champion the betterment of society.[42] But for those who remain convinced, like me, that investor concerns should remain the primary force keeping executives focused on returns, shareholder focus will remain *sine qua non.*

Here's my core concern: Businesses that do not put shareholder interests first will almost inevitably struggle to draw large interest from the community of global investors, both big and small. For that reason, the more fundamental question today is whether we can incentivize shareholder-oriented businesses to place more value on sustainable profit than short-term gain.[43] Our aim, in other words, should be less to forestall the responsibility executives have to drive up short-term profits and more to ensure that a corporation can be judged against its ability to produce sustainable profits into the future. So how do we do *that*?

To begin, we need to focus on standards. In the 1920s, securities could not be properly evaluated or compared against one another because companies too often failed to release truthful accounts of their own situations. New Deal reforms dealt with that simply by mandating that publicly-traded companies audit their books four times a year using standard methods and then release those audits to the public. If a company falsified that accounting, the SEC was authorized to punish it with fines or worse, creating an incentive for honesty, truthfulness, and accuracy. Today the same basic principle should be applied again but in such a way to require corporations to release the long-term impact they are poised to have on society. We need, in other words, an analog to the New Deal reforms that provides for what some call "non-financial reporting."[44]

This is, admittedly, a more complicated and nuanced challenge. But if a corporation is emitting pollutants liable to sicken nearby residents or worsen climate challenges—or if a company is selling unhealthy products or depleting a natural resource such as water—executives should be required to disclose not only the materiality of the risk associated with these activities but also what it is doing to address them. And then we should let the market determine how those broader risks affect the corporation's underlying value.

Already, various efforts have been made to establish non-financial supplements to the quarterly, GAAP-standardized financial statements that companies have released since the SEC issued its mandate nearly a century ago. The Ceres organization created the Global Reporting Initiative (GRI) in 1997, and Dow Jones followed up with Sustainability Indices (DJSI) two years later.[45] But the GRI and DJSI are not yet embraced by every corporation—some companies see these sustainability efforts as little more than marketing ploys and are loath to subject themselves to this sort of rigorous scrutiny. And because no standardization exists across industries and firms, attempts to verify any company's claims are very difficult. The SEC has now released proposed environmental, social, and governance (ESG) disclosure standards for public companies.[46]

Required ESG disclosure will focus corporate leaders on the fact that corporate interests are not adverse to those of society. This "adversity" is what some who inaccurately espouse the Friedman framework want us to believe. In reality, the interests of business and society are interdependent. Society depends upon corporations for wealth creation, jobs, and goods. Corporations depend upon society for an educated and healthy workforce and for natural resources.

I believe a responsible corporation legally must broaden and extend its horizons to societal constituents beyond shareholders. Not only is such a corporation responsible, it is also smart. Such a corporation must do this to survive in the long term. Think about it. It is only because many view the corporation as a purely economic actor that we even ask ourselves why corporate responsibility should be a question at all. A person would not ask such a question about herself or even me.

You might say that I'm not a responsible person or that I'm being irresponsible, *but* your assumption is that I should be responsible or try to be.

Most of us care about the consequences of our actions. And if we don't, tort law can hold us responsible for damages if someone sues us.

But that is not the reason we are responsible people. Most of us do not want to hurt someone else, and if we really don't care and are really indifferent to the consequences of our actions, we are viewed as a psychiatric case or, worse, criminally reckless.

A focus on accurate, required ESG disclosures will make American corporations more responsible—the disclosures will address matters that if ignored by business can harm society—and give investors much greater insight about the business's time horizon, whether short term or long term.[47]

Toward Profitable Sustainability

When the so-called era of globalization emerged several decades ago, corporate executives were often quick to make the most of the consequent opportunities. By reconsidering where they incorporated their businesses, where they hired their talent, where they extracted natural resources, and where they produced their products, they were able to enhance their profit margins and reach new consumers. Many surely felt as though failure to take advantage would be inconsistent with the maximization of profits for shareholders. It would be a dereliction of duty to not sustain profits. Absent shifting production off-shore, they would have paid more for labor. Without establishing factories in countries with less stringent environmental protections, manufacturing costs would have grown. In a world where consumers almost invariably want more for less, globalization created vast new opportunities in the short term, and many executive teams were bent on taking advantage. Stakeholders in both the United States and in the new countries were ignored.

Today, however, many of the corporations that embraced globalization with abandon are suddenly paying a price. It's not just that globalization led many to trim inventories ahead of a pandemic and that a lack of inventory left a range of companies unusually vulnerable to disruptions in the global supply chain like those created by Russia's invasion of Ukraine. It's that, in many cases, the backlash against the *social* impacts of globalization has sparked a worldwide embrace of anti-business populism.

This is a clear example of how short-termism imperils long-term corporate interests. Citizens and government officials are now working to counteract what they see as the deleterious race to the bottom on costs. Donald Trump's emergence as the Republican Party's standard bearer was born in large part from a sense that the American working classes were getting the short end of the modern economic stick. The Biden Administration's pursuit of a global floor for corporate tax rates is born from much the same frustration. And none of this is an accident. Corporate leaders who believed themselves to be doing the right thing by taking advantage of globalization to maximize shareholder profits are now on their heels by a backlash from any number of stakeholders.

This should be an object lesson moving forward. There's a balance to be struck between the view that corporations should be exclusively focused on profits and the notion that a corporation should be exclusively focused on profits in the *short term.* Even if you believe that executives should maintain a focus on the health of their business, they should have sufficient leeway to factor in the interests of various stakeholders: employees, consumers, and community members alike. And that's not because they are altruistic or tenderhearted. It's because failure to honor a company's stakeholders will almost always work against shareholder interests in the long term.

The proof of the pudding is in the eating. PepsiCo's investments in reducing the sugar, salt, and fat in its product portfolio, in conserving water and reducing carbon emissions, in minimizing plastic waste, and in attracting talented employees concerned about work-life balance, paid off in spades. The company's healthier offerings rose from 28 to 50 percent of revenue between 2006 and 2017 even while reducing the use of water by a quarter and raising women up to comprise nearly 40 percent of the company's senior management. All the while, revenue grew 80 percent, and PepsiCo outperformed the S&P 500.[48]

This performance benefited both PepsiCo's shareholders and its stakeholders. Adam Smith, the philosophical father of modern capitalism, got it right when he said the greatest contribution any company can make to society will always be measuring the pie on the table at which we dine.[49]

That's a lesson both for the leadership of corporate America and for those who play a part in setting the incentives for corporate leaders. The corollary to Milton Friedman's axiomatic focus on shareholder primacy is that profitability and sustainability aren't necessarily at odds with one another—and that in the long term they're almost surely aligned. The now long-running debate between those who pit "shareholder primacy" against "stakeholder concerns" generates more heat than light. The greater good need not be adverse to those who care about earnings and profits. In the long run, attending to broader and more global concerns will almost always redound to the shareholder's benefit.

As noted, the world's problems are the corporation's problems because, simply put, we are all in this together. Society needs corporations and corporations need society, at least if they wish to continue to have consumers for their products and services.[50]

As I wrote several years ago in *The Notre Dame Journal of Law, Ethics & Public Policy*, a proper representation of the needs of society, the environment, and the corporation is not the classic Venn diagram of three overlapping circles with a sweet spot where they intersect. It is instead three concentric rings, with the business—which cannot exist except within the society that created and sustains it—in the middle surrounded by society, which in turn is embedded in the environment, apart from which it cannot exist.[51]

Our problems will not be solved in any one person's lifetime. A generation comes, a generation goes, but the earth abides forever (Ecclesiastes 1:4). Because corporations theoretically have perpetual existence, we are most fortunate to have institutions that straddle national borders, that span generations of humankind, that can make a difference for good, and that have the advantage—and the responsibility—of taking a long-term perspective. For me, working toward this objective was indeed a righteous cause.[52]

CHAPTER FOUR

CRIME IN THE SUITES

"Keep It Up"

I was under no illusions when, in the summer of 2002, White House Counsel Alberto Gonzales called and asked me and FBI Director Robert Mueller to brief President George W. Bush on our work combating white-collar crime. By that point, the media had already established the narrative that the President's Corporate Fraud Task Force, which I chaired, was successfully pursuing an aggressive law enforcement agenda. However, some thought our efforts were unnecessarily demonizing business in the public square. So we understood implicitly that some of the President's economic advisers were inevitably angling to get the President to perhaps criticize our work. Gonzales's call, in other words, was less an invitation to a meeting and more the announcement of a coming showdown. And if we were going to continue on, we would have to justify the determined enforcement posture we'd taken against corporate fraud.

The FBI Director, with his security detail, had swung by my office at the imposing building on Pennsylvania Avenue known as Main Justice to pick me up on the way to the White House. Seated together in the back seat of a heavily armored SUV, Bob and I discussed how we might approach the briefing. In broad agreement that our presentation would be less powerful as a discussion of a generalized law enforcement strategy, we decided instead to give the President an unvarnished look at some of the misconduct we had uncovered during the course of our investigative work together while maintaining grand jury secrecy. So rather than lead a strategy session, we decided to structure the briefing as a series of vignettes.

Arriving at the White House, we climbed out of the SUV, passed the marine guarding the door to the West Wing, and walked through a corridor into the Roosevelt Room, the impressive conference room steps from the Oval Office. Several of the President's economic advisers subsequently filtered in, taking seats across the table from the two of us and leaving the chair in the center open for the President. Knowing that several of them were almost certainly the people who I had been told were critical of our Task Force, we nevertheless engaged in some idle chitchat. Neither side knew exactly what the other would present, but everyone knew that the outcome of this meeting would be important to white-collar law enforcement.

Right on schedule, the President walked in. Charming as always, he displayed his penchant for disarming almost any tense situation with a barrage of humorous observations and jokes. But when he then invited us to begin the briefing, the mood of the room immediately became serious. Without anyone saying it explicitly, there was no mistaking in my mind that Bob and I were up against it, with the people on the other side of the table waiting to pounce on any mistake or misstep.

The drama of the stories we told built outrage from one to the next. We walked through the specifics that had defined Enron's recent implosion, the way corporate executives had conspired with outside auditors to give investors the false impression that the company had much more money, and boasted much more impressive profits, than was actually the case. We explained how, when Richard Scrushy, the CEO of HealthSouth, had been told that the company would not meet its quarterly targets, he asked how much "dirt" was required to plug the hole.[53] We revealed how another CEO had lied outright to the auditor who was preparing to report on a company's financial position to the public. And as we told each successive story, two things happened. The advisers flanking the President began to look increasingly sheepish and at times flustered. Meanwhile, the President began to become visibly angry.

Presumably, the President's aides, having expected us to use our time to lay out the legal or strategy theories that justified our approach to dealing with the corporate scandals, had prepared some sort of response. I can only guess at what it was. Perhaps they would have posited the completely unjustified and growing fear that federal prosecution was undermining business confidence at a moment when, in the aftermath of 9/11, the market remained skittish about the nation's economic condition. But the narratives we presented were so stark, the fraud so blatant and rife, that there was very little they could say without looking foolish.

As it was, before anyone on the White House staff could even attempt to counter our presentation, the President gave us a definitive response. He looked at us and then, as if to suggest that everyone on his side of the table must be in agreement, said: "Well, we certainly can't let people get away with this. Good job, LT. Good job, Bobby. Keep it up." The discussion was effectively over. He promptly stood up, winked at us, and left the room.

That was a high point. The Corporate Fraud Task Force would go on to produce solid results in the fight against white-collar crime in the months and years that followed, several of which I'll detail below. But as time went on, I'm sorry to report that the rigor of white-collar enforcement dissipated. Simply put, the federal government over time lost its stomach for the fight. The Bush Administration's approach to keeping corporate executives in line has subsequently been castigated by the left and right alike, though for different reasons. And as a result, even in a moment when the nation is newly focused on crime—generally violent and property crime—the spirit of near-impunity of business wrongdoing that prevailed a quarter-century ago has seemingly gone unaddressed.

That must change. We can't fight crime on the streets while ignoring crime in the suites. Turning a blind eye to white-collar criminality is an affront to the victims of fraud, as those who regularly castigate business are right to argue. But acquiescence also hinders the system of free enterprise because nefarious actors get a leg up on those who follow the rules and because, eventually, corporate America *writ large* pays for corporate crime through stricter and sometimes unwise and/or unnecessary regulatory regimes. Both to satisfy the demands of justice and to prevent a large-scale expansion of the regulatory state, government needs to take a much more aggressive approach to criminal enforcement as it relates to business wrongdoing. And that means taking a comprehensive approach, one that targets bad actors, reckless executives, and bad corporate entities alike.

The Question of Culpability

For those who haven't spent their lives navigating the ins and outs of corporate law, the issue of fraud can sometimes seem inscrutable. It's rarely hard to identify who should be punished when something is stolen from someone's home—the burglar is clearly at fault. But it can be more difficult to assign culpability in cases of corporate fraud. If a business has somehow done something underhanded, whom should the government hold responsible? What if a company misreports its profits in order to drive up its stock price? Should the relatively low-level person in the finance department who unwittingly testified to the figure's veracity take the brunt of the blame? Or the executive who failed to oversee the wayward employee—or even hinted that the employee might be rewarded for fudging the numbers? Or the people who own the company through its shares and therefore hired the executive who oversaw the underlying fraud?

That underlying confusion points to another host of questions. Should the people and institutions that have committed the fraud be subject to criminal enforcement or civil accountability or both? If a pharmaceutical company puts the wrong amount of a given drug in a pill—if, for example, it dilutes a medication in order to increase the corporation's profits—the people running the company stand a good chance of going to prison. If, however, an office supply company sells reams of paper that were all a few sheets short for the same reason, it would not be at nearly so much risk—and rightly so. But what of a company that makes certain people richer and other people poorer by purposely misstating its financial situation? Should the government pursue justice through civil enforcement, which would assign a fine and/or a civil penalty, or through criminal enforcement, which could result in much harsher sanctions?

The answers to these two sets of questions aren't uniform or formulaic, and over decades the answers have evolved. But before even addressing what government *should* do in response to clear evidence of business wrongdoing—or even what it *does* do today—we need to understand what it *can* do. And the answer to that question was delivered more than a century ago in a case known as the *New York Central RR* decision, a case that remains, even today, incredibly important in setting the parameters for how government responds to evidence of corporate wrongdoing.[54]

The economic context for the case is important. In the early twentieth century, a handful of large railroads played an outsized role in the American economy. Most every industrial company with designs to send its wares around the country needed to secure space on the nation's freight trains to bring its products to market. Realizing that the real money to be made from shippers came from securing the business of larger companies, the railroads had begun a practice in the nineteenth century of giving "rebates" to their best customers. The problem, as regulators began to realize, was that the rebates actually perverted the marketplace by giving an unfair advantage to big companies, which were much more likely to get a rebate than their smaller competitors. Rebates amounted to an unacceptable anti-competitive business practice.

To level the playing field, Congress passed, in response, a series of laws empowering Washington to regulate interstate commerce. Among them was clear policy designed to outlaw the practice of rebating. Not long thereafter, investigators uncovered evidence that New York Central had begun offering rebates to the American Sugar Refining Company, which was shipping massive loads of sugar from New York City to Detroit. Typically, the railroad charged 23 cents per 100 pounds on that route. But the New York Central's traffic manager, acting on behalf of the corporation, agreed to what amounted to a 20 percent discount, putting the American Sugar Refining Company's competition at a distinct disadvantage.

The facts of this case may have been routine, but the prosecution was not. Henry Stimson, the lead prosecutor, a historic public servant who would go on to serve both as Secretary of State and Secretary of War, decided to go beyond prosecuting the agents of the company who had agreed to provide the illegal rebate. He decided to prosecute the company itself, the institution that had, by way of proxy, sanctioned the behavior. It was, after all, the New York Central's owners, namely its shareholders, who benefited from the deluge of traffic its agents had secured by offering the rebate. And so, in the government's view, the company itself, and by proxy its owners, should be punished for having failed to guarantee adherence to the law.[55]

In what became a landmark decision, New York Central was not only convicted but was also ordered to pay $108,000 in restitution. The company appealed the case all the way to the Supreme Court, arguing, in essence, that a corporation could not be held *criminally* responsible for the mere behavior of its employees. But the Supreme Court disagreed, ruling in the government's favor that:

> We see no valid objection in law, and every reason in public policy, why the corporation, which profits by the transaction, and can only act through its agents and officers, shall be held punishable

by fine because of the knowledge and intent of its agents to whom it has intrusted (sic) authority to act in the subject-matter of making and fixing rates of transportation, and whose knowledge and purposes may well be attributed to the corporation for which the agents act.[56]

While that ruling did not specify that a prosecutor *must* pursue a corporation in the case of wrongdoing—a rogue agent might alone be responsible—the ruling established a host of possibilities. The doctrine of corporate criminal liability today provides for real consequences—license suspensions, fines, permit denials, and more—when and if a corporation runs afoul of the law. The question remains, however, how corporations might interpret the ensuing implications: Would prosecutors use this new tool to ensure that they changed the behavior of corporations in order to adhere to the law? Or would the potential sanctions simply become something to be almost entirely ignored or, as some might describe it, "the cost of doing business"?[57]

The Evolution of Standards

The public's preoccupation with various categories of crime invariably ebb and flow. During the 1980s, for example, drug enforcement became a pre-eminent focus. In the early 1990s, that concern broadened to include street and violent crime more comprehensively. In the wake of the 9/11 attacks, the American public was overwhelmingly preoccupied with terrorism. But for a few years, largely set in conjunction with the early war on terror, our nation set a certain bright spotlight on corporate malfeasance. That was for a very good reason: Time and again, the public was overrun with examples of executives abusing their positions to enrich themselves at the expense of investors and others. Corporate America seemed to be running amok.

This wasn't the first time that the American public had been made aware of a widespread white-collar crime. Fraud played an important role in prompting the stock market crash of 1929, and the rules that govern corporate behavior today, insomuch as they relate to a public company's finances, are built largely on a foundation of laws established in the 1930s to ensure that securities are traded with accurate information available to all. From time to time during the subsequent decades—during the savings and loan (S&L) crisis of the 1980s, for example—the media tended to focus a bit more attention on white-collar crime even if fraud cases are often relegated to the business section, rather than the front page, of any given newspaper.

In the early 2000s, a series of very high-profile accusations and investigations made clear that widespread criminal conduct had come to prevail across a whole range of companies. Enron, HealthSouth, WorldCom, and Adelphia were among the companies accused of cheating investors and worse. Without having necessarily wrapped their minds around the details, Americans suddenly became aware that a certain number of rich, entitled executives viewed themselves as above the law. So just as I was beginning my service as Deputy Attorney General, the Justice Department was forced to confront a number of highly publicized incidents of corporate fraud. The question then was what to do about it.

This was, of course, before Bob Mueller and I had been summoned to the White House. And no one knew exactly the extent of the damage. So as the deluge of evidence grew to make clear that something was seriously wrong in the nation's executive ranks and corporate suites, we chose to send a signal to corporate America that the Bush Administration intended to bring real resources to bear on corporate fraud. The White House established the Corporate Fraud Task Force that, in my view, was best equipped to push along the sorts of corporate investigations and prosecutions that, for a variety of reasons related in part to the *New York Central RR* case, involved facts, laws, and regulations. And with prosecutors and investigators aligned and coordinated across a whole range of agencies, we got to work.

White-collar infractions are admittedly harder to prosecute than many other sorts of criminal offenses. If an individual is caught burglarizing a house, the perpetrator is subject to a predictable process: He is arrested, then arraigned, and the charges are then either dropped, brought to trial, or pled out. But in a case of corporate fraud, additional complications are the norm.

A prosecutor first has to determine whether the corporation is actually culpable—whether, in other words, the wrongdoing was not simply the fault of a rogue agent. If the criminal activity *is* done in the bowels of a company's operation without the consent or knowledge of any of the corporation's managers or executives, prosecutors can choose to decline prosecution in return for the company changing or clarifying procedures or policies. In other words, if a company suspected of having engaged in criminal activity agrees to, say, terminate rogue employees and establish new ways of ensuring nothing similar ever happens again, a prosecutor may decide to enter into what is typically called a "deferred prosecution agreement," or DPA, which may require the company to basically erect new safeguards against further abuse. Of course, the prosecutor can simply decline to bring a case against the company because the wrongful conduct did not benefit the business.

Deferred prosecution agreements can also serve as an easy way out for corporations who really *should* be held accountable for wrongdoing. And because white-collar cases can be difficult to investigate and prosecute, prosecutors are sometimes too willing to let individual executives avoid accountability. My predecessor as Deputy Attorney General, Eric Holder, issued a memo in the 1990s designed to help line prosecutors think about when and how to deal with companies and executives in white-collar cases. He laid out a series of factors—whether a company's senior management was involved in wrongdoing, whether the company was forthcoming about any internal investigation, whether the company had a plan to avoid future wrongdoing, etc.—that prosecutors could use when deciding whether to charge a company with a crime.

Eric Holder's guidance was well-intentioned. By establishing clear standards, he had hoped to incentivize cooperation by corporations under investigation. If a corporation's legal counsel understood that failure to clear certain hurdles was likely to lead to a federal indictment, he or she might be more willing to advise cooperation with the government. But for a number of reasons, Eric's memo did not, unfortunately, make sufficient impact. In the late 1990s and early 2000s, the horizon of corporate fraud widened, and the depth of wrongdoing seemed only to deepen. This was not the fault of Eric Holder, but it would become my job, as Holder's successor, to deal with the situation.

The Deluge Begins

The fraud revealed inside Enron was probably the most brazen corporate wrongdoing of its era. And despite losing any opportunity to go after the corrupt organization itself—the company went bankrupt soon after the fraud was made public—the Justice Department pursued several individuals, many of whom (CEO Jeff Skilling and CFO Andy Fastow, most notably) served prison sentences. But if Enron came to symbolize the fraud of the era, the company's auditor, Arthur Andersen, was more emblematic of the challenge prosecutors faced then and, in many ways, now. Obscured in the public's memory by Enron's implosion, Arthur Andersen may have more legal importance nearly a quarter-century later.

Again, the context is crucial. At the time of Enron's collapse, Arthur Andersen was a large professional partnership counted famously among the world's "Big Five" accounting firms. The partnership's book of business was not entirely undermined by the Enron scandal—the firm had many other prized accounts. Nor was this the first time that Arthur Andersen had gotten in trouble with the law.[58] And so, as the Deputy Attorney General and the person leading the Bush Administration's Corporation Fraud Task Force, I and my team were largely responsible for guiding the path forward that balanced the nation's broader economic interests with the need for justice and accountability.

To understand the Arthur Andersen story, you need to go back to the late 1920s and early 1930s. At the time, as previously noted, the markets were reeling from a broad sense that the information public companies were reporting regarding their internal finances was not accurate.

That was a large reason the stock market tumbled on Black Friday. And *that* was the reason that Congress and the Roosevelt Administration established a new system, centered on the newly formed Securities and Exchange Commission, that required companies to provide truthful financial information on a quarterly basis and to have the numbers they reported confirmed by an outside auditor. In the years and decades that followed, responsibility for doing that job fell disproportionately to the large accounting firms, an august group that included Arthur Andersen.

As it was, the person heading up Enron's account for Arthur Andersen faced what amounted to a dual mandate. He or she had to make an accurate accounting of the company's finances in any given quarter. But for some audit account executives, including perhaps those heading up Enron's account, there was another business mandate: keep the audit client happy and get more lucrative non-audit business from the client. And, as quickly became clear, those two mandates were in direct conflict. In order to maintain Enron's business, the people working on the energy company's account felt pressure to accommodate Enron while certifying their audit's accuracy.

It would have been one thing if Arthur Andersen's inaccurate certification of Enron's finances represented an aberration from the accounting firm's standard practice. This case might simply have been traced to a single wayward auditor on the accounting firm's Enron team. But, in fact, by the time Enron collapsed, Arthur Andersen had already compiled a long history of problematic professional conduct. As Jesse Eisinger wrote in *The Chickenshit Club*, "Andersen faced thirteen major state and federal investigations over accounting frauds in the years before and just after Enron."[59]

The federal government's previous approach had been telling. After it was revealed in 1998 that Waste Management, one of Arthur Andersen's clients, had overstated its earnings, the SEC chose to act against the accounting firm. But even after developing a strong case, rather than pursuing criminal enforcement, the Department of Justice agreed to let Arthur Andersen enter into a deferred prosecution agreement, a procedure that permitted the firm to avoid admitting any wrongdoing in exchange for a vow to abide by securities law going forward. But Andersen did not abide by its side of the bargain.[60, 61]

Less than a decade earlier, heightened levels of violent crime had compelled federal and state governments alike to impose criminal reforms that amounted to what some called "three strike" laws. If an individual was convicted of three consecutive felonies, legislators began requiring judges to sentence the person to a life sentence on the theory that he or she was clearly beyond rehabilitation. Here we had a professional partnership that had essentially racked up the same record with respect to white-collar crimes. And the question for those of us inside DOJ was whether we would put up with that sort of fraud and resolve yet another instance of wrongdoing civilly, or would we pursue criminal enforcement, recognizing, of course, that the firm was a large one with thousands of innocent partners and employees.

For those of us considering how to handle the case, the path forward appeared fraught. By the standards of justice, many wanted to simply throw the book at Arthur Andersen; these people were angered by Andersen's multiple acts of malfeasance. But Arthur Andersen's counsel argued that a criminal enforcement action, even a deferred prosecution agreement, would be inappropriate. Memories of 9/11 were fresh in the public's mind, and the economy still appeared at risk. Widespread fears of still further corporate fraud risked undermining faith in the market more broadly, and an indictment of a Big Five accounting firm was sure to create a sense of economic apprehension.

Our collective fear of initiating criminal enforcement was driven by another concern as well. Arthur Andersen's core business emanated from the public's trust in its work product. If the company were indicted for fraud, the whole concern could be in jeopardy. And if the firm went bankrupt or closed up shop, the people hurt would spread well beyond those who had worked on Enron's account to include the company's other partners and employees. If the accounting firm collapsed, innocent people could have their careers sidetracked. When you get down to it, Arthur Andersen's counsel were basically arguing, it seemed to me at the time, that the firm was too important to face any type of criminal sanction, including a deferred prosecution agreement, no matter how bad its wrongdoing, including document destruction and obstruction of justice.

I remained torn, but in the end, I thought an out-and-out indictment would be imprudent. As much as I felt strongly that we could not tolerate the firm's wrongful conduct, I worried about the economic implications of an indictment. That did not mean I was against some measure of real accountability; I favored criminal enforcement in some form of a DPA.[62] But Arthur Andersen strongly resisted even that, and the government really had no choice. In my mind, DOJ had been backed into a corner. Andersen was subsequently convicted at trial and forced to shutter. Years later, the verdict was overturned by the Supreme Court on a technicality involving an improper jury instruction. But I believe a clear message of deterrence had been sent. Wrongdoing of the type Andersen engaged in would not be tolerated, and organizations would be held accountable. We would not abide such criminal activity whereby paying subsequent fines in the civil arena appeared to many as nothing more than the cost of doing business.

To Bludgeon or Not to Bludgeon

Because Enron turned out to be just the tip of the iceberg, and Arthur Andersen further evidenced that corporate culture was a significant law enforcement problem, as previously noted, President Bush decided in 2002 to establish the Corporate Fraud Task Force.[63] In ways few realized, the decision was internally controversial. Task forces certainly were nothing new to law enforcement at the time—joint terrorism task forces, for example, existed in many of the nation's big cities. But the idea of bringing resources together from a range of agencies struck some as a kind of publicity stunt in 2002.[64] That was not my intention. So as the Task Force Chair, it was my job to make certain that it was real and would be effective.

Over the course of the next year, those of us at Main Justice were careful not to shift responsibility for investigating and prosecuting corporate fraud away from the line prosecutors who ordinarily would have taken the lead. But even as the Task Force took a light touch on interference, we kept close tabs on various efforts across the country, urging investigators and Assistant U.S. Attorneys not to lose focus. That oversight produced results. Beyond the cases that prompted headlines and news coverage—namely, federal action against companies including WorldCom, Tyco, and HealthSouth—by late May 2003, the Department of Justice had investigated nearly 500 individuals and companies, secured more than 250 convictions and guilty pleas, and obtained more than $85 million in restitution, fines, and forfeitures.[65]

Fortunately, it wasn't just the statistics that changed with the advent of the Task Force. It was also the Department's broader approach to corporate crime. Again, as previously noted, Eric Holder's memo, issued years earlier, had *recommended* that prosecutors use certain metrics and indicators when determining when and if to pursue a corporation's indictment. Had the company cooperated? Had executives taken quick action when realizing that someone was committing fraud on the inside? Had the company accepted responsibility or otherwise tried to obfuscate responsibility?

Several months after the formation of the Task Force, I decided to revise Eric Holder's memo. I created a mandatory standard, meaning that beyond being advisory, my new memorandum directed federal prosecutors to consider criminally charging a corporation under the circumstances outlined in the memo.[66] And I did something else, something that turned out to be quite controversial, much to my continuing consternation: I pushed for greater transparency. That may sound innocuous, but it set off a public firestorm.

When a corporation uncovers evidence of fraud within its ranks, executives often hire outside investigators and lawyers to find any potential wrongdoing. Those lawyers then go through the records and typically interview various employees to find out what happened. In the course of conducting these interviews, the lawyers are supposed to inform employees that whatever the employee shares in the course of the interview is covered by the corporation's attorney-client privilege, meaning that the corporation *could* waive the privilege without the employee's consent.[67] Of course, the employee can then refuse to speak with the investigator. But you can only imagine how that employee's boss might interpret this silence. Failure to cooperate would not be accepted by responsible businesses.

The question then is what happens with the content of those interviews if and when a prosecutor gets involved. In many cases, it's only after the internal investigation is complete that the Department of Justice may become aware of the full extent of any potential fraud. And then, in the course of the government's investigation, the corporation's lawyers generally try to persuade prosecutors *not* to criminally charge a company, urging the government to agree that the company's self-imposed remediation should suffice. Barring that, the lawyers might suggest that prosecutors agree to a DPA instead, thereby requiring the company to institute any number of reforms, pay a fine, or make other amends short of admitting to a crime.

Here's the rub: In the course of trying to convince a prosecutor not to issue an indictment, the company's lawyers may be asked to disclose *facts*. And that's for good reason. The company may be *claiming* that it has taken sufficient proactive measures to deal with previous acts of fraud, but how can a prosecutor know that to be true without truly understanding the facts? Perhaps more to the point: Why would an Assistant U.S. Attorney agree to recommend that a company *not* face a criminal indictment unless the company is entirely forthcoming and he or she understands the facts?

But too often many lawyers sought leniency while being unwilling to share facts. When prosecutors predicated any talk of a deferred prosecution on a company's willingness to share facts, the company's lawyers would sometimes claim that to disclose facts would constitute a waiver of the company's attorney-client privilege that could be used against the company in any subsequent civil litigation arising from the conduct under investigation. This waiver would occur because it was lawyers who were involved in gathering the facts. These lawyers wanted to receive cooperation credit without disclosing to the government the full facts of the investigation.

I want to be clear: I'm wholeheartedly in favor of maintaining the sanctity of the attorney-client relationship. I never wanted lawyers to tell the government what they had advised their clients or what questions clients had asked them. When lawyers are giving their client advice on how to handle legal issues, their conversations should be held in the strictest confidence. But that was in no way what most prosecutors were asking companies to do. Most prosecutors simply wanted to know the facts: Who had done what? What had happened to discipline those people? I didn't think the *facts* should be shielded by the claim of privilege. So here is what I wrote in my new, revised memo:

> One major focus of these revised guidelines is an increased emphasis on ensuring the authenticity of a corporation's cooperation. We have stated that in deciding whether to prosecute a corporation, prosecutors can look to whether the corporation has provided timely and voluntary disclosure. If possible, prosecutors may also consider the corporation's willingness to identify the culprits within the corporation, including senior executives; to make witnesses available; to disclose the complete results of its internal investigation; and in appropriate circumstance to waive attorney-client and work product protection.[68]

That suggestion, however worded in the memo, set off, as noted, a public firestorm like few I have ever encountered. Rarely did the legal community stand up to criticize the sorts of tactics prosecutors use to pressure those suspected of committing street crimes. But what about putting pressure on corporate executives or business organizations seeking leniency or cooperation credit? According to my critics, that was an utter outrage. *The New York Times* claimed that "corporate lawyers . . . contend that the [Thompson] memorandum is being used as a club to bludgeon companies into disclosing legal secrets . . . to avoid being indicted."[69]

To be clear, the employees themselves did not have claim on the privilege. The privilege was owned by the corporation.[70] And the facts that prosecutors sought were far from the types of conversations executives were having about legal strategy with their lawyers. But the critics' sanctimonious outcries could lead some to believe that I had proposed in my memo to rip up the Bill of Rights in its entirety. This criticism has endured. My sons believe that the memo will almost invariably be mentioned in my obituary. And perhaps it will. Nevertheless, I still maintain that my memo was legally sound and necessary. No company should be able to hide the truth and at the same time expect lenient treatment. Moreover, although DOJ policies have removed any reference to attorney-client privilege or attorney work product, disclosure of facts is still required of business organizations seeking cooperation credit.

The Authentic, Conservative Approach to Corporate Fraud

A singular theme dominated the reaction to my memo and more broadly framed a particular critique of the Bush Administration's determination to address corporate fraud as a criminal problem to be dealt with by law enforcement in an aggressive manner. Beyond objecting to the specious notion that we wanted to eviscerate attorney-client privilege, many of the Justice Department's detractors in conservative business circles argued that our law enforcement efforts were demonizing business with a resulting deleterious effect on the nation's economy. I sensed that set beneath a more targeted complaint about attorney-client privilege was an ideological contention centered on the government's role in holding white-collar criminals accountable. And in certain circles—perhaps most notably on the editorial pages of several newspapers and business magazines—that hostility was palpable.

Perhaps most pointedly, an op-ed that labeled my memo "odious" made the argument against aggressive white-collar crime enforcement entirely explicit. Its author, University of Chicago Law Professor Richard Epstein, argued that corporations were the victims of overzealous government lawyers who held all the cards because the specter of indictment was, in the end, worse than the prospect of a conviction:

> The corporation that has strong protections against false convictions—proof beyond a reasonable doubt of the elements of the crime, the ability to examine evidence or cross-examine witnesses—is helpless to protect itself. A conviction carries at most a million-dollar fine, but simple indictment, which lies wholly within the prosecutor's discretion, imposes multibillion-dollar losses. Faced with that kind of pressure, the indictment is all that matters.[71]

Framed in such a way as to suggest that C-suite executives were unfairly targeted and that out-of-control prosecutors had lost all sense of justice, Epstein offered a simple solution:

> The Department of Justice should engage in unilateral disarmament by disavowing the odious Thompson memo, and rethinking why it ever needs to threaten the nuclear option of a corporate indictment. For its part, our new Congress should repeal by statute the doctrines of vicarious liability for criminal conduct in a corporate context—because these give the government unwarranted and arbitrary power over corporations.[72]

As a lifelong conservative, I will admit today to finding Epstein's reasoning at best simply curious because the embrace of this ethos essentially turns a blind eye to business and corporate fraud. That's confounding for at least three core reasons. First, and perhaps most basic, it offends what is typically a more conservative sense of justice. Yes, the center-right's basic embrace of free enterprise suggests, as the famous American aphorism states, "that government is best which governs least."[73] But this, most certainly, does not mean that the law of the jungle should replace the rule of law.

Over the course of my lifetime, it has generally more often been Republicans rather than Democrats who have embraced the basic notion of "law and order." And so unilateral disarmament, as Epstein seems to embrace, of a key tool a prosecutor *could* use to hold rotten corporate entities accountable is in direct conflict with the prevailing conservative notion that wrongdoers should be held accountable. As is often said, if you do the crime, you should do the time, and that basic notion should apply to white-collar criminals and organizations as it does to any other criminal defendant.

Second, businesses that play by the rules are harmed explicitly by letting wrongdoers get away with fraud. Or, to put it another way, Epstein's "unilateral disarmament" would reward bad behavior to the detriment of the corporate world's good citizens. When an executive purposely lies to would-be investors about the financial standing of a company, that executive is stealing the opportunity that honest competitors have of attracting those same dollars. Why would conservatives want to insulate those executives and corporations that may support them from being held accountable? If we're prone to take a "broken windows" approach to street crime, why view corporate crime through a different lens?

Third, and maybe most ominous, these purportedly "conservative" objections to proper and effective enforcement of white-collar criminal conduct almost inevitably hasten the imposition of out-and-out regulation. The free enterprise system depends on the maintenance of certain norms. If those norms are left unheeded—if capitalism becomes a free-for-all where those with special standing in the marketplace can act with legal impunity—society will revolt. When this occurs, society will demand justice from those who previously had special or privileged power. And the new regime will almost inevitably be less free and more regulated than what previously existed.

You don't have to take my word for it. Look at what happened in the wake of the 2008 financial crisis. Government's failure to hold accountable those financial institutions that defrauded various victims through their abuse of mortgage-backed securities led to a broader economic meltdown. And in the wake of the ensuing collapse, Washington passed a broad-based financial reform, Dodd-Frank, that extended new regulations beyond the firms that had been guilty of defrauding borrowers and investors and thereby undermining the economy as a whole. The new regulatory regime also affected all non-financial, Main Street businesses that had absolutely nothing to do with the 2008 financial crisis.[74]

As General Counsel of PepsiCo at the time, I can attest to the thousands of hours and millions of dollars that corporate America was forced to spend to adhere to Dodd-Frank's myriad provisions. One provision, for example, required companies to certify that their business did not profit in any way from "conflict minerals," such as diamonds harvested from war-torn parts of Africa. With a supply chain as complex as PepsiCo's—the company had innumerable suppliers for everything from the ingredients in drinks and snacks to the plastics and packaging that allowed it to deliver those drinks and snacks—this certification became a rather complex and time-consuming exercise. And it had *nothing* to do with the causes of the 2008 financial crisis.[75]

It doesn't have to be this way. The alternative to a vast expansion of the regulatory state is, in the spirit of the Bush Administration's Corporate Fraud Task Force, strict enforcement of existing laws. The choice policymakers need to make is between a nanny state or a guardian state, one centered on sometimes mindless regulation or, alternatively, tough love. As I argued in a speech delivered nearly two decades ago: "Enforcement is not only the right approach, it's the conservative approach."[76] Advocates of *laissez-faire* don't do themselves any favors when they defend a system that will, in the long run, lead almost without exception to more regulation. In the end, strong and aggressive enforcement is the surest defense against arbitrary and mindless regulation.

How to End the Game of Whac-A-Mole—Forever

I remain proud of the Bush Administration's record on white-collar crime. To that end, I still smile when I think of the dour expressions on the faces of those skeptical White House aides when the President offered warm words of encouragement to Bob Mueller and me two decades ago. I don't even regret the controversy stirred by the notorious "Thompson Memo"— indeed, as I wrote earlier, I stand by my original position that it was not an attack on attorney-client privilege. But I'm pained to report two decades after I left federal service that our focus, effort, and determination has not lasted. Worse still, I fear we're continuing to backslide.

As the public's outrage over Enron, Arthur Andersen, WorldCom, Tyco, and a range of other frauds dissipated over the years, so has law enforcement's appetite for appropriate and aggressive criminal enforcement. And over the last two decades, I've watched with dismay from my perch outside government as the culture that opened the door to those scandals has reconstituted itself. Today, in all too many cases, the sense that paying even a large civil fine as a government sanction is "just the cost of doing business" is pervasive in American business. And that has given a proverbial green light to the same sorts of behaviors federal prosecutors and investigators pursued in the Bush Administration's Corporate Fraud Task Force with such vigor in the early 2000s.

This is most evident in the way that many prosecutors today approach white-collar criminal enforcement. These prosecutors are loath, perhaps even afraid, to criminally charge a company. So today, the *status quo ante* prevails. Today business organizations sometimes seem to operate with an air of impunity from criminal enforcement.

The Department of Justice has been very liberal in allowing corporate wrongdoers second and even third chances pursuant to non-prosecution agreements or deferred prosecution agreements.[77] White-collar criminal enforcement has seemingly become something of a perennial game of Whac-A-Mole. Take, as a prime example, the case of HSBC.

Less than a decade ago, HSBC signed a DPA in the wake of revelations that the bank had laundered money for Mexican and Colombian drug cartels. One provision of that initial agreement with prosecutors was that the bank remain clean through 2018. But before the bell tolled, HSBC's head trader was indicted and then convicted for a "front-running" scheme, the act of knowingly trading stocks ahead of the disclosure of news that would affect the price. And yet there were no additional repercussions for the company *despite the previous DPA*. And the story does not end there: In 2019, the company was permitted to sign yet another DPA after having been found to be helping account holders avoid paying certain taxes.[78]

Had most violent criminal offenders received similar leniency from prosecutors, many among the public would be outraged. But when it comes to white-collar crime, this sort of perennial lawbreaking is greeted too often with a yawn. And this is just one example of a growing and pervasive challenge for law enforcement.

Certainly, the root of the problem is in the corporate sphere, where some executives are too often willing to do whatever it takes to win in the marketplace even if it means violating the law. Corporate and business wrongdoing should never be tolerated.

The statistics tell the story. White-collar prosecutions fell by more than a quarter during the first three years of the Trump Administration, according to Justice Department and Syracuse University studies. Duke University Professor Brandon Garrett found that fines fell 76 percent. And the IRS, whose criminal investigators are often the tip of the spear when it comes to white-collar enforcement—they are often the first to discover evidence of fraud—began 36 percent fewer investigations.[79]

If the "broken windows" theory of law enforcement teaches us that minor failures to maintain order invite would-be criminals to be more daring, then this approach is a recipe for disaster in the business world where the rule of law should prevail. This is simply inexcusable.

United States District Judge Jed Rakoff, an eloquent advocate in public life for taking white-collar crime seriously, has written directly about the role of government leniency: "It's easier to make the [civil] case against the company and to have a nice press conference announcing a big fine and all that kind of hoopla. It's much harder to take the two or three years that it typically takes to work your way up the ladder to the highest-level people who were involved in the orchestration of criminal conduct."[80] And Rakoff thinks prosecutors need to get tough again: "It was only twenty years ago that things really changed, and there's no reason that they couldn't easily change back."[81]

Too often, in my opinion, retired government officials look back on their tenure, shake their heads, and argue that those who hold power today would do better simply to emulate their approach way back when. But in this case, I don't necessarily believe that prosecutors need to take exactly the same approach the Bush Administration took 20 years ago. I'm just arguing for more appropriate and aggressive white-collar criminal enforcement as with other types of criminal conduct.

The bad actors in the world of corporate fraud should be subject to vigorous criminal enforcement. Those who oversee them—those executives who are liable to benefit when ill-gotten gains or unreliable numbers define a quarterly report—should also be held accountable. And the corporations themselves—the shareholders who may stand to benefit when a corporation fails to discourage and root out bad behavior—need to know that the company may be held accountable if the executives fail to undertake appropriate oversight through the Board of Directors.

This personal call to action may lead some to believe I'm some sort of ornery, old liberal railing against the private sector. But even if my politics have changed as I've aged (they actually haven't changed), I'm not

Ralph Nader. As a conservative, I'm making this plea in large part because I believe more appropriate white-collar enforcement is the most important bulwark against more regulation, bigger government, and additional restrictions on free enterprise. Simply put, this is in the interest of free market capitalism.

No one can reasonably deny today that we've lost the edge in addressing white-collar crime and corporate fraud. This is not only a loss of a sense of equal justice. It's a blow against a vibrant and healthy economy and a system that rewards those who work hard and play by the rules. Those who would seek to win in the marketplace by cheating, fraud, and other criminal conduct need to be held accountable even in the criminal system if warranted. Surely, the era of failing corporate and executive integrity must come to an end.

CHAPTER FIVE

IT'S THE CULTURE THAT'S IMPORTANT!

The Real Thing

Fourteen months after Joya Williams's first day as an administrative assistant to Javier Sanchez Lamelas, Coca-Cola's Global Brand Director, she was recruited into an obvious criminal conspiracy. Her position at the company's Atlanta headquarters provided her with rare access to a whole range of corporate secrets: strategy documents, marketing plans, even samples of new products. When a couple of her acquaintances realized how valuable this information could be to Coke's competitors, especially PepsiCo, they hatched a plan. The conspirators decided to have Williams smuggle various secrets out of the office and then, using a series of pseudonyms and passthroughs, to sell those secrets to PepsiCo's head of innovation, Antonio Lucio.

When, months later, the conspiracy was exposed and the conspirators indicted in federal court, the FBI's efforts to ensnare them caught the bulk of the public's imagination. The details were undeniably tantalizing. A federal agent posing as a PepsiCo executive had worked out an elaborate scheme to lure the thieves out into the open. The subsequent takedown, which included a clandestine meeting at the Atlanta airport involving both a Girl Scout cookie box stuffed with rolls of $50s and $100s and an Armani bag containing a Coke product sample, seemed like something out of a movie. But in truth, the tradecraft and the police work weren't actually the most interesting part of the story. The most remarkable element was how the FBI caught wind of the conspiracy in the first place.[82]

Law enforcement hadn't relied on happenstance. Nor had Coca-Cola's security department managed to "catch" Williams stuffing documents and product samples out of headquarters. Quite the contrary, law enforcement got involved in the case because PepsiCo, in possession of the conspirators' initial cache of information, had chosen not to take the bait but rather to bring the evidence directly to the attention of the Coca-Cola company. Together, the two companies then approached the FBI. It was only after the two companies had alerted federal law enforcement agents to the conspiracy that the criminal investigators got involved. Which raises the question: Why did PepsiCo blow the whistle?

Nothing would give me more pleasure than reporting that the whole plot was foiled because a high-ranking executive made the brave decision to do the right thing. But the truth is that senior executives at the company's headquarters in Purchase, New York, only played a limited role. When the initial information and material arrived in the mail, it landed on the desk of Antonio Lucio's assistant. When she opened it, she quickly realized something was awry. But rather than consider how PepsiCo might best take advantage of this suspicious information, she did something else: She brought it to the PepsiCo executive primarily responsible for ensuring that PepsiCo followed the law. That is, she brought it to my office.

Of course, I wasn't immediately available—I was hurriedly preparing for a meeting in California. So Lucio's assistant handed it directly to my assistant, Theo Olmer, and Theo, risking my frustration at being interrupted, insisted that I look at the material before heading to the airport. I recall thinking to myself that I had more pressing things to do than look at this stuff. But Theo insisted. I was immediately suspicious—the material appeared fake—but I nevertheless brought the envelope's contents to PepsiCo's head of security, Dave Carpenter, a former Secret Service agent who I believe had previously headed up President Bill Clinton's protective detail. At my instruction, Carpenter then took the material to Atlanta on PepsiCo's corporate jet. Upon arrival, he presented the "stuff" to his counterpart at Coca-Cola. It quickly dawned on them that it was, in the words of one of Coca-Cola's famous marketing campaigns, "The Real Thing." And it was at that point that the contraband was brought to the attention of the FBI.

Credit where credit is due: The FBI agents who designed the sting deployed an ingenious counterplot to identify the culprits. But the *real* heroes of this story were the PepsiCo assistants who, rather than turning a blind eye to the materials, made a decision that foreclosed any chance of this devious scheme being ignored or, worse, being acted upon in the wrong way. These ladies knew that the company's expectation of them was that they would work with honesty and integrity to compete and win in the marketplace without breaking the rules. They knew this was the culture of PepsiCo. And they were absolutely right, subsequently receiving the prestigious Chairman's Award from PepsiCo CEO Steve Reinemund. This "follow your true north" tone at the top is what Steve constantly emphasized and preached, and they clearly got the message.

And that's what's so remarkable. At some companies, employees who turn a blind eye to unethical (but potentially advantageous) behavior are rewarded for their silence. At others, employees would be eager to gain a competitive advantage on a competitor, no matter how wrongful the sinister deed appeared. But at PepsiCo, corporate *culture* successfully steered employees in a different direction. No doubt, that's due in part because PepsiCo worked hard to only hire employees with good character. But it was more than just that. Both of the CEOs I worked with, Reinemund and Indra Nooyi, left no doubt about the ethical standards they expected employees to meet, regardless of the impact on the company's bottom line. Unfortunately, this approach is not uniform in the business world. Within the realm of corporate businesses, culture matters much more than many executives and board members realize or understand.

How to Set Yourself Up for Scandal

Joya Williams's crime, for which she was eventually sentenced to eight years in prison, is at first blush a cautionary tale about how a company can be victimized from within.[83] But within the broader realm of business bad behavior, sabotage or embezzlement are only small subsets. More often, companies are less the victims than they are perpetrators. To get ahead, to make a bigger profit or to outperform a competitor, they sometimes ignore legal requirements or embrace what is plainly unethical behavior. PepsiCo would itself have been culpable had it chosen to accept those stolen Coca-Cola materials for more examination. And that's the larger concern. Beyond protecting companies from wayward employees, we need to better understand why corporate executives so often engage in the sorts of unseemly, unethical, and frequently illegal activity that invariably undermines the public's broader faith in the business community.

When I first began working in corporate law almost five decades ago, concerns about business ethics were circumscribed to the realm of compliance. Corporate executives and Boards of Directors were primarily intent on ensuring that they *complied* with the explicit requirements as set forth in laws and regulations.

This approach continued, and in the early 1990s, when faced with evidence that businesses too regularly failed to comply with basic laws and regulations, the United States Sentencing Commission created a sort of incentive program to make business organizations more compliant. Under new guidelines, if a company was convicted of having failed to comply with a given standard, the company could catch a break of sorts. A fine might be reduced, for example, or a probationary period curtailed if the company demonstrated that it did, in fact, have an effective compliance regime in place.[84] As a result, companies eager to protect themselves needed help standing up and developing compliance programs. And so, like many lawyers at the time, I had a thriving legal practice helping companies write and implement effective compliance programs. And, I must admit, thinking back, that many of these programs were simply put on the shelf after I delivered them to the client.

I don't want to disparage the idea of these packaged compliance programs altogether—there are advantages to establishing clear sets of boundaries around certain behaviors. It is often worthwhile to spell out certain dangerous or unlawful behaviors. But what became clear in the months and years that followed the Sentencing Commission's guidelines—and what was crystalized remarkably well in a groundbreaking article by Harvard Business School Professor Lynn Paine—was that a lot of corporate behavior inevitably bleeds outside the four corners of any compliance program. Paine's argument, carefully crafted but remarkably profound, was that compliance rules were not sufficient in the promotion of corporate ethics.[85] The more crucial element was an organization's *culture*.

Recently, someone told me a story that bears on this very dynamic. Seated on the outdoor patio of a fancy restaurant, this person noticed a group of well-behaved teens chatting at a table several feet away from their parents. Suddenly, a bee descended on the table, prompting a look of terror from one young woman whose back was set against an expanse of grass. She didn't scream—something perhaps she had been told not to do in such a setting. But she did something that perhaps no one would have thought to prohibit in explicit terms: She threw the chicken on her plate ten feet over her shoulder and across the grass in the hopes that the bee would follow.

Now, it's entirely possible that the young woman would have chosen *not* to do that if her parents had explicitly forbidden her to throw food. But that, of course, wasn't precisely the problem. In the course of any single meal, a whole range of behaviors is appropriate, and there is a whole separate set of related behavior that is out-of-bounds. In the same way that a parent cannot be expected to delineate every behavior on each of those two lists, no compliance program can adequately account for every potential employee choice. That's why corporate *culture* is so crucial. It sets guidelines that can be applied outside the four corners of any compliance document or code of conduct.

For many of us who were working in the world of compliance at the time, Paine's argument was a revelation. Once she'd said it, it became perfectly plain that a simple compliance-oriented approach to corporate behavior was broadly inadequate. The dichotomy between what many presumed to be the two loci for bad behavior—individual workers who had gone astray and managers who had failed to properly supervise them—missed the fundamental reality: In ways that defy easy categorization, employees at all levels of a company send and receive messages about what they *ought* to do in furthering the company's interests. And it is those messages that largely determine whether any given organization will perform with integrity in its day-to-day business affairs.

Among others, Paine's article highlighted the case of Sears, which maintained in the early 1990s a chain of automobile repair shops. In 1992, state attorneys general across the country had charged Sears with defrauding customers by regularly selling them services they did not need. Investigations found case upon case of separate repair shops recommending new batteries to customers who simply needed their brakes replaced. The question was why the fraudulent activity was so widespread. Had Sears executives hired legions of cheats to run its repair shops? Had a memo gone out demanding that individual locations begin cheating the company's customers? In point of fact, that's *not* what had happened. Sears had simply adopted a corporate *culture* that tacitly encouraged cheating, all to terrible effect. It had promoted incentives for its employees without telling them it expected the incentives to be accomplished the right way—with integrity.[86]

As Paine noted: "Rarely do the character flaws of a lone actor fully explain corporate misconduct. More typically, unethical business practice involves the tacit, if not explicit, cooperation of others and reflects the values, attitudes, beliefs, language, and behavioral patterns that define an organization's operational culture."[87] That's what had bedeviled Sears. The company's corporate leadership had put so much pressure on individual outlets to garner additional revenue that individual mechanics and salespeople had felt compelled to take advantage of their customers. No one explicitly turned Sears into a bastion of fraud, but the culture made the result unavoidable.

The point Paine stressed—and a principle that has shaped my career moving forward—was that it's not enough to set up a strict compliance regime or to focus solely on the rules. As she quoted former SEC Chairman Richard Breeden in her article: "It is not an adequate ethical standard to aspire to get through the day without being indicted."[88] Rather, to maintain real integrity and, frankly, to avoid the sort of public fall from grace that befell Sears, companies need to mold cultures that encourage individual employees at all levels to behave the right way at all times. Boards of Directors and executives need to set a tone that steers the company on a path where ethics has primacy or else run the risk of a disastrous or embarrassing scandal in the future.

To Win at Too High a Cost

Even insofar as nearly every global industry involves intense globalized competition, automobile manufacturing is unusually competitive. When any one of the world's major automobile companies releases a new model, every element is subject to scrutiny, and the verdicts consumers render on its appeal reverberate up and down the supply chain. Sales figures quickly make clear whether the hundreds of millions of dollars invested on the front end are liable to bear sufficient fruit. And when a newly released vehicle is *not* successful, those involved in its design, production, marketing, and sales are almost invariably in a negative spotlight.

For that reason, it should be no mystery why, in 2006 and 2007, those involved in designing Volkswagen's new fleet of "clean diesel" vehicles felt themselves to be under a great deal of pressure. Not only was it their mandate to design cars that would appeal to carbon-conscious consumers all over the world, but diesel engines were also supposed to draw consumers intent on reducing their individualized carbon footprints. To that end, their work was a touchstone in the company's effort to establish itself as a global leader in environmentally friendly automobile manufacturing.

Initially, Volkswagen's efforts proceeded apace. The company came up with a design for sedans that tested well with consumers. The automobiles were both sporty and comfortable. But the designs were hampered by one significant flaw: To replace ordinary gasoline with diesel fuel, a car's engine must maintain a sufficient supply of an additive known as "AdBlue," which helps curtail emissions. Unfortunately, Volkswagen's engineers were unable to design models where the AdBlue tank was placed anywhere but in each model's trunk. And that hurdle reduced trunk space and forced the company to choose between a distasteful series of options.

The first was to delay release of the new line of vehicles until the engineers could find a workaround, likely costing Volkswagen many millions of euros. The second was to go with the existing design, though the marketing team argued that consumers would not likely buy vehicles with such limited trunk space. Third—and this option was not discussed openly—the company could reduce the size of the AdBlue tank, restoring the trunk to normal size. But this third option had a hitch: Without sufficient AdBlue, the vehicles were bound to spew significantly more toxic emissions. So to adhere to American standards, the company would need to develop software that enabled the car's internal software to cheat, modifying the car's emissions profile when the dynamometer detected that the car was being tested.

As revealed in the massive settlement that Volkswagen entered into with the United States government in 2016—that required the company to plead guilty to three felony counts and pay $4.3 billion in criminal and civil penalties—Volkswagen, unfortunately, chose this latter option.[89] Only after more than half a million deceptive vehicles had been sold to

American consumers, researchers at West Virginia University uncovered the underlying scheme, prompting federal investigators to take a closer look. But even when confronted with evidence of the conspiracy, Volkswagen executives continued to lie.[90] And when the public was finally made aware of the extent of the crime—cars in "cheat mode" would control exhaust, but those in "drive mode" emitted many times the regulatory limit—few could understand how a company with a positive international reputation for engineering prowess to uphold could be so stunningly deceptive.[91]

This is when I became involved. Having spent years overseeing the ethics and compliance program of a large public company and having worked during the full course of my career on the compliance regimes of companies as a defense lawyer in many industries—e.g., finance, banking, health care, and aerospace—officials at Volkswagen and the Department of Justice contacted me and sought my help and involvement. As part of the settlement, Volkswagen and the Department of Justice had agreed to have an independent monitor oversee the company's progress in satisfying the terms of its agreement with the Department of Justice. Volkswagen presented the Department of Justice with a slate of potential monitors. Once Volkswagen put my name forward, the Department of Justice selected me for the role, and a federal judge in Detroit approved my selection. Over the next three years, I became intimately involved with Volkswagen's effort to transform itself. Quite frankly, it was a massive undertaking. And while the bulk of my work under the Plea Agreement and Monitorship remains confidential, the details of the underlying narrative, all of which can be found in the public domain, teach an important lesson.

When I was first approached about taking the Volkswagen position, I reacted immediately and positively. After the better part of a lifetime in corporate life, government service, and practicing law, my so-called retirement was supposed to offer me more "downtime." But there was something about Volkswagen that drew me in. I'd learned to drive sitting behind the wheel of a 1963 Beetle. Volkswagen was at that point the largest manufacturing company in Europe and the largest automobile manufacturer the world over.[92] Having spent decades thinking about and talking about how culture was the key to a successful corporation, I found in Volkswagen an opportunity to put that core belief to work. And so, even after turning down other opportunities to serve as an independent monitor, I accepted the Justice Department's invitation to serve as Volkswagen's Independent Compliance Monitor for three years.

Rule by Fear

It's important to understand from the outset what I was *not* hired to do. The monitorship had not been created to act as another layer of law enforcement *per se*. By the time of my appointment, Volkswagen had already accepted broad-based criminal responsibility for the crimes it had committed and had paid massive criminal and civil fines and penalties. Rather, my role, which I shared with my very talented team, was to verify that Volkswagen was taking the steps required to ensure that something so serious would, hopefully, never happen again. Beyond establishing a new compliance regime with rules designed to ensure Volkswagen's compliance with applicable laws and regulations, I also made it our primary mission to help reform the "culture of the company," to make it so that, even if Volkswagen executives wanted to cheat the public, its workforce would choose not to. In other words, I would assess, oversee, and monitor Volkswagen's compliance with the terms of its Plea Agreement with the Department of Justice and work toward certifying the company efforts to establish a culture of integrity along with an effective ethics and compliance program.

The process began with trying to understand the circumstances that prompted the unlawful and wrongful decision-making. When my team first began interacting with the Volkswagen executive team, we needed to understand why many of the company's middle managers had seemingly been drawn into the conspiracy. What was it, we wanted to know, that had prevented them from raising red flags, from alerting more senior executives, board members, or even the public that something so very wrong was being carried inside the fabled company's "clean diesel" enterprise? And the answer, as it turned out, was not difficult to identify.

This wasn't the case of a few bad apples, though by this point, several executives were already under separate indictment or government investigations. Rather, it was, in the words of the company's then new CEO, Dr. Herbert Diess, a situation where the company's "rotten" culture had gotten the better of the enterprise altogether. Those wayward employees had been under enormous pressure to create a line of automobiles on an entirely unreasonable timeline. That excessive burden had incentivized them to do the wrong thing. And to fix *that* problem, our monitorship could not simply be about establishing new rules. We needed to help this global manufacturing giant fundamentally alter its DNA, its CULTURE.

Consider this mundane example: If your boss told you to build a rocket ship to the moon using only the materials you had in your kitchen—and to do it in the next two weeks—you might tell her that the assignment was impossible. But if an assignment was slightly less outlandish but impossible nevertheless—and, moreover, if your job and livelihood depended on you accomplishing the assignment—you could have a massive incentive to cheat. *You* might choose to do the right thing anyway. But not everyone would. And that was the point. The expectations that permeated the past culture inside Volkswagen pointed employees to do whatever it took to succeed.

It likely began with unreasonable expectations, but the problem with Volkswagen's culture didn't end there. In a wayward paean to "shelf compliance," the company had years earlier established a paper system for reporting illegal and unethical activity outside the corporate chain of command. But far from encouraging employees to use the system, many rank-and-file employees had the impression that their communications would not be confidential, and that they would incur retaliation. One employee noted at one point that there was a general understanding that truth-telling guaranteed you nothing but a career "in a broom closet." As Diess would later explain, before the fall, Volkswagen had "a combination of too much pressure and lack of a speak-up culture."[93]

But perhaps most important, Volkswagen's rotten past culture intimated to its employees that the bottom line was all-important no matter how it was achieved. It's not that the company hadn't previously invested in compliance—it had. But the compliance provisions that it cared about most were those that worked to cherish corporate results, no matter how they were achieved, and not those that promoted integrity, honesty, and candor.

The company's compliance regime, in other words, was designed to protect the top executives rather than the public interest. In the years before the "clean diesel" scandal came to light, doing things the right way had been subordinated to other priorities. And that had made all the difference.

Of course, it took some time for these realities to come to light. But they emerged, with the help of the company, as my team and I dug deeper. During the course of my three-year mandate, I traveled to Germany on a near-monthly basis. That said, some of my colleagues traveled to Germany more frequently, and several members of my team, German citizens or German speakers, lived in the country, primarily in the Volkswagen corporate headquarters cities of Wolfsburg and Ingolstadt, spending so much time there that they were required to obtain work permits from the German government. We attended and observed meetings, interviewed board members and employees from the top down, and performed what we called "risk-based" testing on compliance functions and systems. It was a lot of work.

Perhaps most remarkable, what we discovered initially was that even years after the scandal had been made public, the lessons of the scandal had not been learned. As I recall, in a survey conducted by the company of nearly 800 employees during the early months of our mandate, 31 percent agreed that "if performance is good, then undesirable conduct is indeed tolerated." And so, beyond helping the company set up better compliance systems, we worked to set up a much better "red light" system for bringing problems to the attention of management.[94]

I've appeared in many court sketches over the years. Here, I'm pictured with my partner Wick Sollers (left) and Thomas Nebel (center) in *U.S. v. Nebel* in 1993. (John Bills/WSMV, 1993)

Teaching not only has made me a better lawyer, but it has also been immensely satisfying. I've taught law at the University of Georgia School of Law on and off since 2001, when this first picture was taken. (University of Georgia, 2001, 2016)

When I was first approached to help Volkswagen in its company transformation, I was immediately drawn in. Here I am speaking at the Global Top Management Conference and pictured with Herbert Diess, the Chairman of the Board of Management of Volkswagen Group from 2018 to 2022. (Volkswagen Aktiengesellschaft)

In my time at the Justice Department, I took the lead in helping restore our financial markets following the spate of corporate scandals that started with the Enron bankruptcy. Here, I'm pictured with Securities and Exchange Commission Chairman William H. Donaldson at a press conference in 2003. William recently passed away in 2024, at the age of 93. (REUTERS/William Philpott/Bridgeman Images, 2003)

U.S. Attorney General John Ashcroft and I arriving to the Justice Department before commenting to reporters on the criminal complaint against John Allen Muhammad in the Washington-area sniper case. In the months and years that followed 9/11, all of us at the Justice Department worked carefully to balance various concerns in the pursuit of protecting our nation. (Joyce Naltchayan/AFP via Getty Images, 2002)

In 2004, President George W. Bush and I participated in a conversation about the Patriot Act in Buffalo, New York. (White House official, 2004)

A television broadcast at the U.S. Justice Department in Washington, DC, as I announced that former Enron Chief Financial Officer Andrew S. Fastow had been charged with fraud, money laundering, and conspiracy. (Joyce Naltchayan/AFP via Getty Images, 2002)

When I heard about the case of Sholom Rubashkin, an Orthodox Jewish man from Brooklyn who was sentenced to an outrageous 27 years in prison for financial fraud, I was stunned and volunteered to help. In 2018, Sholom thanked me with an award for my service at a celebration in Spring Valley, New York. Here I am at the celebration and with (L to R) Gary Apfel, Sholom Rubashkin, and the late Phil Heymann.

My wife, Brenda, and our two sons, have always been supportive of my career choices. Brenda and I are lucky to share an interest in art. More than four decades ago, we began our collection. Today, we have several hundred individual pieces, most of them created by African American artists. As of 2023, we've gifted more than 300 pieces to museums across the country. (University of Georgia)

Brenda and I are pictured with Kevin Cole (left), 2020 recipient of the Larry D. and Brenda A. Thompson Award at the Georgia Museum of Art, and Alton Standifer (middle), Vice Provost for Inclusive Excellence at the University of Georgia. (Georgia Museum of Art, University of Georgia)

My parents, Ezra and Ruth Thompson. I appreciate their love and sacrifices. My siblings and I were raised to believe there were no limits on what we could accomplish. I'm lucky. I picked the right parents.

After serving as Executive Vice President, Government Affairs, General Counsel and Corporate Secretary for PepsiCo, Inc. I am now serving as Counsel to the Atlanta law firm, Finch McCranie LLP. (Lindsay Pace/Finch McCraine LLP)

None of this was easy. Over those three years, my team made thousands of document requests and reviewed millions of pages of internal records. We held thousands of meetings with employees in nine countries. We spent extensive time with the senior management. We worked closely with the company as it rolled out new policies, including a new Code of Conduct and a new integrity system.[95] What became clear to everyone was that the decision to cheat was not, in fact, good business. It cost the company billions of euros. But there were other costs. The company's reputation took a huge hit—the cost of which could not be quantified. The company realized that if it was ever going to get past the diesel scandal, its culture and values would have to change. And today, I believe that has begun to happen.

In September 2020, I certified that "the Company's compliance program, including its policies and procedures, is reasonably designed and implemented to prevent and detect violations of the anti-fraud and environmental laws." I also certified the "Board of Management's and senior management's commitment to, and the effective implementation of, the Company's corporate compliance and ethics program."[96] And Dr. Diess subsequently told shareholders not only that the investment the company had made in reforming its compliance regime had been worthwhile, but that, in his words, "Besides abiding by the rules and obeying the law, the key here is always ethics—a clear moral compass."[97] Does this mean that on a going-forward basis, Volkswagen will never experience another integrity problem? Of course not. Volkswagen is a huge company with over 600,000 employees. But it does mean that if something does arise, the company will handle it much differently than it did during the diesel scandal. Simply put, I believe the company has learned that the cost of doing things the wrong way is unacceptable for the kind of great global corporate citizen it strives to be.

After billions of euros in losses born from a wayward attempt to drive the company's profitability, that, of course, had been the point. The executives who had embraced Volkswagen's then prevailing "rotten" culture thought cheating would push the company ahead. Instead, it nearly ushered the company to a disastrous end. A "rotten" culture had in fact been deleterious to the interests of Volkswagen's shareholders. It was unsustainable. And this hopefully is an important lesson for the global business community.

The Volkswagen experience was challenging and yet satisfying. I was proud and honored to have played a role in the transformation of this important company. I was also touched and humbled when my Volkswagen counterparts installed and planted a tree in a grassy area outside the Volkswagen executive office building in recognition of our monitorship.

Beyond the Pregnant "But"

My three-year engagement with Volkswagen represented just the more recent of what has been a long journey for me through the world of corporate compliance. As previously noted, during the decades that preceded my service as Deputy Attorney General, ethics and compliance represented an important part of my law practice. So by the time of my Senate confirmation, the patterns of bad corporate cultures I had experienced were familiar. And this is the root of my present, continued frustration. Decades after Lynn Paine's article informed the ethical landscape of the compliance world, her wisdom still has yet to become fully realized. What we now have, quite frankly, is a massive failure of corporate good sense.

In the wake of any given transgression, the story typically goes like this: Someone on a company's executive team catches wind of a potential violation somewhere within the bowels of the corporation—and in many cases, the government is not even aware that something has gone awry. The executives then hire experienced outside counsel to conduct an internal investigation. Counsel then spends weeks or sometimes even months reviewing the records, conducting interviews, and analyzing the facts. Once they've drawn their conclusions, counsel comes to the executives with a report that is typically a combination of three elements. First, they provide an analysis of how things went awry. Second, they provide some sort of recommendation on how to correct things. Third, they provide some sort of prescription designed to prevent recurrence.

Having been through this scenario as outside counsel on several occasions, I can say with confidence that executives typically receive the first two conclusions with interest and appreciation. They're eager to identify the bad actors inside the organizations they lead, and they're usually keen to rid them from the organization. They also understand that it is important to hold wayward employees accountable. So, to the degree that there's a proverbial cancer metastasizing inside a corporate hierarchy, executives are generally ready, willing, and even eager to act. But when it comes to the third item—namely when counsel begins offering recommendations on how to prevent a reoccurrence—many times, unfortunately, counsel experiences what I call soft resistance.

Generally, counsel outlines a series of proposed institutional reforms. Perhaps a revamped compliance and ethics program. In some cases, a new set of protocols. Sometimes a new code of ethics. More training and more focus. Typically, the executives receiving the recommendations listen attentively. They nod pensively, conveying a sense that they understand the gravity of the situation. And then, when the presentation is over and it's their turn to respond, the CEO will say something like: "I entirely agree with you that ethics and compliance are crucial. Moreover, I'm willing to do whatever it takes to make sure we're operating on the straight and narrow. BUT we can't let compliance get in the way of running our business (or turning a profit, or keeping a step ahead of the competition, etc.)."

Here's what so many executives don't understand: That pregnant "BUT" is the whole ball game. If you aren't going to do what's needed to change a company's culture such that good behavior is explicitly rewarded (whatever the short-term costs) and that bad behavior is universally abhorred (no matter the financial downside), there's simply no way that a company is going to internalize integrity values. Integrity outcomes must be as important as routine business results. In the end, there is no compliance regime, no set of rules, that will keep your company on a long-term sustainable path if ethics and integrity take a back seat to profitability and business results. And as was so evident at Volkswagen, that mentality will eventually become a scourge on your business and even threaten its demise.

That's not to say that compliance should dominate every business enterprise. The point is simply that ethics should be on level footing with a company's other top priorities and functions. In the same way that no public corporation can reasonably shortchange its finance department such that it's unable to compile its quarterly financial reports, a company should never shortchange its compliance and ethics efforts. This is not just because compliance teams need sufficient resources to do their jobs. It's because shortchanging a company's compliance and ethics regime sends a toxic message throughout the company about the sort of culture the company's leadership executives wants.

Here's the bottom line: To inculcate a *culture* of integrity at a corporation—to spread the values that would compel an employee to do the right thing outside the four corners of any rules-based regime—ethics and compliance need to be held in the same regard as innovation, manufacturing efficiency, accurate financial records, and the like. This is not to discount the rules. But, in the end, the right values must shape the answers to every important question. Should I steal this pencil? Should I accept this bribe? Should I grease the palm of this foreign official? Board members and executives should want, in each and every case, employees to answer these questions the right way. And that should be true whether or not an explicit code of conduct provision addresses that particular situation.

The Cracker Jack Test

As a kid growing up in Hannibal, Missouri, I loved Cracker Jacks. Whenever I went to a baseball game, I looked forward to enjoying what has long been perhaps one of the most quintessentially American treats. But the real reason I was likely to choose Cracker Jacks over cotton candy or ice cream was that, beyond the caramel-covered popcorn and peanuts, every box included a toy. The toys were fun. A whistle, a set of dice, a trading card—all were memorable and lasted well after the edible treat was consumed in its entirety.

Fast-forward several decades to a moment when I was at PepsiCo, which owns Frito-Lay, the company that makes and sells Cracker Jacks. We had been made aware of several troubling reports that children were accidentally eating the toys themselves, which then became choking hazards. This, of course, was a cause for intense concern. From our point of view at PepsiCo headquarters, one injured child was one too many. And so, as consumer protection standards were shifting in the United States, PepsiCo replaced the toys with an alternative novelty, namely digital codes designed to let children play a special game online after opening each box.[98]

Now, I need to be honest. Fun as those digital games may be, they would never have made my adolescent self crave a box of Cracker Jacks like the old toys did. And PepsiCo executives understood that dynamic. How many children would now choose the cotton candy or ice cream if they knew they weren't going to get a toy? How many fewer boxes would the company sell as a result? And so PepsiCo executives had a crucial question to answer: Should the company make the same change in markets where the toys were still legal, such as in Mexico and China? Should the company continue packing boxes with the traditional toys when manufacturing and distributing Cracker Jacks abroad?

Here is something that made me proud to be on the values-based executive team at PepsiCo: The latter was never really considered. When it became clear that children were being put in harm's way by the toys, the company decided to replace the toys worldwide despite knowing that the change might affect our bottom line and despite knowing that keeping the problematic toys in the box was legal in some countries. The values of the company—its corporate culture—was to put consumer safety first. These values put consumers first around the world, not just where the rules or laws prohibited toys in the boxes. PepsiCo was going to do the right thing even if it cut against short-term profits. And that wasn't simply a reflection of corporate altruism. The executives knew that, in the long term, consumers would reward the company's commitment to safety.

The question for executives working at any other company, separate and apart from the specific question of a novelty toy in a box of caramel popcorn, is whether they and their peers would make a similar choice given similar circumstances. Would their corporate culture lead them to make a decision that prioritizes doing the right thing over doing the immediately profitable and even legal thing?

Here's why the answers to these questions are so important. Culture, in the end, has long been the special sauce of PepsiCo. By the same token, culture opened the door to the behavior that steered Volkswagen so seriously awry. So it's not just that companies should prioritize ethics as a matter of good citizenship. They should strive for ethics and compliance because the wrong culture can be immensely costly, undermining the loyalty of a company's customer base, making it harder to recruit and retain talent, and opening the door to additional, burdensome regulation.

That's why I remain frustrated that so many business leaders still don't get it. Every organization built to succeed over the long term needs a step-by-step strategy to establish the right culture. And the first step is to make the company's values crystal clear. Every employee, partner, and associate should understand what's expected of them—what prism they are expected to use to analyze each decision they make. The tone at the top matters a great deal as the message filters down. That means a company's values should be spelled out frequently. Ethical guidelines should be everywhere, in marketing plans, strategic decisions, supplier relations, customer care, etc.

Second, those charged with maintaining ethics and compliance need unfettered access to the company's top decision-makers. In too many companies, the "chief compliance and ethics officer" is subordinated to a Chief

Legal Officer or a Chief Operations Officer who buffers the CEO and the Board of Directors. That sends the wrong message. Private sessions with the CEO and executive sessions with the board should be the norm. Whomever it is that is ultimately held responsible for the administration of the company's values should have a direct line to the most powerful people, and that person should be at the table when major decisions that will affect the company's values and business strategies are considered.

Third, integrity—the degree to which any individual lives a company's values—should be a part of every employee's regular evaluations and compensation decisions. Employees must understand and believe that they will be rewarded personally, both in their remuneration and in their opportunity for promotion, if they do the right thing *even if it costs the company some short-term opportunity.* They should want to avoid developing a reputation as someone who does *not* have integrity. And this should be as true of top executives as it is of middle management. Those at the top should not have "waivers" that green-light behavior that cuts against a culture of integrity.

Fourth, leaders need to hold employees to account in ways that other members of the community see and understand. This is not to suggest that wayward associates need to be publicly flogged. But transgressions need to be acknowledged and dealt with in a way that employees view as fair and equal. At Volkswagen, well after the scandal, some employees remained under the impression that those involved with the clean diesel conspiracy were being protected from any sort of discipline or accountability. This, in and of itself, made changing the company's culture much more difficult. Germany's employee-friendly labor laws made terminating high-level wrongdoers difficult, but ultimately Volkswagen made the decision to take action against wrongdoers even in the face of the possibility of reversal in a German labor court.

Finally, hiring decisions, particularly those made at the top, need to be done with an ethics and compliance culture in mind. Dambisa Moyo, who served on the boards of 3M and Chevron, explained this well in a recent interview: "I recommend that the board get much more granular about questions around ethics and the moral compass of the CEO. We tend to focus a lot on financial acumen, operational expertise, leadership skills. All of that is critically important, but a lot more work needs to be done on a doubling down on ethics and moral compass . . . . Traditionally, we would look in a very simplistic way, is something profitable? Is it legal? And that was good enough. But now there's another leg to think about: Is it actually ethical or moral? Does it stand with our values as a company?"[99]

Not long ago, an old friend told me that when a company he advises began searching for a CEO, an ethics and compliance culture turned out to be a crucial part of the board's criteria. Beyond listening to what candidates planned to do with the company—how each applicant might steer the enterprise or invest the company's revenues or shift brand marketing—the board committee wanted to know how a prospective CEO might inculcate ethics into the workforce and the company's broader mission. He noted that the questions board members were asking about values would have sounded entirely out of place just a few years ago. But no one blinked when ethical culture came up in interviews this time around.

This is, in my view, the best news we could have coming out of corporate America today. It's a crucial step forward for capitalism and free enterprise. At a moment when so many Americans, not to mention so many global citizens, are wary of the degree to which competition prompts an ethical race to the bottom, we need ethics and compliance to come front and center. As described in other chapters of this book, some of the pressure required to steer corporate America in the right direction will come from outside—namely from society as a whole, often through the machinations of government. But as my experience as a corporate lawyer and prosecutor makes clear, much of the impetus will have to come from within the organization. Corporate culture needs to incentivize decision-makers to travel a path that emphasizes integrity. It is my hope that this straightforward principle moves beyond the aspirational and becomes the way we all do business.

CHAPTER SIX

RACE: THE EVERGREEN QUESTION

Getting One Over

In 1997, a Coca-Cola bottling executive in Atlanta, Jimmy Wardlaw, retained me to be one of two lawyers defending him in a serious federal criminal case in Atlanta. He and his colleague, Eric Turpin, were accused of conspiring to bribe a Coca-Cola bottling employee in order to subvert a unionization drive among the company's delivery truck drivers. The case was set to turn on the testimony of Jeffrey Wright, a driver who had, during the unionization drive, been lobbying Wardlaw and Turpin for a raise and promotion. Unbeknownst to Jimmy and Eric, Wright had recorded several of their phone conversations and then handed investigators audio files purporting to show that they had offered to pay Wright to undermine the organizing campaign. If the jurors found Wright's testimony convincing, Jimmy and Eric could be convicted and most certainly would face a prison sentence. My co-counsel for Jimmy, Charles Fels, and Eric's defense lawyer, Bruce Maloy, along with myself were tasked with mounting a vigorous defense.

The prosecutors and the FBI investigative team seemed to have adopted a certain narrative of the case—a narrative that would eventually shape their strategy at trial. Without knowing the specifics, it was tempting to presume that Jimmy and Eric, one of whom happened to be white, had tried to manipulate Wright, an employee who happened to be Black, to serve their greed as company executives and win the union campaign at all costs. Moreover, I felt that the government was trying, in many ever so subtle ways, to mount a theme that a white corporate executive, like Jimmy, was trying to take advantage of a Black worker, like Jeffrey Wright. Given that dynamic, there was some understandable reluctance to recommend that Jimmy and Eric take the stand in their own defense. Up against Jeffrey Wright, a man the government was sure to paint as a sympathetic victim, our clients risked coming off in a bad light.

As trial preparation continued, I began to adopt a different view. Reasonable as it was to expect the jury (which, to be clear, comprised a mix of Black and white citizens) could possibly put a halo on Jeffrey Wright, my intuition suggested that another dynamic was at play. During pre-trial discovery, we discovered that Wright had actively manipulated the recordings before handing them over to the FBI, and he'd done so in such a self-serving way as to convince the judge to preclude those recordings from being introduced at trial.[100] That, it seemed to me, was a "tell." It suggested that, handled the right way, we could impeach Wright's credibility and establish doubt in the jurors' minds about Jimmy's culpability. But to get there, we would need to take a more aggressive approach than many defense lawyers might be inclined to do in establishing "reasonable doubt": To impeach Wright's credibility, I believed Jimmy would possibly have to testify.

Eric Turpin did not take the stand at trial. As was his right, he simply allowed Bruce Maloy, a very skillful criminal defense lawyer, to try to poke holes in the prosecution's case. But after Jimmy lobbied strongly for an opportunity to defend himself directly, Charles Fels, my co-counsel, and I decided to go for it—Jimmy would testify at trial. Even though we risked our client coming off the wrong way under cross-examination by two senior prosecutors, we were convinced that the character discrepancy between Jimmy and Wright would become clear when the jurors heard the two men testify. We believed that Jimmy would present as a stand-up guy and that at least some jurors would see Wright for the schemer we believed he was. And that's what happened. After a two-week trial, Jimmy and Eric were both acquitted.[101]

I recount this story for a reason—namely, I think it highlights an underappreciated aspect of the human condition, one that plays a remarkably powerful role in how we each make decisions. What was it that gave me the confidence to pursue what was so clearly a riskier strategy of strongly supporting Jimmy's desire to testify? From where did I glean the insight to believe that we could win by impeaching Jeffrey Wright's credibility? The answer really just comes down to one thing—intuition. My life experience had given me what I think was a special perspective on Jeffrey Wright's character. I had an instinctual sense of how others, *particularly other Blacks*, would react to Wright when they saw him testify at trial. And I employed that instinct to my client's advantage.

I should be clear here: No two people are exactly alike. But in ways that may be difficult to articulate exactly, Wright reminded me of a certain archetype that would be familiar to many, especially Black Americans. Here was a man who understood that, in certain circumstances, white people would be inclined to view him as a victim almost no matter the circumstance. Even if, like every Black man, woman, and child, he had the legacy and contemporary reality of race in America—I'm sure he had been pulled over while driving on false pretenses before, like indeed I have been—Wright presented to me the type of person who would try to take advantage of some sort of "race" sympathy when it wasn't warranted. In a phrase I have used many times and heard even more times, he was the type of guy who would try to "get one over" on the wider world and particularly the white community. And if we could expose what I believed to be his true character to the jury, and particularly to Black jurors, their disgust with Wright's character would undermine the government's case.

Now, from where did that intuition come? I don't know exactly—and I certainly can't say for sure whether another lawyer boasting an entirely different background might have come to the same conclusion. But in my case, I'm convinced that my instincts were rooted in having grown up in a working-class Black community, going to school as a Black kid at a small Midwestern college, working as a labor relations specialist at an automobile manufacturing plant, attending the University of Michigan Law School, and then practicing law in both St. Louis and Atlanta. My background—yes, including my race—had exposed me to certain people I would not have met had I been born and raised in different circumstances. And those experiences, which bred a certain intuition, informed my decision-making in this case. To put it more pointedly, the diversity of the defense team helped Jimmy Wardlaw avoid conviction.

Inadvertent Myopia

Most often when the public discourse takes up the topic of "diversity," many view the term through the lens of how various groups share in the nation's wealth and privilege. This is commonly referred to as "equity." I can certainly understand why. The legacy of racism in America remains, and the continued gaps separating racial groups make the impact of discrimination and prejudice clear. Conservatives, of course, have long bristled at the notion that government should take a significant role in rebalancing the scales. And I have long shared much of that conservative cynicism. I worry that ham-handed efforts to establish racial quotas at public or private institutions or clumsy efforts to redistribute the nation's bounty by skin color could well do much more harm than good. Indeed, early in my career I had to overcome what I felt was the stigma associated with the impression by some that I was a token lawyer at a large, prestigious law firm.

But "social justice" is just one way to understand the value of diversity. As I set forth in 2003 in a speech to the Federalist Society, those who believe in good, old-fashioned notions of competitive free enterprise have a self-serving reason to see value in the notion of diversity. As the Supreme Court has ruled, many efforts to rebalance the scales with quotas don't meet constitutional muster. But by the same token, diversity can be beneficial for institutions of all shapes and sizes. In fact, whether or not employers should do more to hire women and minorities as a means to make up for previous injustice, business organizations are well-advised to hire more women and minorities for one simple reason: Diversity provides their business a competitive advantage.[102]

At least this much should be obvious to every executive by now: If you want your company to succeed in the long run, you must compile a workforce with a range of talents, interests, and backgrounds. And you simply can't do that if you just hire more of the sorts of employees that you already have. You simply cannot have a monochromatic workforce in today's world. As much as Ivy League schools used to bend over backward to admit students from a variety of geographies because they wanted the student body to reflect the wider society—to that end, for example, students applying from Mississippi did not need quite as sterling credentials to get into a highly competitive school as those applying from, say, Manhattan—businesses today should see hiring new and diverse employees simply as a way to become better.

I've seen firsthand how a *lack* of diversity can prompt what might be called "inadvertent myopia." After serving as United States Attorney in Atlanta, I spent 15 years in private practice. Over the course of that decade and a half, I represented a wide range of clients on many matters opposite lawyers from the Department of Justice. I was engaged in matters in at least 15 different U.S. Attorney offices. Admittedly, the bulk of my clients were white. But here's what I can say with almost unshakable certainty about that span: On only a few occasions did the legal team sitting across the table from me and representing the United States include a lawyer who looked like, well, me.

Perhaps, to some, that revelation will not come as a surprise. Perhaps, others will presume, I faced white lawyers almost exclusively because I handled only one sort of case or because the federal prosecutors working around the country were almost exclusively white. But that wasn't the reality. For one, many of my cases involved clients facing matters against prosecutors housed all over the country—Atlanta, New York, Washington, and elsewhere. But perhaps even more striking, I represented clients on matters across a broad range of the Justice Department's litigation divisions. I was involved in criminal matters, civil matters, environmental matters, tax matters, and antitrust matters. Each division would assign a lawyer with a particular expertise in that realm of the law. But in almost every circumstance, whatever realm, the government's lawyers were white.

Fortunately, the racial monochromatism largely ended there. The judges weren't always white. The witnesses weren't always white. The experts called to testify weren't always white. The jurors weren't always white. The journalists covering the cases weren't always white. Nevertheless, in venue upon venue, I was the only Black person on either legal team. And while it's almost always impossible to assign responsibility for any single verdict or outcome to a single factor—the argumentation, the rhetoric, the timing, the racial or gender identities of the lawyers involved, etc.—in most cases, I felt that my race, background, and, most important, experiences gave me an advantage. This is difficult to articulate. That is, I was able to see approaches to the problem at hand from a unique perspective, and I believe that leg up gave my clients an advantage they otherwise might not have had.

I need to be very clear here because I don't want to give anyone the false impression that people with a certain skin color are more capable than people with another skin color or that hiring an attorney with a certain characteristic—race, gender, ethnicity, sexual identity, etc.—is sure to help a client win a certain outcome or gain them an advantage in any given adversarial setting. But I can't help but believe that, in some circumstances—when a witness was being deposed, for example—my background sometimes had an impact on the eventual outcome. Perhaps a Black witness felt more comfortable speaking to me or was more forthcoming in answers to a question from a Black lawyer. Perhaps not. But in a high-stakes trial or investigative matter, both legal teams are often looking to exploit any possible advantage. And I believe today that, more often than not, my background and experience sometimes helped tip the scales in my clients' favor.

That hasn't always been the case, of course. Our nation's history is rife with examples where all-white juries would have rejected out of hand the arguments made by a Black lawyer. And I'm sure in some circumstances today, white lawyers, particularly those who are highly credentialed and have graduated from the nation's very best law schools, still have real advantages. But that's the point of diversity: The legal teams I tended to lead included white lawyers and Black lawyers alike, along with other colleagues from a range of backgrounds.

At King & Spalding, we could assign various tasks and interviews to a variety of lawyers and professionals among us such that, in each case, we were maximizing our advantage. And while everyone on the team was talented—no one at our firm would have been offered a job without having compiled a solid record in law school and a wealth of applicable experience—my experience was that the broader range of talents and backgrounds gave us a real advantage when facing off against the government's overwhelmingly monochromatic legal teams. In fact, moving even farther back in my own career trajectory, that is why, I suspect, I was hired for my first job out of law school.

A bit of background: Typically, corporations building out their legal departments recruit from law firms—they prefer to bring people in house after they've been trained in corporate law or some related legal expertise. But in 1974, the General Counsel of Monsanto Company wanted to try something new—hire a handful of young lawyers right out of law school and see if that might work well for the company. The company set high standards, but when they selected three of us—the other two hires were white—I suspected that my race had played a role. Even back then, Monsanto *sought* diversity. And that wasn't born primarily out of a desire to counteract the legacy of American racism. The company wanted a diverse workforce because it thought having employees with a broader range of perspectives would redound to its benefit in a diverse world of policymakers, regulators, customers, and other stakeholders. And the company was a government contractor. A diverse workforce was something the government looked at when evaluating contractors.

Effectiveness and Equity

By now, diversity "initiatives" have proliferated through much of corporate and academic America—and some have worked to great effect. But in too many cases, even the most well-intentioned programs have prompted a backlash. Those who have been passed over for a position or, for that matter, rejected from a degree program argue that they face tougher sledding explicitly because they are *not* part of an underrepresented group. That feeds a sense of grievance.

At the same time, those of us who have been hired are often subject to what I call "whispered doubt." As noted previously, those individuals who diversify an organization's workforce are sometimes tinged with the notion that they weren't actually the best qualified for the position they obtained but instead were selected because of their race or gender. It's entirely possible that some of my colleagues at the Monsanto Company quietly questioned whether I was up for the job I got in the law department right out of college. I don't know.

Don't get me wrong—I'm sure that, in some circumstances, people who are less adept at a certain task performed by those hired to fill any given position are, in fact, given jobs. But that's true in all sorts of hiring decisions. Perhaps one lawyer is better at doing research and writing briefs, and another is better at handling oral arguments in court. If only one position is open, it's incumbent on the hiring committee to prioritize one set of attributes over the other, and the final decision may rest on a question of what best complements a firm's existing capacity. If a firm has a panoply of erudite litigators, perhaps it hires the star researcher. If it has a great bench of scholars, perhaps it chooses the lawyer with great advocacy skills. That's not affirmative action—it's just good business.

That's what gets lost in this discussion of racial and gender diversity, particularly among conservatives. Quite simply, there's a very strong business case for broad inclusion. Rather than being some sort of socioeconomic palliative measure, we all need to think of diversity as an asset, making an organization more *effective*, beyond making it simply more *equitable*. And for that reason, to do diversity right, companies need to shape strategies that benefit the enterprise as a whole, rather than those that simply seek to attempt to right historical wrongs.

This important distinction has played a crucial role in my professional career. Just as I returned to public service in 2001, the Supreme Court took up a pair of lawsuits emanating from the University of Michigan which, together, set the stage for the justices to rule on whether and how public institutions could perhaps favor minority applicants for various opportunities. As the newly confirmed Deputy Attorney General serving in an administration that was explicitly opposed to affirmative action based on racial or gender quotas, I was keenly aware of the high stakes.

As it was, the justices issued two rulings that broadly aligned with my thinking. They explicitly rejected Michigan's undergraduate admissions process because it had awarded minority candidates extra points in the process of ranking candidates—points that white applicants explicitly could not receive. This, the justices deemed, was too similar to the racial quota system that a previous decision, *Bakke v. California,* had prohibited decades earlier.[103]

But in the second case, which involved the University of Michigan Law School—as it happened, my law school alma mater—the Court greenlit a process by which administrators could work to compile a broader range of students explicitly because diversity would benefit the students and the law school alike. As Justice Sandra Day O'Connor put it: The Constitution "does not prohibit the law school's narrowly tailored use of race in admissions decisions to further a compelling interest in obtaining the educational benefits that flow from a diverse student body."[104] In other words, diversity was a worthy goal insomuch as it benefited everyone, but institutions could *not* discriminate on the basis of race simply as a means to rectify past wrongs.

Having become so intimately acquainted with the Justice Department's lack of diversity while in private practice, this policy guideline made sense to me. Perhaps more important, it appeared to open a door to change within the government itself. As I made my rounds to various departments, talking to lawyers and others assigned to various divisions and offices, one deficit became increasingly clear: The notion I had that many offices within the Justice Department were *not* diverse applied across the Department as a whole. Places where the government would have benefited from being represented by lawyers who were more familiar with the rhythms of the local community were nevertheless staffed by lawyers who lacked any kind of diversity. As a result, I strongly believed that the Department wasn't able to serve the nation's interests as effectively as it otherwise might have.

This was most readily apparent at the nation's southern border. Like in various pockets all over the country, certain communities in Texas, New Mexico, and Arizona were overwhelmingly Latino. That meant that when a federal crime occurred in the area or an environmental issue, immigration question, or civil lawsuit arose, many involved in the judicial proceedings in these areas were Latino—the litigants, the experts, the judges, the witnesses, the jurors, and more. Nevertheless, the lawyers representing the government were generally not representative of the diversity of the involved judicial districts. And even though the "Anglos" speaking for the DOJ were very good lawyers, this put the Department, and by extension the public interest, at a distinct disadvantage.

The previous administration had begun to cobble together a diversity initiative to tackle this very problem, but their ideas were never implemented. So at Senator Rob Portman's (R-OH) suggestion, I hired a special adviser, Stacey Plaskett, to develop a comprehensive program designed to bring more diverse talent into the Department's pipeline. Plaskett, who would later become the Virgin Islands delegate to Congress, reported back to me with a long list of well-developed and thoughtful proposals, each designed to strike a blow for internal diversity. After a healthy debate about each one, I endorsed the initiative.

Before taking my position public, I wanted to run some traps, just to make sure I was not getting on the wrong side of the Bush Administration's broad skepticism of social justice-oriented affirmative action. I ran the ideas past Solicitor General Ted Olson, who agreed that having a broader range of lawyers would make the Department more effective. So not long thereafter, and perhaps to the surprise of many of our liberal and conservative critics, I unveiled a comprehensive program in front of the entire Department's top brass, including Attorney General John Ashcroft, who introduced me during remarks delivered in the Great Hall of Main Justice and broadcast throughout the country in the various United States Attorney's offices. I stated without equivocation that our administration would "strengthen the Department of Justice's attorney workforce by intensifying outreach to individuals from a wide range of racial, ethnic, economic, and geographic background, and by creating incentives to enter and remain in public service."[105]

The initiatives we packaged under a single umbrella differed significantly from one to the next. We committed to investing more time and resources recruiting students and lawyers into the Department, partially through the Attorney General's prestigious Honors Program. We began expanding opportunities for lawyers internally to fill more coveted vacancies. We augmented the Department's loan repayment program, established a mandatory mentoring program, and instituted a new regime of diversity training to "prevent stereotyping and other subtle forms of identity-related employment issues."[106]

But it didn't end there. We stood up a formal career development program in collaboration with the Office of Personnel Management, established a norm of conducting exit interviews when lawyers decided to leave the Department (primarily in order to see when and if an individual's identity had played a role in their decision to resign), and set up a program to monitor our progress across the whole initiative. Perhaps most important, after our initiative was up and running, we managed to have it transferred from the political realm into the civil service side of the Department, installing it within the Justice Management Division so that our changes could not be easily unwound by future administrations.[107]

In my long career in both the public and private sectors, few moments have provided as much satisfaction to me as that speech in the Great Hall. I look back with particular pride on that moment because I know, in ways that we'll never be able to identify with exact precision, that we were setting the Department up to be more successful in the future. We were setting the Department up to better serve the public's interests. Diversity is not just code for equity—it's a proactive strategy to make an organization more effective. And our efforts to diversify the Department of Justice's attorneys would have almost certainly ensured that the American people were better served by their government in the years that followed.

The Business Case for Diversity

The diversity initiative I led at the Justice Department may have been revolutionary because it did not just focus on identities, but it was by no means the first time that the government molded its personnel to face a new challenge. As Department officials sought to combat gangs in the 1980s, they sought to hire agents and attorneys who understood life on the street. As the Department's leadership turned to focus on the threat of terrorism after 9/11, it recruited agents who understood the nature of organizations such as al-Qaeda. In other words, as the challenges facing the country evolved, so did the mix of personnel working in the public interest. Diversity in that sense strengthened the Department; my contribution simply extended the same logic to another realm. The same basic principle applies in any organization—and, in fact, shaped my own career when I left the Department.

On to PepsiCo

PepsiCo's then CEO, Steve Reinemund, was searching for the company's next General Counsel. Intent on hiring someone with broad experience, he was also interested in leveraging the new hire to drive some important shifts for the company moving forward. For example, beyond the typical work of a law department—negotiating contracts, ensuring compliance, handling corporate litigation—Steve sensed at the time that a burgeoning corps of activists would aim to get the government to adopt punitive measures directed at the company's products—on salty snacks and sugar-sweetened drinks. As such, the next General Counsel would have to understand Washington and the public policy process. Steve also knew that PepsiCo's growth depended in large part on its expansion overseas, so the new head lawyer would have to be familiar with international law. Steve knew that PepsiCo's executive ranks were overwhelmingly white and male, so he wanted to use this hire to enhance the executive suite's gender or racial diversity. These factors would *all* play a role in determining his selection.

I obviously can't say exactly why Steve ended up choosing me for the job. I know he interviewed a whole range of candidates, and I'm sure that many were terrific lawyers and that some certainly would have boasted skills or experiences that I did not have. But my candidacy was, by the same token, fairly unique. I had been a U.S. Attorney. I had spent 16 years in private practice before returning to public service. I had been the second-ranking official in the Department of Justice at a time when white-collar law enforcement was a top government priority. I had significant experience in dealing with government agencies and in dealing with Congress. I was from the Midwest, and I had subsequently grown some southern roots. Finally, I was, of course, Black. I suspect that *all* of these elements of my identity strengthened my appeal.

To the degree that PepsiCo's decision was tied in any way to my race, Steve's notion that diversity would help the corporation's bottom line had been borne out in research. It's not just that PepsiCo has long been purposeful—both under Steve and under his successor, Indra Nooyi, a woman of color herself—in harnessing a wide range of employees in order to support broad-based employee diversity. It's that, as PepsiCo realized early on and as more rigorous studies done over time of a whole range of global corporations have proven, corporations that invest in inclusion and diversity set themselves up to be more successful. PepsiCo wanted to stay ahead of the competition.

McKinsey, the global consulting company, has done a series of studies on this topic that are remarkable because of both their breadth and depth. In 2014, McKinsey began harvesting insights from more than 1,000 companies scattered across 15 different countries. McKinsey's professionals analyzed corporate efforts on diversity, incorporating results from a process they call "social listening," designed to measure sentiments within a company's workforce. Then having gathered sufficient data to understand how the companies approach various realms of diversity, they compared the companies' financial performances. What they concluded was powerful: One study found that a 10 percent increase in ethnic and racial diversity among senior executives corresponds with a nearly 1 percent increase in earnings.[108] In other words, diversity and inclusion aren't just good for society as a whole—they're important to a company's bottom line.[109]

But it's not just that diversity helps drive success. McKinsey's research found that the diversity of a corporation's workforce can be a differentiator when stacked against the competition. Gender diversity is important: In 2014, those in the top quartile of an index rating each company's success in hiring a mix of men and women were 15 percent "more likely to have above-average profitability than companies in the bottom quartile." In 2017, that rose to 21 percent. By 2019, the figure was 25 percent. But *ethnic* inclusion was even more influential: By 2019, those with ethnic and culture diversity were a stunning 35 percent more likely to outperform the competition.[110] *

I was thrilled and honored to work at PepsiCo for almost a decade. And I can say, without a doubt, that I drew on all aspects of my experience and identity at various moments through my tenure. PepsiCo's vaunted competition with beverage and salty snack giants across the world demanded a workforce that was among the world's best across a whole variety of realms—product development, quality control, distribution, sales, and more. And as I spent years leading the company's law department and government affairs function, I realized that we needed not only competent lawyers and other professionals but also personnel from a whole range of backgrounds. So much as Steve Reinemund had leaned into inclusion when hiring me, I made it my mission to expand the diversity of our internal workforce and, most important, our outside counsel and advisers. I emphasized to my colleagues, many of whom stayed on after I retired from the company, that PepsiCo's fortunes rested in no small part on ensuring that those who represented the company's legal and regulatory interests comprised a broad range of diverse voices.

That mentality really resonated within PepsiCo, and after I left, it unexpectedly emerged as one of the most important elements of my legacy at the company. In 2016, after I retired, PepsiCo created a diversity and inclusion summer program for aspiring lawyers entering their second year in law school. The ten-week internship is designed to aid lawyers emerging from underrepresented communities to get their feet in the corporate door, no matter whether, upon graduation, they intend to join PepsiCo's workforce. The point, broadly speaking, is that when PepsiCo seeks out legal counsel—even when it is hiring outside lawyers—the company will benefit if the nation's retinue of lawyers draw on a broader range of backgrounds.[111]

---

* Admittedly, these figures reflect correlation and not causation. Nevertheless, they are important data points for managers who want to drive success.

Today that program, renamed the Larry D. Thompson Legacy of Leadership Fellowship Program, is thriving at PepsiCo, and I am humbled to have it bear my name. The program has by now received applications from students at more than 90 law schools and has grown from four to seven spots each summer. As with all hiring, academics and performance are key considerations when PepsiCo selects the Thompson Fellows each year, but they're not the only considerations. PepsiCo seriously weighs how selecting any one applicant will bear on the long-term diversity of the legal profession. And that's not just good for PepsiCo—it's good for the nation's corporate interests as a whole.[112]

A Knowing Look

Several years ago, while a partner at King & Spalding, I was asked to lead the defense team in a criminal trial located outside Atlanta but still in the South. I recall thinking early in the trial that the odds were stacked against us—the prosecution had a very strong case, based upon the testimony of a shrewd convicted felon, and it would take a little short of a small miracle to convince all 12 jurors that my client was not guilty of *anything*. So, even while preparing to make the best case I could in his defense, I kept an ulterior strategy in the back of my mind: I would work to turn at least one juror into such a strong believer in our case that he or she would "hang" the jury even if everyone else was prepared to convict my client. I'm certain many defense lawyers reach this point in defending a criminal case.

The hunt for a hung jury requires a defense lawyer to seek a more intense connection with targeted jurors—and that sort of connection is uncertain and not guaranteed. Fortunately, this connection is not impossible. This trial lasted for about four weeks. During all that time, lawyers are generally able to develop some rapport with at least some of the jurors.

These sorts of connections are almost inevitable. Lawyers will give knowing looks to their favorites in the box. The jurors will also betray their emotions by the looks on their faces at crucial moments in the trial. In ways that would seem entirely mundane in most social situations, trial lawyers get to know jurors despite the prohibition against direct communication. And if you've ever spent any time with a trial team, you would know that after court adjourns each day, the lawyers speak among themselves about what they've gleaned from the jurors' reactions to the day's proceedings.

This particular jury comprised a wide mix of people, white and Black, male and female, old and young. And as the prosecutors laid out their case, I watched several of their faces, concluding in several instances that various individual jurors were probably beyond my ability to reach—they appeared convinced that my client was ultimately culpable. But there was one juror, a Black woman, who seemed, by my reading of her body language, more predisposed to take an open-minded approach toward my client or, perhaps, a more questioning approach to the government's case. Early on, I decided that if I was going to get a hung jury, I needed to convince this one woman that she could stand her ground in jury deliberations and hold to her position that the government had not proven its case against my client beyond a reasonable doubt. I never gave up on trying to exonerate my client before the entire jury—but by some measure, my focus from some point in the trial was geared to an audience of one.

Consider, for a moment, how that might have changed your approach if you had stood in my shoes. As a good lawyer, you would almost certainly have taken pains to take notice of even the slightest reaction from this single juror. When did she smile? When did she scowl? Which witnesses prompted her to furrow her brow—and which elicited a wry smile? Which lines of argument got her scribbling in her notebook—and which steered her to daydream? Moreover, you would have paid her some special attention when speaking to the jury as a whole. As a lawyer fulfilling your responsibility to do everything possible to advance your client's interest, you would have pressed every permissible advantage.

I will never know why, in the end, we got a hung jury in that case. After initially complaining that they could not come to a unanimous verdict, the judge implored the jury to keep deliberating, but they came back time and again reporting that they were at internal loggerheads. Eventually, the judge declared a mistrial because the jury could not reach a unanimous verdict. We were never given an opportunity to "poll" the jury, namely to ask the jurors individually how they had voted while in deliberations. Several years later, I learned that the jury was hung eleven to one to convict my client. I remain convinced today that the one Black, female juror I'd identified was the lone holdout. And to this day, I believe that her view of the case was likely impacted by the interpersonal connection we forged over the course the trial. Indeed, my "source" for this information also believes this one Black woman was the holdout. Was that connection forged in some part on the basis of our shared identity? Was she more open to my argument because, as a Black woman, she felt more at ease listening to points made by a Black man? It's impossible to know for sure. And even if we knew for sure which juror held out, it would be impossible to disaggregate for sure which elements influenced any individual juror's decision. To me, this shows why diversity matters so much—it allows a team, like ours, to forge different sets of relationships. And those relationships can work to an enormously powerful effect.

There is a place today to debate the legacy of discrimination, prejudice, enslavement, and more in America.[113] But for all we may want business corporations to make decisions using a moral compass, hiring a broad range of employees need not be an exercise in corporate self-sacrifice. To succeed in the contemporary marketplace, it's important that leaders of organizations embrace and enhance their internal diversity. At the end of the day, it's difficult to determine how either racial animus or benevolent diversity have affected my career. I do know I've been allowed the opportunity to work hard many times under a great deal of stress and earn my place in the profession in pursuit of what some would say has been a successful career. But I also know we haven't completed the mission yet.

I'm enormously proud of the role I've played opening doors for those following behind me. And I hope, in the years to come, that the diversity trajectory—the pace by which we ensure that people of various backgrounds have access to every possible professional opportunity—heightens to the point that Americans of every race, ethnicity, and gender believe that they have, in earnest, the capacity to open every door and become successful.

CHAPTER SEVEN

ESCAPING THE POLITICAL RHETORIC OF CRIME

Two Tragedies in Atlanta

In the summer of 2020, just a few short weeks after a young man named Rayshard Brooks was killed by police officers in the parking lot outside an Atlanta Wendy's, a child was made the victim of another senseless act of violence. Secoriea Turner was riding in the back seat when her mother steered innocently into a parking lot with the intention of turning the vehicle around. Unfortunately, amid the demonstrations over Brooks's killing, the parking lot had been barricaded by a group of young people. When some among the group mistakenly assumed that the car posed an incoming threat, several drew guns. Within seconds, shots had been fired, wounding little Secoriea. In the panicked moments that followed, she was rushed to the Atlanta Medical Center.[114] But to no avail. She died later that night, her young life taken away at eight years old.

Brooks's killing garnered national attention, largely because it came on the heels of George Floyd's murder in Minneapolis. The officers involved were promptly fired, the police chief quickly resigned, community anger began to fulminate, and reporters converged on Atlanta in anticipation of demonstrations.[115] Brooks's death appeared to fit a narrative many knew all too well: an unarmed Black person killed, seemingly for no good reason, by an overly aggressive white police officer. What followed has come to be almost routine. A whole range of voices—members of the mainstream media, many scholars inside the academy, and even a range of leaders within the Black community—attempting to explicitly connect the shooting to what they view as wanton and racist violence perpetrated by white police officers against innocent Black people. This represented another clarion call for nationwide reform.

Secoriea's murder, by contrast, received a mere pittance of attention. Neither the media nor leaders of the Black community itself gave it much attention. Local reporters made mention of the crime—but the national networks certainly did not send camera crews to report on the moment-by-moment developments in the case. The pundits and experts who oftentimes help the nation make sense of current events did not cite her shooting as evidence of a broad trend that society would have to address. In the broader scheme of things, Secoriea's murder was little more than a blip on the community's radar. And that was, in my opinion, for one simple reason: Secoriea was Black, and so were her killers.

To be sure, it's not my view that the relationship between America's law enforcement community and the nation's Black citizens is entirely as it should be. I am well aware that those who are employed by the government have a special responsibility to serve and protect. Because of that, I believe that abuse at a police officer's hand is a special kind of horror. To that end, I was shocked and dismayed by George Floyd's murder, and I've experienced my fair share of worrisome moments over the years about the fates of my two sons, both of whom are Black. Like many Black parents, when they were coming of age, my wife and I gave them "the talk," urging them to be abundantly humble and nonconfrontational throughout any interaction with the police. They were told in no uncertain terms not to react to rude or even arbitrary, unjust treatment by police officers.

But I don't believe that the fear Black people, and Black men in particular, have of being abused by members of the law enforcement community should distract us from other prevailing realities in our communities. Because if we focus on this fear to the exclusion of so much else, we begin to lose perspective. Today our society's nearly exclusive emphasis on the singular fear of racially oriented police brutality is muting the alarm that should be sounding over a much more pervasive threat: the rising spate of violent crime committed by Black people against other innocent, law-abiding Black people. It is a shame what happened to Rayshard Brooks. But what happened to Secoriea Turner is no less horrific. In fact, it's worse.

I can already feel the blowback that last paragraph is likely to elicit among those laser-focused on police brutality. Some of my friends, colleagues, and readers will be tempted to ask: How could any educated Black man compare instances of a police officer killing an innocent civilian with any given crime done by one ordinary citizen against another? How, they might add, could I deign to distract the public from the extraordinary threat of police violence? Maybe most cutting: How, as a Black man, could I muddy an issue that unites the Black community in favor of directing more focused attention on one that is almost sure to divide us?

But that's exactly what I intend to do, and for one simple reason: I think those who hope to steer the Black community toward greater prosperity and security make a grave mistake by ignoring stark realities in pursuit of convenient or false cohesion.

Among those who hold political positions of authority in minority neighborhoods, there are many advantages to highlighting the plight Black people face when confronted by white police officers. We're drawn together as a community when our brethren are upset with law enforcement. But that doesn't obviate the reality that so many of us know so well: The most potent threat to personal securities for most Black people in this country comes from . . . other Black people. We're simply not safe in our own communities. And that's not primarily because the police are apt to abuse us—though that is, of course, sometimes the case. We're not secure because we are not sufficiently protected from the predatory and reckless within our own community. To be sure, crime in some predominately white communities has increased and is unacceptable. This crime is being condemned by political leaders in a high-profile manner. However, I focus here on crime against innocent, law-abiding Black people that many leaders are reluctant to address honestly and effectively.

If we as a society intend to protect future generations of Black Americans from the violence that too often upends their lives, we're going to need to shift a great deal of our focus to what some call "Black-on-Black" crime, no matter how divisive that issue may appear to be. Addressing that reality with open eyes may not pull us together as a community united against a threat from the outside. But it will, at long last, protect more ordinary citizens from the sorts of horrors that ended Secoriea Turner's young and promising life and the lives of so many other innocent Black people in our country.

Hiding the Dirty Linen

The discrepancy between perception and reality predates this moment. I began my career in law enforcement in the early 1980s—I was appointed in 1982 as the U.S. Attorney for the Northern District of Georgia. The office headquarters were in Atlanta and much of the same dynamic prevailed then, if not in quite as stark a contrast. Leaders in the Black community, which is, in and of itself, diverse and often riven by division, were loath to call out the Black men and women who were making victims of their neighbors. And the media, which thrives on conflict and often finds self-serving reasons to play up interracial violence, reflected the same bias.

As U.S. Attorney, I was able largely to turn a deaf ear to the distortions shaping public opinion. It didn't matter to me whether the media covered the indictments my office brought in federal court, or whether leaders in the Black community were criticizing our efforts in public speeches. This was perhaps proven by the fact that the Civil Rights icon, Rev. Joseph Lowery, once labeled me an "equal opportunity prosecutor." My office went after criminals with the same seriousness of purpose no matter the race of the victims or suspects.[116] That said, when I returned to private practice after serving as U.S. Attorney and took a seat on Atlanta's Metropolitan Crime Commission, I was struck by the chasm separating popular impression from reality, and I became increasingly concerned about the effects those distortions tended to have. And they have persisted even as crime numbers have ebbed and flowed.

Today we sit at what I fear may be the tail end of a truly remarkable trend in American history: Until recent years, for more than three decades, beginning during the presidency of George H. W. Bush, violent crime had been in retreat. Many younger Americans today don't understand the force that crime had psychologically among those of who were born earlier. Crime reached a point where some believed there was no way out, and members of the Black community—many of whom lived in neighborhoods that were disproportionately affected by high crime rates—wondered if anything could be done.

But that's not what we heard from community leaders at the time. Far from being focused on the way crack dealers and crack users in particular were terrorizing law-abiding Black Americans (again, to a disproportionate degree), the politicians, preachers, and pillars of our communities, including the media, too frequently took pains to highlight only crimes perpetrated across the racial divide. Blacks in a poorer section of Los Angeles were more likely to be murdered or beaten by other Blacks than they were by officers wearing an LAPD badge, but it was the beating of Rodney King in 1992 by LA police officers that led to widespread rioting. And that outlook typified the prevailing approach in communities across the country.

To give you a sense of how distorted the attention was even back then, in 1988, a quarter of the nation's households included a victim of crime—one in four. But the threat wasn't evenly spread across the races. White men had a one in 179 chance of being murdered that year—too high, of course, but fairly remote. Black men, by contrast, had a one in 30 chance. In other words, Black men were at much greater risk. But the alarming rate of victimization failed to spur the Black community's leaders to provide an accurate accounting of the underlying threat. At the time, 94 percent of violent crimes Blacks endured were perpetrated by, well, other Blacks.[117] And yet the disproportionate cause for alarm within the Black community centered on police brutality and injustice.

Some understood the nature of the problem at the time, Democrat and Republican alike. As I sat in Atlanta befuddled by the failure to focus on the true nature of the nation's crime problem, the then junior Senator from the State of Delaware, a member of the Judiciary Committee, issued this statement:

> We must take back the streets. It doesn't matter whether or not the person that is accosting your son or daughter, or my son or daughter, my wife, your husband, my mother, your parents—it doesn't matter whether or not they were deprived as a youth. It doesn't matter whether or not they had no background that would enable them to have, to become socialized into the fabric of society. It doesn't matter whether or not they're the victims of society. The end result is they're about to knock my mother on the head with a lead pipe, shoot my sister, beat up my wife, take on my sons. So, I don't want to ask, "What made them do this?" They must be taken off the streets![118]

Now, President Joe Biden was absolutely right at the time. It wasn't just that so much of society was *ignoring* the nature of the crime in the Black community—it was that many were making excuses for it and choosing in many cases to focus on other challenges. Reasonable as it might have been to cite poverty, or prejudice, or historic injustice as an *explanation* for someone falling into a life of crime, that explanation should not then, and should not now, shield them from culpability. Those who do wrong need to be held to account or else those who *could* otherwise live a peaceful existence may begin to presume that they can hurt others—white and Black—and get away with it. And that we should not, and cannot, abide.

In ways that are even more amplified today, often to the point that they are deafening on the national political stage, fear of what I call "airing the dirty laundry" appears to be spurring Black leaders to turn their backs on the problem afflicting our neighbors and peers to a vastly disproportionate degree. Black criminals, while victimizing other Blacks, have come to be viewed in the abstract as victims of broader social injustice. In this narrative, the situation cannot be reversed unless broader social dynamics are addressed—dynamics born in decades and centuries of prejudice and discrimination. Then, as now, many Black leaders have been drawn to temptation; eager to build cohesion *within* the community, they focus on threats from the outside. To use a term that is popular in today's parlance, this is simply a form of "wokeness."

Pointing out the deep distortion born of this strategy isn't to deny the horrors perpetrated by members of law enforcement on the Black community. The so-called "politics of crime" in America have always been inextricably linked to the "politics of race." Where systemic racism *does* exist, it should be eliminated, root and branch. But the tendency born decades ago to ignore the culpability that individual Black men have for crimes against people in their own community, and indeed in any community, needs to be called out for what it is: a deep and harmful injustice. If we are going to protect Black people from crime, we need to have the temerity to call out all predators and hold them responsible.

A Familiar Threat Emerges, Once Again

More recently, two things have happened. First, after falling for decades, crime has begun to tick back up. Not all crime rose through the pandemic—certain categories, including property crime, remain near record low levels. But violent crime has spiked in ways that will feel terribly familiar to those who lived through the 1970s and 1980s. In 2020, murder rose by nearly a third, marking the biggest jump since Dwight Eisenhower was President. The nation saw aggravated assault rates grow by 12 percent. And while some of the rise can be ascribed to the disruption wrought by Covid-19, some of the shift actually predates the novel coronavirus.[119]

The most notable jumps occurred in America's big cities. In Seattle, murder investigations jumped by nearly three-quarters between 2019 and 2020, even as the city's police force hemorrhaged officers. In my hometown of Atlanta, the murder rate jumped 62 percent over the same period, making crime the central focus of the 2021 mayoral campaign. But the media and many among the country's Black leaders, including those most tied to the Black Lives Matter movement, remained focused on officer-related violence. Yet, among many others, including many in the Black community, another concern has emerged as a result: the risk of being victimized by an ordinary criminal.[120]

The second shift is related to that discrepancy. Among those focused on the fight for social justice, the crusade against "systemic racism" has become more than a cause—it has emerged, in Columbia Professor John McWhorter's estimation, as something more akin to a "religion." As he put it in his book *Woke Racism*: "I do not mean that these people's ideology is 'like' a religion. I seek no rhetorical snap in this comparison. I mean that it actually is a religion. An anthropologist would see no difference in type between Pentecostalism and this new form of antiracism."[121]

McWhorter's point is exactly right. For too many now at the forefront of efforts to eliminate prejudice and the legacy of discrimination in America, balance and reason have taken a back seat to dogma and blind faith.

Every bad thing that happens to a person of color now can, it seems, be explained by the legacy of racism. And that means that even as Black people are victimizing other Black people through crimes of violence, some can continue to hold the view that the perpetrators are themselves victims of a broader injustice.

In the public discourse, fights over "cancel culture" and "political correctness" sidestep what is a more fundamental issue: the vast disparity that separates society's focus on different categories of crimes, one that inflates the prevalence of police brutality far beyond reality. And that's not just true among the so-called "woke," some of whom prevail at the top echelons of the nation's great academic institutions. It's true among some leaders of the Black community who choose to direct undue attention to white-on-Black violence seemingly as a way to unite people of color.

I was worried about just this sort of distortion early in my career. After my stint as U.S. Attorney, I wrote an article for the Heritage Foundation on "Black-on-Black" crime that became a cause of some turbulence during my Senate confirmation hearings more than a decade later.[122] But the divide has become much starker today, and the repercussions for taking a dissenting view—namely, in demanding more protection against the sorts of crimes that ordinary citizens, Black and white, commit against other citizens—are much more drastic. It's not just that certain voices in the public dialogue would like to steer more attention to officer-related violence. It's that any deviation from that focus is sometimes considered racist—even meritless or misguided—in and of itself.

Take the case of Lee Fang, as an example. Fang reports for *The Intercept*, an online news source with a decidedly progressive slant. In 2020, he traveled to California amid the nationwide outcry from George Floyd's murder and attended demonstrations that were understood broadly to be part of the Black Lives Matter movement. He videotaped an interview with a young Black man named Max, whose two cousins had been murdered in East Oakland. In an emotional moment, Max asked Fang: "Why does a Black life only matter when a white man takes it? Like, if a white man takes my life tonight, it's going to be national news, but if a Black man takes my life, it might not even be spoken of."[123]

After Fang posted the interview, a colleague of his at *The Intercept* took exception. In her view, his decision to give voice to Max's query undermined the central message of the underlying demonstrations. Fang was, to her view, crossing a line simply by choosing to cover an element of the crime story that did not comport with the narrative that she considered most important. And while Fang stood by his reporting initially, he eventually apologized for doing something that, to my view, was entirely in keeping with the practice of good journalism. He was exploring a deeply textured topic in order to give his readers a more complete and nuanced view.[124]

In fact, I take an even stronger view. I believe that Max's view should be kept front and center and that the pervasive focus on the instances where white officers abuse Black citizens should be put in a context that provides the public with a real sense of what's happening in the Black community. Police should not be allowed to abuse civilians—but nor should anyone be misled into believing that police misconduct or worse is the primary threat to Black men and women today. Everyone should be made to understand that the most important challenge is to get the bad guys and to ensure that would-be bad guys are not tempted to victimize their neighbors and others. The race of those criminals and would-be perpetrators should not matter even one iota.

Make Room for the Criminals

As a U.S. Attorney from 1982 to 1986, I made it a mission to ensure my office was viewed as a partner by Georgia's local and state prosecutors. Most violent crimes—murders, robberies, etc.—are traditionally handled by State District Attorneys. The Justice Department, by contrast, tends to focus on more complex cases: organized crime, for example, and white-collar crime. But insofar as local, state, and federal prosecutors frequently compete for opportunities to handle high-profile cases, I wanted instead for my office to support local efforts whenever appropriate.

As I testified during my confirmation hearing in 2001, the Department of Justice "must work creatively, think outside of the box as it is sometimes referred to, and work with local law enforcement agencies and perhaps even some private organization to attack the problem of violent crime."[125] Ultimately, in my view, it was the responsibility of government, whether local, state, or federal, to protect innocent civilians from those who would do them harm, and government would more likely be successful in that effort if there were meaningful cooperative efforts.

For good and for bad, in the years since I served as the U.S. Attorney for the Northern District of Georgia, the American criminal justice landscape has changed in drastic ways. Governments employed a whole range of strategies to counteract the criminal activity that had metastasized during the 1970s and the 1980s. Law enforcement agencies added beat cops, embraced "broken windows" policing, established civilian complaint boards, and more. But perhaps most notably, governments at all levels toughened their sentencing guidelines and, in some cases, imposed mandatory minimums for criminal activity that appeared like a gateway to violent and other antisocial behavior. This approach applied in particular to drug offenses.

There is, today, ample room to debate whether this was wise. In general, I believe that government should deal with criminals with a firm hand and that those who break the law should be subject to penalties that are commensurate with the seriousness of their crimes. Tougher sanctions, including more mandatory jail time, were not the sole reason that crime finally began to fall in the 1990s—but I'm yet to be convinced that tougher sanctions did not play an important role. And, had I not been compelled by circumstance to turn my attention more squarely to the challenges of terrorism and corporate fraud during my tenure as Deputy Attorney General in the early years of the Bush Administration, I almost surely would have proposed using additional federal resources to meet this very challenge. What I testified to before the Senate during my confirmation hearing reflected my strong desire to confront violent crime.

That said, the resulting explosion in the population of prisoners in the United States has had a material impact on the strategies that policymakers and law enforcement have taken when trying to keep our communities safe. We need to think closely about whether the *right* criminals are incarcerated for the *right* amount of time. And what has become increasingly clear over the last two decades is that our priorities have been completely lost in the rush to throw more and more Americans behind bars.

At the federal level, the shift has been dramatic. In the 40 years that began in 1940—from the Roosevelt Administration through the Carter Administration—the *federal* prison population held roughly steady at 24,000 inmates. Since then, however, for the reasons stated above—most notably a focus on drug crimes that ensnared more and more minor characters in the drug trade—the budget and burden borne by the Federal Bureau of Prisons (BOP) has grown dramatically. As of 2016, there were more than 200,000 federal prisoners, and the BOP's costs have risen dramatically from a not insubstantial $330 million the year Ronald Reagan was elected President to $6.9 billion.[126]

This long-term trend, one that is reflected at the state level as well, has had three major effects. The first is that the sprint to toughen the criminal code has now gone too far—people who really should be given reasonable sentences for relatively minor crimes spend too much time locked up. The federal government's desire to combat the drug trade was worthy, and narcotics kingpins should still be subject to harsh justice. But a mother who "assists" her abusive husband to sell drugs on the street for fear of being further abused should not be forced behind bars for years at a time. The impulse to disincentivize drug activity by making sentences harsher has gone too far.

Second, that impulse to be punitive has reshaped the goal of the nation's criminal justice systems. In many states, prisons are run by a

"Department of Corrections," a title designed to suggest that the time that incarcerated individuals spend segregated from the rest of society should be designed to give them the tools required to succeed without resorting to a life of crime when they leave prison. But with the prison population growing so dramatically, any real effort to establish time behind bars as a fresh start has been lost. The concept of rehabilitation has gone away. Prison shouldn't be cushy—but neither should the government seek simply to warehouse lawbreakers. The cost of doing so is unacceptable and deleterious to society as a whole.

Third, and perhaps least understood by the wider public, the tendency to fill *federal* prison cells with fairly low-level drug offenders has hampered the role that U.S. Attorneys *should* be able to play in combating drug crimes. In instances where state and local prosecutors are overwhelmed— places where violent offenders are liable to be granted bail simply because state and local jails don't have space to keep accused criminals before they are put on trial—federal prosecutors should be able to step in, charge those same criminals federally, and then keep them off the street. Unfortunately, in cases where the federal facilities are overwhelmed as well, federal prosecutors are sometimes unable to offer this safety valve. This enhances the possibility that a violent criminal, charged but not yet convicted, will be returned to the streets.

But if too many people are unnecessarily held before conviction, we need to be careful about whom we let out of jail without bail. In a strange turn of events that also emanates from the fact that law enforcement, until recently, has proven so effective at combating crime, many so-called progressive district attorneys have now taken great pride instead in demonstrating how lenient or attuned to social justice they have become. As *The Wall Street Journal* has editorialized: "Local prosecutors now brag about how few crimes they prosecute. California has effectively decriminalized shoplifting." Referring then to local bail reform initiatives that have had the effect of making it much easier for violent criminals to return to the street after being charged with violent crimes, the *Journal* wrote: "In hindsight, perhaps releasing thousands of repeat offenders from jails and prisons to alleviate overcrowding wasn't such a good idea."[127]

The challenge then is to strike the right balance in embracing reform. The lesson to be learned from the efforts to make our criminal justice system more punitive as a deterrent—an effort that likely played a role in reducing crime but quite clearly drove a needless deluge of incarcerations—is not to overcorrect for the problem. Legitimate concerns about how the government is too harsh should not be taken as license to go too far in the opposite direction. What we need, instead, is what might be called simultaneous "front-end" and "back-end" reform. That is, we need to be more discerning about who is actually put in prison, and we should do a much better job ensuring that those who are *not* a threat to society are given opportunities to re-enter society with the tools required to live a law-abiding life.

Fortunately, and perhaps surprisingly, bipartisan efforts in Washington point the way forward. During the Trump years, Bob Goodlatte, Chairman of the House Judiciary Committee, and longtime Democratic stalwart Rep. John Conyers worked collaboratively on the First Step Act, which tamped down mandatory minimums for certain drug crimes, shaved down the punitive impact of the so-called "three strikes" laws popularized in the early 1990s, and expanded the scope of judicial discretion. It was clearly a major bipartisan piece of legislation passed during President Trump's four years in office.[128]

A Balanced Approach

More than three decades ago, during a period when the nation's capital was viewed from much of the outside world largely as a den of crime and poverty, the Chief Judge of the Superior Court of the District of Columbia revealed the depth of his outrage when sentencing a young criminal. Judge H. Carl Moultrie was a Senior Black Judge and a beacon of wisdom to citizens of all backgrounds in Washington and around the country. But looking down from his bench at a recalcitrant and unrepentant young offender, he said what many others, including many Black Washingtonians, were thinking about his ilk: "He's just a criminal. He's just damn mean. They don't give a damn. Your life to them is nothing. I would like to see the death penalty. I would use it."[129]

If any judge, let alone a white judge, were to say that today, the comments would spark outrage. The use of the word "they" would be interpreted as a slight to all young Black men. Judge Moultrie's sentiment would be interpreted by many pundits and activists as further evidence that the criminal justice system is "systemically" racist. His unvarnished disgust for the underlying behavior would be understood as a window into how those in power generally view minorities and young Black men in particular. No wonder, many would say aloud, that gross disparities exist between the nation's races. And in some instances, that sentiment would be dead-on accurate. Racism *should* be excised from the criminal justice system.

But the "woke" outrage would likely look past the crucial context for Moultrie's comment: The young Black thugs he had grown so accustomed to seeing in his courtroom—and I am perfectly well aware of how loaded the word "thug" is today—weren't engaged in an effort to help Black communities in America climb out from the decades and centuries of abuse and prejudice that had forced them to the margins of society. Quite the opposite, they were overwhelmingly victimizing other Black people. Their violence was being perpetrated on other Black people. They were instilling fear in other Black people. Whatever systemic issues were at play, their thuggish behavior was itself victimizing the Black community. And as anathema as it may have been then for leaders of the Black community to indict members of their own communities for the communities' broader struggles, Moultrie's comment laid the truth bare.

Today, of course, it's not enough to act on Moultrie's sentiment. Changes made since the 1980s require us to balance an effort to be smarter about the approach we take to less serious offenders with other initiatives designed to tighten the screws and protect the public from violent offenders regardless of race. Federal prosecutors, for example, should become more actively involved in sharing the burden of addressing violent crime with local prosecutors. When it seems likely, for example, that a violent offender will be released on bail by a local judge despite the possibility of committing additional crimes, federal prosecutors should actively offer to assist their state colleagues. Moreover, the Department of Justice should help establish additional violent crime task forces so that prosecutors at all levels of government are in more active and constant coordination.

The Biden Administration is steering the Department of Justice in this direction explicitly. A May 2021 memo from Deputy Attorney General Lisa Monaco established a standing Violent Crime Reduction Steering Committee that reaches across the Department's various silos to coordinate the federal government's efforts to combat violence in communities. Perhaps most important, Monaco put new emphasis on a Department-wide program known as Project Safe Neighborhoods, which directs local U.S. Attorneys to play a more active, strategic, and coordinated role with local and state law enforcement officials to combat violent crime, providing resources, technical support, and accountability for those on the front lines.[130] As Attorney General Merrick Garland said upon release of Monaco's memo: "In this endeavor, we will engage our communities as critical partners. And through our grantmaking, we will support programming at all stages—from the earliest violence interruption strategies to post-conviction reentry services."[131]

But beyond what prosecutors can do to stem the most recent uptick in violent crime, ordinary citizens, like me and you, can do much more to shift our focus onto the challenge as it is rather than as we might want it to be. As Justice Robert Jackson once said: "It is not the function of government to keep the citizen from falling into error, it is the function of the citizen to keep the government from falling into error." If policymakers, responding to the will of the people, remain focused so overwhelmingly on the threat police officers pose to innocent members of minority communities, we probably will not be able to address the more pervasive threat posed to members of the Black community, namely the criminals who live in their communities.

There is no doubting the horror of George Floyd's murder or the sorrow wrought by Rayshard Brooks's death in that Atlanta Wendy's parking lot. But Secoriea Turner's killing, though at the hands of Black men, was no less tragic. As a Black man, I am not inured to the threat of racism, but neither am I blind to the fact that my sons are less likely to die at the hands of a police officer than they are of being killed by someone who shares their skin color. In the end, what matters is that all law-abiding citizens of our great country remain safe on the streets and in their homes, no matter the color of their skin. And to get there, or at least to get us closer to that ideal, we all need to direct our attention and resources to the challenges we face together as a society, not to the challenges most gratifying to our sense of grievance or community.

CHAPTER EIGHT

LIFE

I HAD TRAVELED FROM Atlanta to make a pitch for an interesting investigative matter for General Motors. General Motors had been a client of mine, but this matter was a complex one and required me to present how I would handle it to General Motors' in-house counsel. I was in the office of Tom Gottschalk, the highly respected General Counsel of General Motors, and his assistant came in and said to Tom, "Mr. Thompson has a call. It's the Governor of Georgia." What a shock! I don't know to this day what Tom Gottschalk thought of that call—he did have a puzzled smile on his face as I left his office to take it—but General Motors did retain me to handle the matter.

This is how my legal career has played out over the years. It has been an exciting mix of pure legal work, work in public policy, and, yes, politics. It has been, at times, a very challenging, but always satisfying, run.

And, by the way, I was being called by Governor Zell Miller, a Democrat, to join the State of Georgia Board of Education. I was recommended to the Governor by my good friend Johnny Isakson, a Republican, who went on to become a great United States Senator from Georgia who was beloved by Republicans and Democrats alike.

As noted at the beginning, the intended purpose of this book is to show how various episodes of my life and career shine a light on some of the challenges we face today and how we, as a society, can successfully address them. But there's something else that has run through my thoughts while working on this project. If we lawyers are to truly play a constructive role in society as we serve our clients, we should strive to be wise and understand—even enjoy—LIFE. Keith Richards of the Rolling Stones titled his expansive book simply, *Life*.[132] And, Life is what I think is important. For me, lawyers must understand Life beyond our narrow, professional vistas. If you understand Life, you understand that giving legal advice is a serious, nuanced, and even quiet process. Not a loud or fist-pounding one. I strongly believe that in most instances, the lawyer should not be the central figure in the process. She is simply trying to help her client solve a legal problem. My mentor, Judge Griffin Bell, often said that the job of a lawyer is to solve his client's legal problems and not necessarily vanquish an adversary. That is what I've tried to do in my legal career while, at the same time, understanding Life.

Important to me and this understanding is dealing with the WHAT MIGHT HAVE BEENs in my career. We all have them. I have two that I think are important.

When I joined PepsiCo in 2004, CEO Steve Reinemund and I had a "handshake" agreement—an understanding that I would remain at the company for at least five years. About two years into my job, I received a call from an executive recruiter who told me that officials at Apple had reviewed information about me and wanted me to travel to Cupertino, California, for an interview. Although working for Apple at the time was considered a tremendous job opportunity, I thought about my commitment to Steve and my PepsiCo executive team colleagues. After consideration, I informed the recruiter that I would not take the interview but would remain at PepsiCo. Now, I have absolutely no idea whether, after an interview, I would have received a job offer at Apple. Nevertheless, I have no regrets.

That decision, made some 17 years ago, represents the essence of what I've tried to do in my career, and that is to be a person of my word.

———

After Justice Sandra Day O'Connor announced her intention to retire from the United States Supreme Court, I received a call from a senior official in the White House asking me if I was interested in being considered for nomination to the Supreme Court. The official told me that President Bush liked me. I told the official it would be an honor to be considered, and he told me I would be getting a call soon. The call never came, and I did not know what happened until years later after reading Jan Crawford Greenburg's book *Supreme Conflict: The Inside Story of the Struggle for Control of the United States Supreme Court*. To be sure, I realized at the time of the call that I was a long shot. I knew that Senior White House Counsel Harriet Miers and United States Circuit Court of Appeals Judges J. Michael Luttig and Samuel Alito were being considered. But Greenburg describes in her book a dinner between Leonard Leo of the Federalist Society (I was a member of the Federalist Society at the time) and Alex Azar, the General Counsel of the Department of Health and Human Services. Azar speculated that President Bush might nominate me for the Court. Greenburg noted that even though I was a good friend of Supreme Court Justice Clarence Thomas, some conservatives worried that I "lacked a clear philosophy and would move left like Justice Kennedy."[133] Now the reason why I never received the call was clear. I did receive a memorable call, related to a potential Supreme Court nomination, in my PepsiCo office from Senator Edward Kennedy of Massachusetts. Senator Kennedy said he supported me to replace O'Connor and wanted to know whether he should publicly praise me or condemn me. I responded, "If you want me on the Supreme Court, Senator, you had better condemn me." Soon after, the Senator did just that.

Again, no regrets. As a practicing lawyer I represented individual clients sometimes facing prison or business entities sometimes facing extinction.

I felt no need to speak out on the hot-button issues of Second Amendment rights or abortion. Again, I kept to what I believe was my essence: a practicing lawyer who always put his clients' interests first.

Looking back on my career, there is no doubt in my mind that, to the extent I've been successful, it's because I've always been interested in not only the law but the broader and wondrous implications of Life.

The Wisdom of Cicero

Life, even as I practiced law actively and intensely and at the highest levels of government and the private sector, has come into sharper focus as I approach my 49th year of law practice. I recently read a little book, *How to Grow Old*. It was written by Cicero in 44 BC and was brought to my attention by the columnist Jonathan V. Last. Several passages resonated with me.

"He plants trees for use of another age."[134]

Cicero is quoting Caecilius Statius, who said that for a well-lived life, we must continue to work and cultivate the field. The old can contribute their wisdom and experience to help those who follow. For me, this is why it has been so important and gratifying to teach law at the University of Georgia School of Law on and off since 2001. Teaching not only has made me a better lawyer, it has been immensely satisfying. Receiving a note from a former student about her experiences in my class is, simply put, a great joy. And I hope this effort will also be a "tree" that will guide lawyers and other leaders to work toward a better, safer, and more just society.

"So there is truth in Solon's verse . . . in which he said that as he grew older he learned more and more every day. Surely there can be no greater pleasure than the pleasure of the mind."[135]

Michelangelo famously once said, "I continue to learn."[136] That's what has happened to me. I now focus more on the things that make life more meaningful and even enjoyable than when I was practicing law full time. I can now selectively accept matters involving challenging legal problems and help clients solve them while continuing to focus on passions that have enlightened me in the past and made me, I think, a better person. In the process, I continue to enjoy, in the words of Cicero, "The pleasure of the mind."

"The particular fruit of old age, as I have said, is the memory of the abundant blessings of what has come before."[137]

I have been a very, very lucky person. For this, I'm grateful.

Over the years, I've given several commencement speeches, and I almost always include the life lesson I once heard from the writer Alex Haley. It goes like this: Haley and a friend were walking down a long and winding path that was adjacent to a tall, beautiful wall constructed with a polished, slick stone. As they were making their way down the path, Haley noticed a large turtle sitting atop the wall. And he thought to himself, *This is very strange for a turtle to climb all the way up this slippery wall.*

So Haley turned to his friend and asked, "How do you suppose the turtle got up there?"

The friend thought for a moment and then said, "I don't know, but you can bet on one thing—he did not get there by himself."[138] This story really sums up my life. I've had so many good friends and mentors who have supported me and made my life and career possible. This is now the time to enjoy the memory of these "abundant blessings." An important aspect of these "blessings" is to recall all the people I have helped in my legal career, people and institutions who entrusted their most complex and sensitive legal problems, and even their lives, to me. Following my formal swearing-in ceremony as Deputy Attorney General in 2001, my guests were in line to greet me and Attorney General John Ashcroft, who was standing next to me. As one of my former clients was about to shake John's hand, John asked him, "How do you know Larry?"

My former client replied, "He saved my butt!" This is the time to reflect and enjoy such moments that chronicle my life's work.

Seeing the World Through Other Eyes

One of the "pleasures of the mind" that gives me great joy and meaning is art. More than four decades ago, my wife, Brenda, and I began collecting art. In fits and starts, in between moments of distraction, often for me centered around the press of my work, but with an enduring seriousness of purpose and commitment to the pursuit of beautiful, historic art, we now have a substantial art collection. Taken together, we have today several hundred individual pieces in our collection, most of them created by African American artists. Our collection includes paintings, etchings, sculptures, and some photographs.

While this decades-long passion has given us a great deal of purely aesthetic pleasure—both of us enjoy looking at our art just for its beauty—we've been driven by other considerations: We believe that the stories of African American artists, and the stories told by their lives' work, are underappreciated and, in many cases, unknown. This is unfortunate. Great art by these artists remains largely unknown, and these artists' stories serve to help us understand American art in general and how Black artists have created beauty under very difficult circumstances. The art world will clearly benefit from this knowledge. So, with the benefit of our good fortune, we decided to try to collect as many of these stories as possible and share them widely.

Our art collection is the result of a serious effort. Maintaining it is a lot of "work." We have a registrar who catalogs and maintains the collection. We share our collection. As of 2023, we've gifted more than 300 pieces to museums across the country, including the Georgia Museum of Art in Athens, Georgia, the Phillips Collection in Washington, DC, the Saint Louis University Museum of Art in Saint Louis, Missouri, the University of Michigan Museum of Art in Ann Arbor, Michigan, the Detroit

Institute of Arts Museum in Detroit, Michigan, and the David C. Driskell Center at the University of Maryland in College Park, Maryland. We also lend our art to museums and galleries across the country for exhibitions.

For me, the process of building our collection has been joyous. Selecting the art, learning about the artists, and in doing so learning about their lives and struggles and accomplishments—the entire process has had a profound impact on me both as a lawyer and personally. I've been rounded by art. I've come to appreciate the fact that many artists, especially Black artists, continued to create beauty and meaning in the face of very difficult, and even hostile, circumstances. Art has become food for my soul.

We have also enjoyed the personal contact with scores of artists in our collection. Our relationship with Vertis Hayes is memorable and illustrative. Mr. Hayes (as we always called him) lived in Los Angeles when we met him. He died in 2000 but had been a part of the Harlem Renaissance art scene. He was very dear to us. When we traveled from Atlanta to Los Angeles to meet with him, he talked to us about the lack of opportunities for Black artists to obtain recognition or economic support for their art. We purchased several pieces of art from Mr. Hayes, and my wife, Brenda, tried, without success, to get galleries and museums interested in his work. Frustrated by this lack of attention he said one day to us that "it will be through [my] being in [your] collection that people will know my work." We were flattered at the time but saddened because he may have been correct. In 2009 the David C. Driskell Center at the University of Maryland organized an exhibition of our collection called *Tradition Redefined*.[139] There were over 70 paintings and sculptures in the exhibition, including two paintings by Mr. Hayes, and it traveled to several American cities, including St. Louis, Houston, and Jacksonville, Florida. In 2012 we gifted all the pieces in the exhibit to the Georgia Museum of Art at the University of Georgia. One of Mr. Hayes's paintings, "The Lynchers," is very moving in the way it depicts a horrific event. Mr. Hayes only painted the people who were observing the lynching, including children. The victim is not visible in the painting. It is now one of the most popular paintings at the Georgia Museum of Art and is in demand for lending to other museums. Brenda and I visited a major exhibit in Memphis where Mr. Hayes's painting was prominently featured. If Mr. Hayes was correct in his assessment of the role our collection would play in introducing the public to his art, then our collection is, as Brenda has stated in an essay written for the *Tradition Redefined* catalog, "Truly a mission accomplished."[140]

Another example: Our son, Larry Jr., attended law school at New York University. At a reception for students and their families, Naila Williams, a first-year student, introduced us to her parents, William T. and Patricia Williams. Brenda immediately recognized William T. as a prominent artist and greatly admired his work. Since then, we have not only enjoyed owning William T.'s wonderful work, we have also learned so much from his perspectives on art in general and his understanding of art by Black artists in particular. One of the favorite abstract pieces we own is by Jack White, now deceased, from New York City. I had not heard of Jack White until one day William T. said to us, "You need to see Jack White. He can paint his butt off."

In the decades before he was taken from us by Covid-19, David Driskell established himself not only as one of the nation's premier African American artists, but also one of our greatest African American art historians and collectors of art. After years of collecting, my wife and I had an opportunity to get to know David personally, initially as little more than curious art collectors but eventually as friends. Before the pandemic, he visited us at our home in Sea Island, and we spent a delightful several days with David and his family.

David was just a remarkable person. He had a deep understanding of the African American art experience and channeled that understanding into the art he created. He was a font of knowledge and a national treasure. He was also warm and personable. Most remarkable, his fervent belief that the story of American art could not be told without a greater understanding of African American art crystalized our shared notion that the key to understanding in so many situations demands that each and every person invest in building bridges to each other.

Several months ago my wife and I were involved in a gathering of art collectors in Atlanta. One of the topics of the session was art by African American artists. Amalia Amaki, a highly respected artist and academic, was the presenter. One of the attendees—a collector who knew a great deal about American abstract expressionism and who could have recited chapter and verse on the career of Jackson Pollock, perhaps the most famous modern American abstract artist—told us privately in the course of the discussion that he had never heard of Norman Lewis, an African American abstract artist featured prominently in Amaki's presentation. That might have been an understandable oversight for a novice collector. But Lewis is a major figure in modern American abstract art. He was the only African American in attendance at the famous Studio 35 meetings in Manhattan.[141] Although his work was largely overlooked by white art dealers and gallery owners, he did exhibit at one time with Mark Rothko, the preeminent white abstract artist. Lewis went on to help found the Spiral Art Group with leading African American artists such as Romare Bearden and Hale Woodruff. Today some of Lewis's work has sold for over a million dollars, but still much less than the work of Pollock and Rothko!

There's very little likelihood that I would ever have met David Driskell or the many other artists, curators, gallery owners, and educators with whom I've interacted had I not been involved in the art world. My life has clearly been enriched by my relationship to collecting art. Beyond the sheer joy I've experienced from collecting art, there is absolutely no doubt in my mind that I'm also a better lawyer because of my rich life experiences like teaching law school and collecting art.

Understanding the totality of the human condition is a key to solving legal problems and being an effective advocate. It is the key to understanding and relating to all kinds of people. And, in the end, law really is a people profession.

Rendering unto Caesar

I'm a Christian, but I'm definitely not a theologian. My faith is important to me, if for no other reason, because it helps me deal with the many mysteries of life. I rely on my faith to a point that on a handful of occasions, with clients facing intractable legal circumstances, I've joined with them in prayer. This is also why I've been humbled a few times in my career to witness legal miracles that, to my point of view, can't be explained by good lawyering or even luck.

That has never been clearer to me than in the case of Sholom Rubashkin, an Orthodox Jewish man from Brooklyn who had moved to Iowa to run a kosher meat-processing plant. Determined to run his plant the right way, Sholom adopted protocols for hiring workers at the plant in accordance with the law. Unfortunately, in 2008 Sholom was arrested for violating immigration laws when the authorities discovered illegal workers at the plant. When Sholom decided to go to trial and defend himself against the charges, prosecutors filed a superseding indictment against him on multiple counts of financial fraud. The charges alleged that he had inflated the value of collateral on a loan application, that he had falsified invoices, and that he had channeled some customer payments toward the cash needs of the business instead of into a "sweep account." Sholom was convicted, and even though he had no prior criminal history and his crime had no real, personal victims of fraud, he received a higher sentence than the convicted Enron executives—27 years in prison! Seventy-five law professors and former federal prosecutors signed a letter urging Attorney General Holder to investigate prosecutorial misconduct.[142] Compare what happened in this case to the wrongdoing admitted to by the large American banks and the billions paid in penalties during the financial crisis of 2008. Yet not one bank executive spent a single day in jail!

When I heard about the case from Rabbi Zvi Boyarsky, a young rabbi from Los Angeles, I was stunned. This was clearly a miscarriage of justice, and I volunteered to help.

In the years that followed, I worked closely with a terrific attorney from Los Angeles, Gary Apfel, in pursuing justice for Sholom. His appeal to the Eighth Circuit Court of Appeals, filed by terrific lawyers, was denied.[143] His petition for *Certiorari*, filed by another group of excellent lawyers, was denied by the Supreme Court.[144] Following these formal appeals, Gary Apfel and I traveled across the country and met with numerous Department of Justice officials, members of Congress, and others, seeking post-conviction relief for Sholom in the form of a pardon or clemency given the level of prosecutorial misconduct we believe occurred in his case. As Sholom's lawyers, Gary and I were compelled at each juncture to relay the news to Sholom's daughter, Rosa, and also to Rabbi Boyarsky, who was coordinating our efforts to seek justice on behalf of our client. And what was so remarkable about this was that, despite our frustrations, Rabbi Boyarsky responded to each setback with poise and equanimity. He never lost faith. What we relayed to him was not bad news to his ears. He told me countless times not to worry and that God would provide justice for Sholom.

And the Rabbi proved to be right. At the end of 2017, President Trump granted Sholom clemency and commuted his sentence to time served.[145] To this day, I don't understand why President Trump made this decision. This case involved allegedly illegal workers, which was a hot political issue at the time. I've seen this movie over a dozen times, and it never ends this way. Sholom was free after nearly eight years in prison. But in the days that followed, after watching thousands of people in Brooklyn celebrate the unlikely news of his release, I was convinced of at least one thing: The commutation did not come about solely because of our legal work, relentless as the Rabbi, Gary, and I had been in pursuing every angle. Something more powerful had intervened on Sholom's behalf. To my mind, his freedom was an act of God. To this very day, this is what I believe.

I relay this story not to suggest that we should expect Divine intervention in every case. We shouldn't. However, unexplained mysteries or even miracles do happen. We lawyers should be humble about the limits of what we can accomplish. It is healthy to accept this reality. As I grow older, I understand clearly that there are at times limits to what I can accomplish for a client. However, that does not mean I give up. As Rabbi Boyarsky has demonstrated to me, you always have God.[146]

The Power of Community

More than any other place I've ever been, the Chautauqua Institution, a picturesque community located on Lake Chautauqua in Western New York, combines the two extralegal themes I've discussed here—the need to experience the world beyond the narrow lens of the law and the importance of engaging in the process of discovering the mysteries of life. Founded more than a century ago by Lewis Miller, an Akron, Ohio, inventor and the father-in-law of Thomas Edison, and John Heyl Vincent, a Methodist minister, as a place devoted to "the highest ideals of the spirit and the intellect," it went on to become a beacon for what we now call lifelong learning.[147] I spoke at Chautauqua in 2004 at the invitation of my former law partner, Bill Goodell. It was my first visit to the Institution, and I have returned every year since. Now we even own a home on the grounds of the Institution. For me, Chautauqua represents the human desire to learn together and to explore the wider world in the spirit of community. It's a magical place, one in which differences, for the most part, are respected rather than feared. And, in many ways, it represents what America *should* aspire to become.

To a degree you might not expect from an Institution founded by Methodists, a broad range of faiths are now represented within Chautauqua's gates. There are denomination houses for every mainline Protestant denomination. There's also a Catholic house, a vibrant Jewish heritage center, and even a house where Orthodox Jewish patrons worship. Like many such places in our country, Chautauqua's population remains largely older and white. But the Institution has embarked on a serious effort toward diversity and inclusion. Progress is being made. An African American Heritage House is now in place. And Chautauquans are truly engaged in lifelong learning. Issues are discussed actively, seriously, and, most important, civilly. For example, I recently witnessed a serious discussion about how we can depoliticize issues related to climate change and come to some sort of common understanding about how we can move forward. This is a good example of how our larger society can benefit from what is going on at Chautauqua. In addition, a season at Chautauqua is also a wonderful mix of beauty and joy—the visual arts, dance, theater, classical music, opera, lectures, worship, and more. Chautauqua is truly unique and cannot be replicated.

As I write these words, I'm struck and saddened by the state of American society at this moment. I was floored when I read the following in the August 13, 2021, edition of *The Wall Street Journal*: "We're in a moment in which there's incredible disagreement about whether democracy is a good idea in the first place, what a good democracy looks like, what civility looks like and what truth looks like."[148]

We seem to be losing a sense of common ground, common purpose, and even common facts. Despite what former Attorney General of the United States William Barr said, despite what high-ranking officials from the FBI and Department of Homeland Security said, and despite the rulings of many Republican-appointed federal judges, many Americans still believe there was widespread fraud in the 2020 Presidential election. In fact, this view continues to be promulgated by former President Trump without much pushback from many members of his own political party.

At Chautauqua, led by President Michael Hill, the exploration of ideas and differences is welcomed and even celebrated. Efforts at finding common ground are made and mostly pursued in a civil manner. I've learned over the years that not much is accomplished through red-hot debate or screaming matches.

This may seem unrealistic, but Chautauqua was established to bridge political and life differences. We all need to continue learning. We all need to practice civility. We all should appreciate our larger humanity through music, the arts, and religion.

So at the end of this work about my life *in* the law, I want to conclude on a point that centers on the realities we all face outside it. Shortly after I became Deputy Attorney General, I had lunch with a young Justice Department lawyer who told me that we really do not need to be of one mind all the time as long as we are of one purpose. I found this profound. To me, based on my Chautauqua experience, that one purpose is understanding each other through civility. I believe, notwithstanding our considerable differences, that there is a strong fabric in American society that will ultimately hold us together.

America is *not* perfect—we all know that. But it boasts a greater promise of prosperity, freedom, security, and happiness than any other society in the world today. We should prize this, invest in it, and work to pass along to future generations a better version of America than the one we inherited. This is what I have tried to do during my years as a lawyer and as a citizen. I've enjoyed successes and suffered failures in both areas—and that's okay. I believe this effort to make a broader contribution beyond the law has made my life's work more satisfying and more meaningful. If I had one piece of advice, it is for all of us, especially lawyers, to join in this broader commitment to make certain our great country is a more prosperous, just, and democratic one.

ACKNOWLEDGMENTS

MY EXPERIENCE WITH RABBI Boyarsky reminds me of how rich and blessed my life and career have been. It would be impossible here to note all the people whom I would like to mention. But there are some individuals whom I must thank for their enduring friendship and support.

Former United States Senator Mack Mattingly, who nominated me at age 38 to be U.S. Attorney for the Northern District of Georgia.

Supreme Court Justice Clarence Thomas, whom I practiced law with straight out of law school at Monsanto Company in St. Louis, Missouri, and who encouraged me to consider a career in the growing city of Atlanta.

Anthony Welters, a former client and now dear friend. Tony was introduced to me by Justice Thomas and is a brilliant businessman.

Alphonso Jackson, whom I met in St. Louis and who has been a friend and confidant over the years. He is a former Secretary of Housing and Urban Development. Alphonso, Tony, Justice Thomas, and I continue our friendship and meet regularly.

FBI Director Christopher Wray, who is a great public servant. Chris worked with me in Washington as Principal Deputy Attorney General. He was an invaluable partner.

Senior Partner Paul Murphy of the King & Spalding law firm. Paul is an extremely talented lawyer and also worked with me in Washington as Associate Deputy Attorney General. Paul, too, was an important partner.

Senior United States District Judge Richard Leon. Judge Leon worked with me on several significant legal matters over the years, including the Judicial Review Commission on Foreign Asset Control.

Peter "Bo" Rutledge, Dean of the University of Georgia School of Law. Bo is a wonderful Dean and a brilliant lawyer and has been a steadfast supporter of my teaching efforts and this book project.

Richard Hendrix, a great lawyer and Senior Partner at Finch McCranie, which has been so good to me in my "retirement" years.

Lane Dennard, my former partner at King & Spalding who has made enormous contributions to the justice system through his pro bono work following retirement.

King & Spalding, my former law firm. A great firm and where I learned to practice law.

Steve Reinemund and Indra Nooyi, CEOs of PepsiCo to whom I reported. My efforts at PepsiCo would not have been successful without their support and trust.

Attorney General John Ashcroft, who allowed me to partner with him in overseeing the operations of the United States Department of Justice. John is a good man.

Scott Marrah, Benjamin Wilson, Michael Sullivan, and Michele Edwards. They were my leadership team during the Volkswagen Monitorship and helped me and our amazing team bring this important and complicated effort to a successful conclusion.

Dan Bryant, from whom I learned so much about public policy formulation and strategy. Dan has deep experience and terrific wisdom. I worked with Dan at the Department of Justice and PepsiCo. He's now a senior Walmart executive.

President George W. Bush, who nominated me to be Deputy Attorney General and who assigned me significant responsibilities after 9/11 and the corporate scandals that started with the bankruptcy of Enron.

Joseph Vining, one of my law professors at the University of Michigan Law School. Joe ignited a spark in me and my interest in corporate and criminal law. He's a good friend, mentor, and supporter.

Judge Griffin Bell, Jimmy Carter's Attorney General. The wisest lawyer I've known. I learned so much from him.

My wife, Brenda, and our two sons, who have been supportive of my career choices. Without their encouragement and support, any one of the cases and positions I've taken could have been fraught with conflict. They have not only been supportive but have helped me maintain a healthy balance of family and career, for which I am truly thankful.

APPENDIX

I HAVE OVER 400 speeches I've delivered over the years digitized. Some are simply handwritten notes and others are more fulsome and typed. I spent a lot of time thinking about and preparing the speeches regardless of the format in which they are memorialized. Here, I include an arbitrary number of speeches, 15, that are meaningful and memorable to me.

OPENING STATEMENT AT CONFIRMATION HEARING FOR DEPUTY ATTORNEY GENERAL

I WAS VERY EMOTIONAL. *It was hard for me to imagine how a kid from Hannibal, Missouri, whose parents had not graduated from high school, was on that day appearing before the Judiciary Committee of the United States Senate. I will never forget the complimentary remarks of Senator Dianne Feinstein when I concluded my opening remarks.*

Mr. Chair, Senator Leahy, and other members of the committee, it is a great honor to be here today as the nominee to become the Deputy Attorney General of the United States.

I would like to thank my home state Senators and friends, Senator Cleland and Senator Miller, for their introductions and support.

Let me first introduce my wife of thirty years, Brenda Thompson.

My father is deceased, and my mother is 83 years old and somewhat ill. She lives in Hannibal, Missouri. I have two sons: Larry is 26, a chemical engineer and a first-year law student at New York University. Gary is 22 and is a senior at Kalamazoo College in Kalamazoo, Michigan. My cousin, General Donald Scott, Deputy Librarian of Congress, and his wife, Betty Scott, are here with me today. We grew up together in Hannibal, Missouri.

Mr. Chair, it is a privilege to be considered for this position, and I would like to thank the members of the committee and their staff for the courtesies extended to me over the past several days and providing me an opportunity to meet with many of you in the course of the confirmation process. It has been very helpful to learn what issues are of concern to you and to begin a cooperative and working dialogue that I pledge to continue if I am confirmed.

At the risk of introducing what might be considered sentimentality into these proceedings, I cannot help but think, as I appear before you today, what a great nation we live in and how fortunate I am to have had the parents I did. I was born and raised in Hannibal, Missouri. My father worked for the railroad as a laborer. My mother was a part-time cook and housekeeper. I attended a segregated school for eight years where I had dedicated and stern teachers. But I also had wonderful and supportive teachers after integration. All of this is to say that I simply could not have imagined 40 years ago, when my father was living, that I would be sitting before this great body today as a participant in these proceedings.

I have been practicing law for almost 27 years. Nineteen of those years have been primarily dedicated to the federal criminal justice system, either as a prosecutor or defense lawyer. I have worked with, and learned from, a number of great lawyers. Chief among them is my senior law partner, former Attorney General, Judge Griffin B. Bell.

As U.S. Attorney under President Ronald Reagan, I managed and led an office covering Atlanta and over 40 counties in north Georgia, an area with a population of over three million people. During my tenure, the U.S. Attorney's Office conducted several successful investigations and prosecutions relating to government program fraud, prescription drug diversion, public official corruption, illegal tax protests by supremacist organizations, and terroristic acts by members of the Ku Klux Klan that led to criminal civil rights convictions.

Also, as United States Attorney in Atlanta, I established and led the Southeast Organized Crime Drug Enforcement Task Force. The Task Force covered five states and involved 12 different U.S. Attorneys' Offices, including the office in Mobile, led by Senator Sessions, the FBI, the DEA, ATF, IRS, and the U.S. Marshals Service. The Southeast Task Force had many law enforcement successes, but none I'm more proud of than the convictions of leaders of a large cocaine smuggling and trafficking organization that smuggled over five tons of cocaine into the United States during a 15 month period between 1982 and 1983. This investigation involved coordinating with a number of law enforcement and intelligence agencies, both at the domestic and international levels. At the time, this was the largest cocaine smuggling organization ever to have been destroyed and brought to justice.

As U.S. Attorney, I learned to respect, admire, and even love the many energetic, talented and hardworking prosecutors and agents with whom I worked. Many of these people literally put their lives on the line every day in order to make our communities safe places to live. Some of the things I witnessed, for example, in dangerous undercover operations, were literally heroic.

I obviously admire the Department of Justice as an institution, and if confirmed, look forward to returning and serving a leadership role in it. Since serving as U.S. Attorney, I have maintained an interest in public service, even while continuing to practice law privately. I was honored to serve as a replacement Independent Counsel for Judge Arlin Adams in the Samuel Pierce and Department of Housing and Urban Development investigation. Most recently, I was honored and privileged to serve Congress as Chair of the Judicial Review Commission on Foreign Asset Control, which was a bipartisan commission established by Congress to study certain issues relating to the Foreign Narcotics Kingpin Designation Act.

As a defense lawyer, I have represented individuals, rich and poor, and entities, large and small, accused of wrongdoing. I have handled cases throughout the country, from Boston to Los Angeles. Many of these cases involved complex and lengthy investigations. And, in many of them, I have had to work hard and creatively with the government in order to resolve my clients' legal problems without resorting to trial. These resolutions always had as their foundation the mutual respect and trust between me, as private counsel, and the government.

Also, as a defense lawyer, I have represented citizens who believed that governmental power was being misused or was even unrestrained by law. Some of these clients, individuals, and entities have doubted the fairness of our criminal justice system.

All of these experiences, I believe, have prepared me for the challenges I will face as Deputy Attorney General.

I would now like to briefly identify for you what I hope to accomplish as Deputy Attorney General, if confirmed, under Attorney General Ashcroft's leadership.

I would like to discuss three important objectives.

First, and most important, the Department of Justice must continue to earn and maintain the trust and respect of all our citizens. To do this, the Department must operate in a non-partisan and impartial manner. We must be as open to the public as legitimate concerns for privacy and investigative and grand jury secrecy allow.

As we go about accomplishing this important objective, I take my guidance from a speech delivered by Attorney General Robert Jackson at the Second Annual Conference of United States Attorneys in 1940. General Jackson noted: "The prosecutor has more control over life, liberty, and reputation than any other person in America. His discretion is tremendous."

Instructing the assembled prosecutors on how to conduct the public's business, General Jackson noted that a good prosecutor displays "a sensitivity to fair play" and further pointed out: "The citizen's safety lies in the prosecutor who tempers zeal with human kindness, who seeks truth, not victims, who serves the law and not factional purposes, and who approaches his or her tasks with humility."

I have always followed General Jackson's counsel.

I believe that because of my record of vigorously, but impartially, enforcing the laws, I have been honored to receive support for my nomination from both the Fraternal Order of Police and the National Association of Criminal Defense Lawyers.

Second, we must continue to make certain that the traditional role of federal law enforcement is carried out with vigor and effectiveness.

Federal law enforcement must attack such critical crime problems as large multi-state and international drug trafficking organizations, complicated fraud schemes, civil rights violations, serious environmental violations, terrorism, and espionage.

Sometimes these areas overlap. For example, a leader of the large cocaine smuggling organization my U.S. Attorney's Office prosecuted in 1984, who was an admitted Marxist and an associate of the M-19 Guerrilla Movement in Columbia, wrote the following in a letter that was intercepted by law enforcement: "I hate all governments so much. I want to destroy them. I guess in my own way, sending drugs into the U.S. was one of my ways of fighting."

We need to continue to direct the tremendous federal law enforcement resources at individuals like this who, if unchecked, will wreak havoc on our nation.

Finally, the third objective is one not necessarily associated with traditional federal law enforcement but does involve helping our citizens achieve a greater sense of personal security and safety in their homes and neighborhoods. This involves violent crime, which is especially important to some of our minority and low-income citizens against whom violent crime has a disproportionate impact.

Of all our important civil rights, the right to be safe and secure in one's home and neighborhood is perhaps the most important. We must work creatively, think outside of the box, as it is sometimes referred to, to work with local law enforcement agencies and perhaps even some private organizations, to attack the problem of violent crime. I certainly do not have all the answers now but do believe that we must continue to encourage and support local law enforcement efforts that take violent and repeat offenders out of circulation, especially those who use guns in committing their crimes.

Many of our citizens continue to be literally terrorized by violent crime. The federal government should play a leading role in attacking this problem. At stake is the well-being of millions of citizens and even the lives of some of them.

In accomplishing these objectives, I will be guided by what Attorney General Ashcroft has committed the Department of Justice to do. We will listen to Congress and to others and try to find common ground with people of widely diverse viewpoints.

I thank President Bush for his confidence in me.

Again, I am honored to be here, and I look forward to working with you. Of course, I will be pleased to answer any questions that you may have.

FORMAL SWEARING-IN CEREMONY AS DEPUTY ATTORNEY GENERAL

July 11, 2001

This was a very special time in my career. It gave me an opportunity to reaffirm my deep and abiding respect for the Department of Justice.

I look out into this wonderful audience and see so many people with whom I have worked and who are friends. People who mean a lot to me. And I would really like to say something about each of you, but obviously time does not permit that. But I would like to acknowledge and thank some of you who are here and even some who could not come.

My family: thank you for being here. You know I appreciate the support you have always given me. My mother: She has meant so much to me and my brothers and sister.

My colleagues in the Atlanta U.S. Attorney's Office with whom I worked in the 1980s: You are great public servants and great lawyers whom I respect a lot. My former associates and partners at King & Spalding: You are my friends and professional colleagues. I have enjoyed practicing law with you over the past 20 years and am very proud of the things we have accomplished for our clients and the Atlanta community.

My colleagues in the Criminal Defense Bar: Because my practice focused on white-collar criminal defense work, I know some of you thought I was only a marginal criminal defense lawyer. But I am proud of having been counted among the members of the Criminal Defense Bar. I know the difficulties and frustrations associated with what you do. But I also know and understand that your good and professional work is absolutely indispensable to our criminal justice system.

I have observed over the years that there is actually more civility between prosecutors and criminal defense lawyers than between private practitioners in civil cases. I certainly hope that kind of relationship continues.

My former clients: I am deeply honored by your presence at this ceremony. You entrusted me with some of your difficult and sensitive legal problems. Some of you even entrusted me with your lives. I appreciate all the wonderful friendships that have developed over the years.

Senator Mattingly, you deserve a very special thanks. You had a really special confidence in me back in 1982 when I was a young, relatively unknown lawyer in Atlanta. You recommended me to President Reagan to be U.S. Attorney for the Northern District of Georgia. That decision obviously had a profound impact on my professional life. Thank you, Mack.

Attorney General Ashcroft, you have a wonderful vision for the Department of Justice. One of your objectives is to make certain that all Americans, regardless of their backgrounds, have trust and confidence in our justice system. Your trust in me is very important, and I am proud to help you achieve our objectives.

Ted Olson, we served together in the Reagan Administration Justice Department, where we both caught the same disease—an abiding love and respect for the Department of Justice. I am pleased to count you as a colleague again.

My friends and colleagues at the Department of Justice, thank you for your warm welcome and your complete dedication to the important work you do for our country. And the work you do is not only important—it is absolutely necessary.

Whether it be international drug trafficking organizations, serious environmental violations that threaten the public safety, or terrorism, crime is a clear and present danger to what our Constitution calls the "domestic tranquility."

In order to combat the enemies of our way of life, we in the Department of Justice have been granted a tremendous amount of power. At the Second Annual Conference of U.S. Attorneys in 1940, Attorney General Robert Jackson urged government lawyers to exercise this tremendous power in ways that are "dispassionate, reasonable, and just."

And that is what the professionals in this great institution strive to do—day in and day out. This is illustrated by a note I received from a career lawyer a few days ago. This lawyer has spent over 30 years with the Department. In his note, the lawyer reminded me that the work we do in this building, and the way we go about it, is why this institution is named the Department of Justice rather than the Department of Federal Prosecutors.

I mentioned my clients earlier. And now my client is the United States of America, perhaps the greatest client any lawyer can have, and one I pledge to represent zealously. But in doing so, I will always remember my responsibilities as a government lawyer as set forth more than 60 years ago by Justice Sutherland of the U.S. Supreme Court. Justice Sutherland's observation was also mentioned by former Attorney General Griffin Bell when he spoke to Department employees in 1977 in this great hall; that is, our responsibility as government lawyers is not just to win cases, but to do justice.

And as we go about our work, it is also good to know that it is the strong fabric of this wonderful institution that will hold us together. As a young Department lawyer, Heather Epstein, told me recently when we were having lunch, we really need not be of one mind all the time, as long as we are always of one purpose—to do justice.

Thank you.

REMARKS AT ANTI-DEFAMATION LEAGUE SOUTHEASTERN LEADERSHIP MEETING

March 10, 2002

After 9/11, most of my work as Deputy Attorney General was tactical. It involved how the Department of Justice could best protect Americans from further terrorist acts.

I spent a great deal of time thinking about this speech and was trying to understand why the terrorists attacked us and what I could say about it. What I most remember about this speech is that I did not use my prepared remarks. I spoke extemporaneously and from my heart. I'm certain most of what was in these prepared remarks made its way into my actual speech.

It is a pleasure to be back home in Georgia and a distinct honor to address the Anti-Defamation League, which has been a preeminent leader in the civil rights efforts that we all hold dear. I am also glad to have the opportunity to share some of my experiences in Washington with you, particularly with the onset of the war against terrorism and the challenges this war has posed for the Department of Justice and the nation at large.

Since September 11, I still hear a number of people say that we are having trouble getting back to normal; many find it difficult to get into an acceptable routine. But I have noticed something remarkably normal—and quintessentially American—in our common reaction to this great tragedy.

I'm sure you have noticed it too. It is our spirit. We have all pulled together to support each other, to preserve our way of life, and to rise to the challenges that this new struggle has thrust upon us. People from all over have called and/or emailed, volunteering to do whatever they can. What a tribute to our country!

There is a common sense of purpose—that we as a nation will prevail against terrorism. And we do face a challenge. We have not been hit again, but threats still exist; they are real. Terrorists are still plotting and attempting to commit acts of mass murder against innocent Americans.

Nevertheless, the events of 9/11 have had a transforming effect on DOJ—and a personal transforming effect. This is as righteous of a cause or case as I have ever worked on. There is a great effort put into strengthening domestic security, the magnitude and intensity of which I have never seen. Think about this: The potential loss of civilian life by mass murder, by a foreign enemy, on American soil, is unprecedented.

To be sure, DOJ continues to investigate crimes of 9/11 with an eye toward prosecution in appropriate cases. But the overriding imperative of DOJ is to disrupt and prevent terrorism, a little like a cop on the beat: save lives. The most essential function of any government is to secure the safety of our fellow citizens.

Investigators and prosecutors are used to handling information and evidence in a certain way. Attorney General Ashcroft has given strict instructions to investigators and prosecutors: Make pertinent information available to appropriate officials if sharing information can disrupt or prevent a terrorist attack, even if it means compromising potential criminal prosecution. In essence, there is a new challenge at DOJ and a new paradigm to meet the challenge.

The Justice Department has undertaken several new efforts in our fight against terrorism. First, we have established special task forces nationwide to initiate and coordinate swift preemptive actions by federal, state, and local law enforcement. The federal government does not have enough eyes, ears, and feet available to investigate all terrorist threats.

Second, we have substantially improved coordination between the FBI, INS, and our intelligence agencies.

Third, we are ensuring that the names of foreign nationals seeking entry to the United States are checked against law enforcement and intelligence databases for potential indications of terrorist associations or activities. This has led to the creation of the Foreign Terrorist Tracking Task Force. Among other things, this Task Force carefully monitors student visas and considers the use of biometrics in our immigration entry system.

Fourth, we are detaining foreign nationals with suspected links to terrorist organizations.

Fifth, we are conducting voluntary interviews with several thousand additional foreign nationals to gain information about potential terrorist operations in the United States.

Sixth, we are intensifying efforts to enforce judicial orders of deportation against fugitive aliens from certain countries.

Finally, we are reexamining and revising administrative regulations where appropriate to be more aggressive in investigating the threat of terrorism.

Some commentators and lawyers have raised concerns over some of these measures. As a public official—and as an attorney who, for many years, represented criminal defendants—I share the concern that the struggle against terrorism not change the essential character of our nation.

During my tenure as United States Attorney for the Northern District of Georgia, and now as Deputy Attorney General, I have seen firsthand how dearly Americans cherish their heritage of liberty under law and their keen awareness of how the rule of law makes our democracy possible.

In the months since the tragic events of September 11, we have recognized that the Justice Department's success in defeating terrorism depends on public confidence that we can ensure the fair and impartial administration of justice for all Americans while carrying out our essential national security mission.

Indeed, it is our very open democratic and just society—whose hallmark is our concern for civil rights—that has made us the terrorists' target. Our civilization's freedom is grounded in the rule of law. Our freedoms, our laws are the envy of the world and the perennial winner in the global marketplace of values and ideas.

It is precisely because the terrorists' ideas cannot compete in the open marketplace that they have turned to violence and horror. They attempt to achieve through mass murder what they will never be able to accomplish in a free exchange of ideas: to subvert our freedoms, freedoms for which millions of Americans—from our Founding Fathers to our immigrants from every quarter to our civil rights marchers—have strained and sacrificed.

They target us simply because we are Americans. They make no distinction between rich and poor, Black and white, Jew and Christian. Because they fear our freedom, they resort to terror.

But we will prevail because of our sacrifices and the strength of our laws safeguarding freedom. We are certainly not the first nation to be assailed by terrorists bent on its destruction.

The state of Israel, which has struggled for its existence from the day of its founding, has, in the past year, suffered a virtually ceaseless onslaught from terrorist attacks. We have much to learn from Israel's success in combating terror while holding fast to the very democratic values and civil rights that define both of our nations.

The shared struggle of the United States and Israel against terrorism raises many uncomfortable questions: At what point does the protection of society trump the rights of the individual? Must rules fashioned for the protection of citizens in time of peace apply to terrorists who murder civilians indiscriminately?

The Israeli Supreme Court confronted these issues in a recent decision on the propriety of so-called "moderate physical pressure" in interrogating terrorism suspects. I met with retired Justice Gabriel Bach of that court recently in my office in Washington and was literally mesmerized not by his keen intellect, but by his wisdom.

The Israeli court decided to prohibit such techniques, recognizing that: "A democratic peace-loving society does not accept that investigators use any means for the purpose of uncovering the truth. At times, the price of truth is so high that a democratic society is not prepared to pay it." The Israeli court's conclusion applies equally to our country that: "This is the destiny of democracy, as not all means are acceptable to it, and not all practices employed by its enemies are open before it. Although a democracy must often fight with one hand tied behind its back, it nonetheless has the upper hand. Preserving the rule of law and recognition of an individual's liberty constitutes an important component in its understanding of security. At the end of the day, they strengthen its spirit and add to its strength and allow it to overcome its difficulties."

This same reverence for civil rights inspired the Attorney General immediately after the terrorist attacks to challenge all of us in the Justice Department to "think outside the box" in fighting terrorism but caution us: "Don't think outside the Constitution." We also take to heart then Attorney General Robert Jackson's cautionary admonition that government lawyers exercise their tremendous power in ways that are "dispassionate, reasonable, and just."

As a longtime career employee of the office reminded me soon after I began this job, this is the reason that we are the "Department of Justice" rather than the "Department of Federal Prosecutors." That said, we are duty bound to zealously represent the United States "with earnestness and vigor" and to obtain justice through every constitutional and legal means at our disposal.

This is the way I represented clients in private practice. And this is the way I believe I should represent the public interest.

The initiatives I have outlined, to borrow the Supreme Court's phrase from *Berger v. United States*, strike "hard" blows against terrorism, not "foul" ones. They are aggressive, and we must be aggressive in confronting a threat of this magnitude. Yet, these measures are balanced, and in all cases, subject to judicial review. They do not change the essential character of the legal protections available to criminal defendants.

We can discuss in detail a couple of our measures in this important fight.

Detention of aliens: Let me address, in particular, the concerns that have been expressed regarding the detention of foreign nationals and the possible monitoring of conversations between terrorist inmates and their attorneys. The detention of foreign individuals suspected of terrorist ties is consistent with applicable law and constitutional precedent. The detainees are either already wanted for crimes, or in violation of their immigration status, or have testimony material to the ongoing investigation.

All detainees have the right to be represented by an attorney and to have their detention reviewed on legal grounds.

Monitoring of communications between inmates and attorneys may occur only in those few, but critical, situations. This monitoring requires that the head of a law enforcement or intelligence agency certify that reasonable suspicion exists to believe that the inmate may use those communications to further or facilitate terrorist acts. The Supreme Court has long held that such communications could not, in any case, be privileged. The monitoring is not surreptitious. It is conducted only after written notice to the inmate and the attorney. The team monitoring the conversations is barred from any connection with the further prosecution of that inmate. Without court approval, the government cannot use the information for purposes other than preventing a terrorist act. All of SAMS, including the ones relating to attorney communications, only apply to about 20 out of over 150,000 inmates in federal custody.

At the same time that the Department has shifted its focus to prevention and disruption of terrorist attacks, we have continued to take aggressive measures to ensure that the American public's sensitivities to the terrorist threat do not boil over in a way that results in discrimination or violence against our fellow Americans of Middle Eastern descent or who worship in the Muslim faith.

Since September 11, the Department's Civil Rights Division, the Federal Bureau of Investigation, and United States Attorneys' Offices have investigated approximately 300 incidents involving violence or threats against Arab-Americans and other individuals perceived to be of Middle Eastern origin. Federal indictments have been brought in several cases, and federal assistance to state and local prosecutors has facilitated the prosecution of more than 60 additional cases.

Just one example of our aggressive response to a hate crime precipitated by the events of September 11 occurred in Utah. Two days after the terrorist attacks in New York and Washington, an individual attempted to burn down a restaurant owned by a Pakistani-American family. The owners and patrons were inside the restaurant at the time. The perpetrator was federally charged and later pleaded guilty, admitting that his crime was "in retaliation" for the terrorist attacks. He was sentenced to four and a half years in prison.

While we have aggressively pursued all such cases wherever they have occurred, as an American, I am pleased that such incidents of hate-motivated crime based on individuals' perceived Arab-American heritage have been extremely rare.

Let me close by recalling the words of Martin Niemoller in remembering that we must band together in this national and global fight against terrorism. As you know, Niemoller was a Protestant minister in Germany before and during Hitler's rise to power and was sent to a concentration camp.

After the war, he gave the famous warning about division in the face of evil: "When Hitler attacked the Jews, I was not a Jew; therefore, I was not concerned. And when Hitler attacked the Catholics, I was not a Catholic, and therefore, I was not concerned. And when Hitler attacked the unions and the industrialists, I was not a member of the unions, and I was not concerned. Then Hitler attacked me and the Protestant church—and there was nobody left to be concerned."

We must be concerned. We and our friends across the world must all be concerned about the threat of terror and seize on every legal means to annihilate it. I pledge to you that we will move aggressively to defeat terrorism wherever it exists and defend citizens' rights whenever they are threatened. I can assure you of that.

Thank you.

APPENDIX 4

FINAL SPEECH OF THE DEPUTY ATTORNEY GENERAL AT UNIVERSITY OF MICHIGAN BUSINESS SCHOOL

January 31, 2003

Following the corporate scandals of 2002—Enron, Adelphia, WorldCom, and others—President Bush established the Corporate Fraud Task Force and named me to head it. The Task Force adopted an aggressive, enforcement approach to corporate fraud. This approach was criticized by some in the financial media as demonizing business and also by many conservatives as government outreach. This speech at the University of Michigan was delivered to show that the true, conservative approach to corporate fraud was tough but fair enforcement and not endless regulation.

Good afternoon. It is good, as always, to be back at the University of Michigan. I spent three great years here studying law, so I think it is good to be back here in Ann Arbor to talk to this distinguished gathering about one of the rather momentous issues that now face us at the Department of Justice.

Although on a day-to-day basis, I devote much of my time to the war against terrorism that we are fighting both here and abroad, I do not plan to address those matters today, at least not directly. Instead, I will say a few words about a subject near to my heart as both a prosecutor and a former white-collar defense lawyer of many years, and that is the role that swift and strong prosecution decisions should play in maintaining a vibrant business environment.

I could talk about a number of aspects of what we are doing at the Department of Justice to address the spate of corporate scandals that rocked the nation and our economy several months ago. President Bush established the Corporate Fraud Task Force, which he asked me to head. We have had, in my opinion, remarkable success. Since the Task Force was established, we have opened over 130 investigations, charged over 160 individuals, and obtained convictions of over 50 individuals. We have frozen or forfeited over 30 million dollars. I could also talk about my direction to our prosecutors to not hesitate to charge a business entity itself under appropriate circumstances consistent with DOJ guidelines, and also to look at the role professionals play in these matters carefully. Instead, in this setting, I would like to offer some observations about what we are doing as prosecutors.

Few among us, even the most extreme advocates of *laissez-faire* economic policy, will argue that government should take no role in policing the market—that the law of the jungle should replace the law of contracts. Rather, it seems to me that the debate tends to focus on the nature and degree of government intervention.

Where you come out in this debate depends on your faith in the ultimate resilience of our capitalist system. If you join with me in the belief that Adam Smith's "invisible hand" best allocates resources to the improvement of our society as a whole, then you will want to limit the extent of policing, since every government intervention tends to carry an economic price tag.

Over time, many critics have attacked this proposition, from the mercantilists to the Marxists to today's anti-globalization protesters. What these critics have in common is the conviction that some group of experts divorced from the rough and tumble of trade can do a better job—that they can achieve what the economist Thomas Sowell derisively refers to as a "cosmic justice."

Capitalism's critics pounced on the recent spate of corporate scandals to pronounce our system deeply flawed and in need of a thorough and intensive regulatory overhaul. But it is important to remind ourselves that as traumatic as these massive frauds have been for investors and for the confidence of the markets, such events are not new.

The dustbin of history is littered with the sensational exposure of massive frauds. Just within recent memory, we had the devastating savings and loan bankruptcies of a decade ago. Less than two decades ago, we had the high-profile insider trading scandals and the spectacular collapse of the junk bond schemes. Three decades ago, we discovered that some of our prominent corporations were engaging in corrupt foreign practices that would have been intolerable in the United States. The list goes on with depressing regularity through the stock manipulations of the 1920s and the antitrust conspiracies and the robber barons of the early twentieth century to the real estate scams that marked the dawn of the Republic.

The lesson here is not that greed and criminality have always been with us, although, clearly, they have. Rather, the lesson is that Americans have overcome each of these jolts, and our economy has remained the envy of the world. Each fresh business scandal has brought calls for more regulation, tighter rules, better weapons to fight the last war, to make certain that the chicanery used so successfully in the scheme just past can never be used again.

Some regulations have been exemplary. Those that promote transparency can give the market more uniform and accurate information. But overzealous and sometimes mindless regulation can also prove to be a very bad thing. Too many regulations, rules that become Byzantine in their complexity or rules that seek to advance social policy preferences unrelated to the general economic welfare—these rules can seriously stifle innovation.

As commentators from Milton Friedman to Philip Howard, author of *The Death of Common Sense*, have pointed out, we are already suffering some of the ill effects of over-regulation. Companies must hire legions of experts and consultants merely to comply with their dictates. These regulations' frequent shifts and virtual immunity to legislative recourse make the future business climate more difficult to predict and further increase the cost of capital. Start-up businesses are deterred from even entering heavily regulated industries. Companies choose the safest course, not the one that might pay dramatic returns.

While it begins with the well-intentioned impulse to close the barn door after the horse is gone, the problem is that the over-aggressive regulatory system becomes progressively more comprehensive with each ensuing scandal. Regulations gradually expand to encompass every possible abuse—except the next one. This is what I call the hyper-regulatory "nanny state" that grows ever closer to central planning and to the substitution of a government-driven policy for individual initiative.

Rather than the "nanny state" model, criminal fraud prosecution represents the "mommy and daddy state." It is the "tough love" antithesis of over-regulation. The criminal law has the unique ability to concentrate the minds of corrupt businesspeople and to deter those teetering on the brink of letting greed supplant responsibility. The enforcement of the criminal statutes that punish fraud send the message that deviant behavior will be dealt with in a way that the offenders find particularly unpleasant: going to jail, and going to jail for a long time.

Our job at the Department of Justice is to make clear that the consequences of criminal conduct are severe and virtually certain. Our struggle has been to quickly and decisively prosecute corporate criminals so as to demonstrate both to the wrongdoers and to other potential wrongdoers—as well as to the investing public—the direct connection between the crime and its consequences.

The massive frauds that we are now investigating and prosecuting have compromised the integrity of a wide range of companies—from multi-billion-dollar communications giants to tiny internet start-ups. And because the vitality of our increasingly complex economy rests on the free and fair exchange of information, these crimes are particularly pernicious and appropriately the subject of intense—and that is what they are getting—law enforcement focus and action. They affect not only institutions, but shareholders and employees and pensioners. They harm average folks as well as major investors, Main Street as well as Wall Street.

In discussing these crimes, it is important not to underestimate the stigma that appropriately attaches to criminal conduct and thus not to tar, with too broad a brush, the overwhelming majority of corporations that operate morally and productively in the best and highest interest of their shareholders and the country. Yet, I believe you will agree the breadth and extent of these recent scandals do demonstrate intolerable legal and ethical misdeeds that require our comprehensive response.

The alternative to the broad campaign of criminal prosecution is an even broader and more minutely intrusive regulatory framework that more closely directs individuals' conducts. Yet, regulation alone can never be a sufficient deterrent because the truly corrupt will always view the violation of these rules as merely the cost of doing business. My colleagues at the Securities and Exchange Commission, for instance, would be the first to recognize that their jobs get easier and regulatory compliance gets much better if individuals realize that willful violations mean prison and stigma—not merely fines and lawsuits.

The same holds true for entity or corporate criminal liability. Regula-tory sanctions simply do not have the power of criminal penalties to change corrupt corporate cultures. Large business organizations, particularly public companies that are already regulated in myriad ways, sometimes have the disappointing tendency to view civil sanctions as merely the "cost of doing business," a cost that can be passed on to customers and shareholders.

Vigorous criminal enforcement is thus more harmonious with the healthy economic development to which we aspire. The criminal laws set a standard whose transgression is—and ought to be—swift and, yes, terrible. But they do not, by and large, creep toward inserting the government as the decision maker and undermine the entrepreneurial spirit. A strong regime of criminal enforcement leaves the honest businesspeople free to compete while weeding out those few—and I emphasize few—who break the law.

Of course, by my comments here today, I do not mean to undermine the regulatory structure now in place: Certainly the rules that require the open disclosure of financial information are invaluable tools in helping investors to value companies and in revealing criminal wrongdoing. Neither do I wish to disparage the valiant efforts of the regulators themselves. What is clear, it seems to me, is that the vigorous enforcement of the criminal laws, in support of the rule of law, is appropriate for punishing fraud while preserving economic freedom.

Almost 60 years ago, the philosopher Friedrich Hayek recognized that "while every law restricts individual freedom to some extent by altering the means which people may use in the pursuit of their aims, under the rule of law, the government is prevented from stultifying individual efforts by *ad hoc* actions. Within the known rules of the game, the individual is free to pursue his personal ends and desires."

We at DOJ will continue to uphold those rules to keep the game open and competitive. We will continue to strike decisively with our powers of criminal enforcement to ensure that the liberties we cherish do not give way to corruption.

Thank you.

DEPUTY ATTORNEY GENERAL REMARKS ON DIVERSITY AT THE DOJ GREAT HALL

February 5, 2003

It was clear when I became Deputy Attorney General that the Department of Justice's attorney workforce needed to be more diverse. Department attorneys interacted every day with judges, jurors, and law enforcement officials who were becoming increasingly diverse. The Department was losing cases I thought it should have won, and I suspected lack of diversity of Department attorneys was a factor.

I recruited Stacey Plaskett to the deputy's office and one of her primary responsibilities was to help me develop a Department of Justice diversity effort that would be completely within the spirit and letter of the law. Stacey did a great job, and she is now a member of the U.S. House of Representatives from the Virgin Islands.

This is one of the most important and satisfying speeches I've given. In the midst of two anti-affirmative action cases then pending before the U.S.

Supreme Court, on behalf of the Department of Justice, with the full support of Attorney General John Ashcroft, I announced the Department's first ever comprehensive attorney outreach and diversity effort.

Thank you, General Ashcroft.

How fitting it is that we gather today in this great hall, a symbol of our stewardship of justice. In the men and women of this Department reposes the trust of a great people to achieve justice under the rule of law.

Our pursuit of justice is stronger, and the fulfillment of our national mission more effective, when we bring to bear the experience, judgment, and energy of colleagues from a wide spectrum of racial, ethnic, economic, and geographic backgrounds.

To succeed fully in our mission, we must earn and retain the trust and confidence of all Americans in how we fulfill our responsibility as custodians of justice. And that trust and confidence is a function of the American people's understanding that the Department of Justice draws on the finest legal talent from every quarter of this great nation.

As the Attorney General announced, today we embark on a series of initiatives that will enhance our ability both to pursue justice and to demonstrate to the American people our commitment to justice. These initiatives differ in form and substance. But all of them have a common purpose: namely, to strengthen the Department of Justice's attorney workforce by intensifying outreach to individuals from a wide range of racial, ethnic, economic, and geographic backgrounds, and by creating incentives to enter and remain in public service.

Of course, in understanding these initiatives, we will continue to demand that the attorneys who comprise and represent the Department of Justice meet the highest standards of excellence and professionalism.

These, I believe, important initiatives are as follows: First, we will make a more aggressive and focused effort to reach out to and educate law students and young lawyers, especially minority students and lawyers, about the benefits of a career at the Department of Justice, and to make information more readily available about employment opportunities at the Department, both at main Justice and in the field. This effort commenced last year when a number of senior Department officials, myself included, visited law schools throughout the United States to recruit applicants for the Attorney General's Honors Program.

In the coming months, we will expand this initiative to include the placement of advertisements about careers at the Department of Justice in publications aimed at minority audiences, as well as in state and local bar publications throughout the United States. In addition, we will increase the number and regional distribution of appearances by senior Department officials at conferences and symposia attended by minority attorneys. Overseeing this initiative will be a new deputy for recruitment in the Office of Attorney Recruitment and Management, whose responsibility, among other things, will be to proactively identify ways to recruit a diverse and talented applicant pool for the Attorney General's Honors Program and lateral vacancies at the Department.

Second, we will make information about attorney and supervisory vacancies more transparent and accessible both to attorneys outside the Department, and to our own personnel. Within 30 days, all attorney and supervisory vacancies, including vacancies at U.S. Attorneys' Offices, will be posted on the DOJ intranet, thereby facilitating lateral movement on a competitive basis within the Department. In the coming months, we will take steps to broaden the applicant pool for the Attorney General's Honors Program and lateral vacancies by requiring that all attorney and supervisory vacancies be posted on the internet.

Third, to make public service more financially viable, we will take advantage of longstanding regulatory authority to institute a program of student loan repayment for all qualifying new attorneys entering the Department under the Honors Program or laterally, and as a mechanism to retain experienced attorneys. Under OPM regulations, federal agencies can pay up to $6,000 annually toward the repayment of qualifying federal student loans for an employee who meets the requisite criteria, up to a maximum of $40,000 per employee. According to the law, individuals receiving the benefit of this loan repayment program will, in turn, have a minimum three-year service obligation to the Department of Justice.

For fiscal year 2003, we have reallocated $300,000 from the Dependents' Special Projects Fund to begin immediate implementation of the loan repayment program, enabling the Department to defray the burden of loan obligations for as many as fifty graduating law students and practicing attorneys. Beginning in fiscal year 2004, we expect to double our annual financial commitment to $600,000, enabling the Department to provide financial assistance to as many as 100 qualifying individuals.

The Office of Attorney Recruitment and Management will administer the loan repayment program and make determinations regarding eligibility. Individual components and U.S. Attorneys' Offices will continue to make their own hiring decisions. Within the next month, application forms for this loan repayment program will be available online on the Department of Justice website.

Fourth, we will institute a mandatory mentoring program for all incoming attorneys. This program will be in place within all Department components by the fall of 2003, when the next incoming class of the Honors Program enters on duty.

Fifth, we will initiate diversity training throughout the Department in the coming months. This training will focus on ways to prevent stereotyping and other subtle forms of identity-related employment issues in order to help managers create a positive workplace climate in their components. Training will be provided to section chiefs, senior supervisory attorneys, component heads, and Department leadership.

Sixth, we will establish a formal career development program for all Department attorneys in collaboration with OPM. This program will be aimed at assessing managerial potential and developing the skill sets and qualifications in attorneys necessary to assume management responsibility at the SES level.

Seventh, we will take appropriate steps to monitor our progress in achieving the goal of a more diverse attorney workforce. Among other things, we will engage outside expertise to help us administer periodic internal surveys to assess our progress in improving the Department's diversity environment.

And finally, we will conduct exit interviews with all voluntarily departing attorneys to determine their reasons for leaving and to develop strategies to promote increased retention.

I would like to thank Attorney General Ashcroft for his steadfast leadership on this issue. In addition, I would like to thank Deputy Assistant Attorney General Joanne Simms, Acting Director of OARM Lou DeFalaise, and Department Comptroller Eugene Schied for their assistance in shaping these initiatives. I would also like to thank and recognize OPM Director Kay Coles James for her valuable counsel and guidance.

The initiatives we announce today represent an investment in the most important asset of this great institution—its people. They will require sustained leadership and commitment not only from the Attorney General and the Deputy Attorney General, but from component heads and supervisory attorneys throughout the Department, both in Washington and in the field. These initiatives, simply put, recognize the importance of inclusion. And it is the spirit of inclusion that has made this country great.

Working together, we will further strengthen the fabric and foundation of this Department and continue to earn the trust and confidence of all Americans. I have been affiliated with (as a prosecutor) or working with the Department (as a defense lawyer) for over twenty years. These are worthwhile efforts.

DEPUTY ATTORNEY GENERAL STATEMENT FOR DOJ PRIDE MONTH CELEBRATION IN THE GREAT HALL

June 19, 2002

This was supposed to be a routine, brief, ceremonial speech. When it was ascertained that I had spoken to a gay pride event, a firestorm erupted. As you will read in the speech, I made no reference to lifestyle or sexual orientation issues. I simply congratulated a DOJ employee group for their hard work. I was summoned to appear before a top White House official who told me, "I'm proud of you." That was the end of this fire drill.

Thank you for the invitation to speak with you today.

I have now been serving as the Deputy Attorney General for more than a year, and that experience, while trying and arduous at times, has been greatly enriched by attorneys, investigators, and other professionals I interact with on a daily basis in the Department.

During these difficult times, I have been privileged to work with so many dedicated employees of the Department who have sacrificed much to serve our country. Experience has shown that, although we come from many different backgrounds, our common responsibility as trustees of America's freedoms holds us together.

The work done by the employees of the Department is not only important—it is absolutely vital. Whether you are combating terrorism, international drug trafficking organizations, serious environmental violations that threaten the public safety, or one of the many other challenges that confront us, you and your fellow professionals of the Department play a critical role in protecting the safety and well-being of the American people as never before.

We must, of course, bear in mind the tremendous authority and discretion vested in the Department of Justice. That tremendous power brings with it an equally immense responsibility. As former Attorney General Robert Jackson cautioned at the Second Annual Conference of U.S. Attorneys in 1940, Justice Department attorneys must exercise this power in ways that are "dispassionate, reasonable, and just."

Yet even these great powers will not safeguard the Republic if we lose the unity of purpose that we share. Now, more than ever, we at the Department must stand together to preserve our nation's liberty in the face of a relentless and deadly adversary. The nation and the world must know that we are united in the defense of our civilization.

When you think about why we are being targeted by the terrorists, you realize that our freedoms and values are the envy of the world and the perennial winner in the global marketplace of ideas. It is precisely because the terrorists' ideology cannot compete in the open marketplace that they have turned to violence and horror. They attempt to achieve through mass murder what they will never be able to accomplish in a free exchange of ideas to subvert our freedoms, freedoms for which millions of Americans have sacrificed.

I want to thank each of you for your dedication and hard work over the past year and urge you to steel yourselves for the many challenges we have before us. I am sure you feel as I do that together we can rise to these challenges and continue to fulfill our sacred trust to this great nation.

Thank you.

REMARKS AT THE THURGOOD MARSHALL U.S. COURTHOUSE DEDICATION IN NEW YORK

April 14, 2003

This was to be another routine speech. However, when I started to read about Thurgood Marshall's life, I was fascinated with his dedication to the profession and his sacrifice. Marshall's life also fit into some speeches I was reading about the legal profession authored by former Supreme Court Justice Robert Jackson.

Also at the time, I was talking with my dear friend William Coleman, who was the former Secretary of Transportation under Gerald Ford, about his interactions with Thurgood Marshall. As a young lawyer, Bill Coleman worked on the Brown v. Topeka Board of Education *case with Marshall. I included in my remarks a wonderful story Bill told me about a conversation he had with Marshall.*

We are gathered to dedicate this courthouse to the memory of a remarkable American lawyer. Just as this building has withstood the trials of six decades, so too does the memory of Justice Thurgood Marshall.

After the passage of 70 years, the legal world into which Thurgood Marshall emerged as a new lawyer in 1933 is unrecognizable in many important ways. Justice Marshall had been barred from the University of Maryland by racial discrimination. He lived and worked in a world and profession perverted by segregation.

It is to his undying credit—and in large measure, it is the reason that we pledge this courthouse to his memory today—that Thurgood Marshall dedicated his life to remaking our world in the image of equality and tolerance that the Constitution requires.

Our praise today can merely echo the resounding effect of a lifetime of work that resulted in demonstrating how the Constitution could serve our nation's modern needs in a diverse society. Unlike many here today, I was not privileged to know Justice Marshall, so the quality of my reminiscence may necessarily be poorer than many others'. But my admiration is rich for what he achieved, what he stood for as a lawyer, and the sacrifices that he made.

Thurgood Marshall was one of the most impressive lawyers of the twentieth century, and not just in the famous Supreme Court cases, but in the hundreds of matters he handled all over the country for the NAACP.

But Justice Marshall was more than just a brilliant advocate. I remember him for the passion he had for the profession, for his public service and his strong sense of how both could positively impact our great nation.

In 1942, Supreme Court Justice Robert Jackson described the ideal lawyer as a lawyer who loved his or her profession and who had a sense of dedication to the administration of justice. To this ideal lawyer, the law was like a religion, and its practice was more than a means of support; it was a mission. This completely describes Justice Marshall and his career.

Today, I and many others are concerned about the practice of law becoming simply another white-collar industry where the non-economic aspects of the profession, which were once considered responsibilities, are ignored. We are also concerned about the seeming reluctance of many lawyers, especially younger lawyers, to enter public service. Not so with Justice Marshall.

Shortly after he began his law practice in Baltimore, Justice Marshall's teacher and mentor, Charles Houston, cautioned him not to neglect the development of his own practice for the work he was doing for the NAACP on the side. Fortunately for all of us today, Justice Marshall did not listen to this advice and told Houston in 1935: "Personally, I would not give up these cases here in Maryland for anything in the world, but at the same time, there is no opportunity to get down to really hustling for business."

Justice Marshall's career was never about how much money he could make as a lawyer. Instead, James Freedman, one of Justice Marshall's former law clerks when he served on the Second Circuit Court of Appeals, has said that Justice Marshall's career was one of commitment to the public profession of the law.

That Justice Marshall clearly understood how this commitment to the law could impact our nation, is illustrated by a brief story that my friend William Coleman provided me.

On their way in a taxi from the hotel to the Supreme Court building on the day Justice Marshall was to argue the Brown case, Bill Coleman said to Justice Marshall to relieve the tension, "You are going to have to be as good as Touissant L'Ouverture" (who defeated Napoleon's generals in Haiti). Justice Marshall replied, "You still don't get it. This issue is not one of Them against Us; it is an issue where, if we win, they will benefit as much, or even more, than we do—we fight for both, and equal rights and liberties for all."

With his obvious legal prowess, it is clear that Justice Marshall could have won himself a fortune in private practice. Instead, and to the betterment of our nation as a whole, Thurgood Marshall became the embodiment of the spirit of public service.

For that service, I want to thank the members of the Marshall family who are here today. We look forward to Thurgood Marshall's name honoring this storied courthouse—and inspiring both bench and bar—for many years to come.

Thank you.

REMARKS OF PEPSICO GENERAL COUNSEL AND SVP OF GOVERNMENT AFFAIRS BEFORE THE STATE BAR OF TEXAS CORPORATE COUNSEL FORUM

June 16, 2006

I was a bit upset and angry when I gave this speech. I was no longer a government official and had served as PepsiCo's General Counsel for almost two years. Nevertheless, I observed many lawyers on the wrong side of trying to help their client organizations establish good, ethical cultures. Many in the profession continued to be fixated on privilege issues and continued to advance arguments that were unsupported in the law. I settled down and gave, I believe, a dispassionate and professional speech encouraging lawyers to do better.

I've been asked to talk generally about how a business or a corporation can have, as a part of its culture, the right ethical tone at the top. This topic is obviously very important in today's post-Enron corporate enforcement environment.

Before I try to tackle the subject of tone at the top, let me make an observation about corporate cultures based on my experience as a defense lawyer and prosecutor. Distinctive corporate cultures do exist. I think we all know and have experienced corporate cultures that are good; the majority of them are, in my experience. But unfortunately, there are also bad corporate cultures. Almost all organizations, including corporations, develop their own set of attitudes and practices that guide employees' thoughts and behavior. This establishes the culture of an organization. In most corporations, the culture instills respect for the law and ethical conduct. In a minority of organizations, a culture develops that breeds contempt for the law and prizes business results regardless of means. And, of course, there are other corporations where the culture is uncertain because there has been no clear tone at the top set to guide employees' behavior.

So with this backdrop, I'll review with you this morning some observations about setting the tone at the top of a business organization. What is the right tone? Exactly why is tone at the top important? How do you achieve the right tone at the top?

Next, I'll review the role of lawyers in establishing the right tone at the top. I'll discuss common mistakes I've observed lawyers make in representing business organizations that have aided in establishing bad cultures in those organizations. Finally, I'll briefly explore with you whether the current, rather rigid fixation on privilege issues by some in our profession is an impediment to establishing the right tone at the top of business organizations, especially in today's post-Enron and post–Sarbanes-Oxley environment.

Although I have drawn on my own practice experience in preparing these remarks and observations, I've also been aided by the work of two academics who have published some thoughtful and thought-provoking works. They are Professor Lynn Sharp Paine of the Harvard Business School and Professor William Simon of Columbia University Law School.

Establishing the Right Tone at the Top

Now let's consider what is the right or correct tone at the top of a business organization. It is obvious that it is far easier to say you should have a certain tone at the top than to spell out in detail what that tone should actually be or say. One commentator in the field has noted that the answer to the question of what is the right tone at the top is similar to a famous line in the 1964 obscenity decision, *Jacobellis v. Ohio*, provided by Justice Potter Stewart, when he noted that while we can't define pornography, we know it when we see it.

For Professor Paine of Harvard, the right tone at the top goes beyond compliance systems that are prevalent in many corporations today and that focus on the avoidance of legal sanctions. The right tone at the top involves a system of organizational integrity where the business organization has a set of guiding values that are understood and support ethically sound behavior by all employees. These ethical values are the responsibility of all employees, not just lawyers or compliance officials.

Professor Paine's work was published in 1994, well before the Sarbanes-Oxley legislation enacted in 2002 and the revisions of the organizational sentencing guidelines that went into effect in November 2004. So while having the right tone at the top seems to be the smart and responsible thing to do, there are legal reasons for doing so as well.

Sarbanes-Oxley mandates that public companies adopt a code of ethics for their principal executive officers and senior financial officers. Among other things, the required code of ethics should have provisions that promote honest and ethical conduct as well as provisions that promote full, fair, accurate, timely, and understandable disclosure in public reports and documents. In other words, Sarbanes-Oxley calls for complete transparency in a corporation's dealings.

But establishing the right tone at the top means much, much more than compliance with post-Enron legislation and regulations. Establishing the right tone at the top is the best way to preserve a business organization's good reputation, which can be easily destroyed when employees act unethically. Also, business organizations with the right tone at the top are, in the long run, winners in the marketplace. As one expert in the field has noted, these companies attract and retain the best talent. They are also the corporations other corporations do business with, attracting the best suppliers, customers, and business partners.

Professor Paine has outlined five factors that are critical to establishing an effective integrity or ethics strategy in a corporation. First, the guiding values of the organization must make sense and be clearly communicated. Employees at all levels must take responsibility for them. At PepsiCo, a cross-divisional, cross-functional global team of more than 40 employees worked for over a year to develop a set of core values and guiding principles that could apply across all of our diverse businesses and in more than 200 countries.

Those values have been rolled out across the world in thousands of in-person training sessions. Management constantly reinforces our values through town hall meetings, newsletters, posters, and other types of communications. Our values are personal—they articulate who we are and what we stand for as individuals and as a company. And we expect each employee to take personal ownership for living our values.

Second, an organization's leaders must be personally committed, credible, and willing to take action on the values they promote. This is the essence of setting the right tone at the top. Corporate executives must visibly embrace the corporation's values. They cannot be mere mouthpieces.

Third, a corporation's other systems and structures must support its existing values. For example, a performance appraisal system should be sensitive to means and not just reward ends. At PepsiCo, executives and managers are rated every year through a 360-degree process, not just on the results that they achieve, but on how they achieve those results.

Fourth, the corporation's values should be integrated into the normal channels of management decision-making and are reflected in the company's critical decisions. For example, marketing plans, strategic decisions, dealings with customers and suppliers, and people decisions should all reflect a company's values. Two of PepsiCo's core values are to care for customers, consumers, and the world we live in, and to sell only products that we can be proud of. We continually review our products, our marketing and advertising programs, and our operations to measure progress against these core values.

Fifth, managers throughout the corporation should understand the values and be empowered to make ethically sound decisions on a day-to-day basis. A system of ethics training is usually needed to achieve this factor. At PepsiCo, we just completed training over 20,000 employees worldwide through a multilingual web-based course on our code of conduct. The course was interactive and scenario-based and provided employees with practical advice on how to handle real-life ethical dilemmas.

To me, when you cut through it all, setting the right tone at the top of a business organization is simply communicating to employees that everyone, from the CEO on down, is expected to conduct the company's business in accordance with high ethical conduct and absolute integrity. This is so because it is what it takes to be a great, successful company, and not just because the law mandates it. And this is everyone's job, not just the lawyers or the compliance officers.

Once you've set the right tone at the top—established the values that guide business decisions day in and day out—how do you know that your message is taking hold in the organization? At PepsiCo, we conduct electronic surveys whereby our employees can respond anonymously about the effectiveness of the values message they are receiving from the top. Early last month, our CEO, Steve Reinemund, sent a message to all PepsiCo employees asking them to complete our biannual Organizational Health Survey. Steve told our employees that the survey is one way "we assess how we're holding ourselves accountable for living our values."

The Role of Lawyers

While establishing the right tone at the top involves more than setting up a compliance program, everyone in this business recognizes that we lawyers play a key role in developing and promoting an ethics regimen that will always have legal compliance as one of its critical components. Certainly, in the face of some very high-profile abuses by just a few corporations, we've come to understand that some lawyers have made mistakes when advising corporate clients, especially on issues relating to ethics and compliance. Based on my experience, lawyers tend to get into trouble in this area when they make one or both of the following mistakes:

First, some lawyers fail to give corporate clients their independent professional judgment. That phrase, "independent professional judgment," is, and ought to be, redundant. A professional lawyer, by definition, is a person who renders independent judgment pursuant to his or her professional responsibilities.

Giving independent judgment should be more important than job security. Independent judgment is the only thing we lawyers, as professionals, have to offer. Think about this: Without it, we are merely hired guns who trade off the reputation of our great profession.

Second, some lawyers in the corporate context forget who their client is. We all know from our first corporate law class, and now from Section 301 of the Sarbanes-Oxley Act, that the client is the corporate entity. It is not just the CEO or, if you're in a law firm, the General Counsel who hired you. A 2002 survey conducted by an organization of General Counsel found that more than 20 percent of the General Counsel surveyed felt that their corporate cultures were such that they emphasized "senior management" as the client, as opposed to the corporation itself. Yes, this is a minority view, but it is sufficiently large to put at risk billions of investor dollars at plenty of companies.

To me, these mistakes illustrate how we lawyers may sometimes inadvertently impede setting the right tone at the top of corporations. I submit we need to get past this type of thinking and behavior and understand that, as corporate lawyers, we represent the corporation as an entity and have a professional obligation to zealously protect the interests of shareholders. In corporations with the right tone at the top, lawyers' professional obligations are co-extensive with the executive team's, which is to ultimately be responsible for the interests of the shareholders. For example, as all of you know, we presently have the debate about the privilege going on, primarily amongst ourselves. It is interesting to some, emotional for many, and somewhat puzzling to others, including myself. It involves the attorney-client privilege and its waiver in the context of government investigations.

Professor Simon of Columbia University Law School provocatively challenges this almost unthinking devotion to the privilege in connection with government investigations. He calls this the confidentiality fetish. For Professor Simon, claiming the privilege to keep factual information from regulators or enforcement officials is inconsistent with the notion of openness and complete transparency in today's post-Enron world. It also flies in the face of Section 406 of Sarbanes-Oxley.

Most corporations, when faced with a government inquiry, retain lawyers to conduct internal investigations to determine what happened and to give the corporation legal advice on a going-forward basis. Oftentimes, factual information the government believes it needs to complete its investigation is withheld from the government because divulging it, in the opinion of these lawyers, could constitute a waiver of the privilege and work to disadvantage the corporation in any subsequent litigation with third parties.

The debate about what to do in this situation is very complex, and I simply do not have the time this morning to get into all the issues about whether government policies actually coerce corporations into waiving the privilege. But I do want to emphasize that I understand that the privilege is absolutely essential to a lawyer's ability to effectively represent a client and protect the attorney's advice to a client in our adversary system. And I do believe the Department of Justice policies enacted in 2003 did not envision or contemplate privilege waivers for purposes of a corporation establishing cooperation except in limited circumstances when the factual information needed by the government could not be obtained in any other way.

I refer you to an excellent article on the subject of corporate internal investigations by George Terwilliger, the former U.S. Deputy Attorney General, and Darryl Lew. The article discusses the sophisticated investigative techniques that should be used in today's enforcement environment, an environment that favors a corporation's cooperation with government investigations. The authors also recommend legislation supporting a limited waiver, which would protect a corporation from adverse litigation consequences associated with waiver of the privilege when cooperating with the government.

For me, when representing a corporation, much of the debate about waiver of the privilege in the face of a government investigation is misplaced. The privilege belongs to the client, the corporation, not to me, the lawyer. My client's policy—one important part of the ethical tone at the top—is to cooperate fully with government investigations. In my view, that means making the necessary facts available to regulatory or enforcement officials, and to the company's internal and outside auditors, not using the privilege to prevent disclosure of relevant facts. I want to stress here that I'm referring to facts and not an attorney's advice to a client, which is, I think, almost sacrosanct and should only be requested by, or disclosed to, the government in limited, very special circumstances that are clearly articulated in the law. But when it comes to facts, not legal advice, the attorney-client privilege shouldn't trump the full and complete disclosure of the necessary facts, even if there are potential consequences in future civil litigation.

As a prosecutor, I witnessed lawyers representing corporations refuse to provide factual information to the government for fear of a disclosure that might constitute a waiver of the privilege. I never really understood this because I could not even fathom a situation in which it would not be in the interest of a corporation, which had an ongoing, viable business, to do anything but fully cooperate with reasonable requests by the government for factual information.

I have heard the argument in favor of doing things a different way. It goes like this. Without the confidentiality of the privilege, corporate officials would avoid lawyers or withhold information from us. As a result, we lawyers would not be able to properly advise the corporate officials on how to obey the law. However, one problem with this view is that it assumes an employee is bent on disobeying the law. This is usually not the case in my experience. But if it is, a lawyer has another set of problems relating to his or her duty of loyalty to the corporation and not the employee or official who is bent on disobeying the law.

But as Professor Simon points out, the rationale for preserving the privilege at all costs completely collapses when you understand that it is absolutely clear under *Upjohn* that the privilege belongs to the corporation. In fact, employees interviewed during the course of an internal investigation should be informed of who owns the privilege during the standard *Upjohn* advice to interviewees. No corporate executive can assume that everything he or she tells the corporation's lawyer, especially during an investigation, will remain confidential forever. A corporation may direct its counsel to waive the privilege in the face of a government investigation, despite potential adverse civil consequences, in order to get the matter under investigation quickly behind it. In fact, this is exactly what happens oftentimes, and corporations certainly do not need lawyers standing in the way of their ability to fully cooperate in a government investigation and receive the appropriate credit for doing so.

So closing on the tone at the top theme, the right tone at the top, in my view, does not, in today's environment, involve having lawyers keep factual information from investigators, from its internal and outside lawyers, and from government officials during investigations. This approach runs counter to the interests of the corporation and its shareholders.

And this is not to say that we lawyers are always on the wrong side of the equation in these circumstances. I've seen lawyers play literally heroic roles in representing corporations where the culture and tone at the top were bad and caused the corporation to get into a lot of trouble. These lawyers literally saved their corporate clients and brilliantly represented the interests of the corporation's shareholders.

So we all know that having the right tone at the top is critical. Notwithstanding my concerns regarding the privilege, I'm absolutely confident that lawyers will play a pivotal role of most corporations in setting the right tone at the top. This is as it should be and is consistent with high standards of integrity in our profession.

REMARKS OF PEPSICO GENERAL COUNSEL AND SVP OF GOVERNMENT AFFAIRS AT LOYOLA MARYMOUNT UNIVERSITY'S JOURNALIST LAW SCHOOL PROGRAM

May 31, 2013

I was on my second tour of duty at PepsiCo when I gave this speech. I returned after teaching at the University of Georgia Law School. At Georgia, my legal research detailed the history of the corporate form and pointed out how advocating for a purely economic outcome for corporate performance was inconsistent with the legal and historic foundations of the corporation. My research was a forerunner of what we today call stakeholder capitalism. This speech was my attempt to present these legal concepts to laypeople, albeit very smart journalists.

Now, to those of you who've had experience covering investor calls, you know about safe harbor announcements.

So let me start with a safe harbor announcement or disclaimer of my own, and my goal is for it to be the only part of my speech that sounds like an investor call. The opinions I'll express today are mine. I'm here today representing myself, not any employer, present or past.

Okay. Safe harbor announcement over.

Now, on behalf of all those who engage with the law, and the media, almost every day, thank you for coming, for taking the initiative to attend this program. Seeing the "course of study" you're taking here, I believe you'll leave better prepared to find, understand, interpret, and share the facts.

Corporate Law: "A Responsible Corporation . . . What Does That Entail?"

We learn from others and, at this conference, experts. We can't be experts at everything. You don't have to try to be a superwoman or superman to be an expert at everything. This truth reminds me of a story I once heard about former heavyweight boxing champion Muhammad Ali.

I grew up in Hannibal, Missouri. And Hannibal's most famous son, Mark Twain, a reporter himself for a number of newspapers, had some advice for his fellow journalists: "Get your facts first," he said.

"And then," he added, "you can distort them as much as you wish."

Now, that may have been Twain's experience with the fourth estate. But it hasn't been mine.

Throughout my career, in both the public and the private sector, I have, countless times, interacted with journalists off the record, and on background, to help them understand the context of a story.

I have never once been burned, never once been misquoted. The journalists I know, and I'm sure this applies to you, are truth seekers, above all else, and honorable in the pursuit of truth.

So in that spirit, in the spirit of seeking the truth and getting facts straight, today I'd like to tell you the facts and context about one aspect of law.

There is one aspect of this field that I've been particularly interested in for several years—since a meeting I had with PepsiCo's CEO and my boss, Indra Nooyi. This area is generally defined as corporate responsibility.

Back in 2007, Indra and I were discussing refinements to PepsiCo's "Performance with Purpose" agenda: a plan to, among other things, make our products healthier, our communities stronger, and reduce our impact on the environment while, at the same time, maintaining a high level of financial performance.

There were some cynics. And that's when Indra turned to me and said, "Larry, I simply want to be a responsible corporation. From a legal standpoint," she asked, "what does that entail?"

Now, that question alone tells you something about our company and my boss. Chief Legal Officers and General Counsel are expected to win cases, do deals, and prepare complex contracts and regulatory filings. Not many GCs are asked to do research on the legal basis of a responsible corporation.

The Misquotation of "Engine Charlie"

In fact, I'd like to start with one story I've uncovered—one that brings together all the elements we're here to discuss—business, journalism, and the law. It's the story of "Engine Charlie."

In the early 1980s, two men, both named Charles E. Wilson, ran two of the country's largest corporations. The first Charles was nicknamed "Electric Charlie" because he was CEO of General Electric. The second was nicknamed "Engine Charlie" because he was the CEO of General Motors.

Then—like now—General Motors was a behemoth, an iconic American company. During World War II, Engine Charlie's GM had secured the largest government contract of any corporation. And after the war's end, GM controlled 50 percent of the domestic automobile market and employed over 600,000 people, equivalent to one-tenth of Michigan's population.

So when President Eisenhower needed to select a Secretary of Defense, a post that controlled 60 percent of the federal budget, Engine Charlie seemed like a natural choice. And an uncontroversial one—uncontroversial, at least, until the confirmation hearings.

In 1953, Engine Charlie sat before the Senate Armed Services Committee and was asked if, as Secretary of Defense, he would be able to make decisions that were in the national interest but were adverse to GM's interests. According to the newspapers, Charlie responded with one of the most infamous political gaffes ever.

"What is good for General Motors," Wilson reportedly said, "is good for America." "What's good for GM is good for America" became a cultural proof point, indicative of a sort of arrogance of the business community.

But here's the thing about that line: Engine Charlie never said it. In fact, he had said the opposite, and I quote, "I cannot conceive of a situation [where America's interests and GM's do not align]," he'd told the committee, "because for years, I thought what was good for the country was good for GM."

According to historians, journalists covering the hearing had misquoted Charlie. Some may have wanted to believe his track record at GM fit into a preconceived narrative about the apathy of the business class. They saw him as a symbol, not an individual.

But as it turns out, the individual and the symbol couldn't have been more different. Engine Charlie wasn't a heartless number cruncher. On the contrary.

Before Engine Charlie was Engine Charlie, he was a card-carrying member of the patternmaker's union. When he became CEO, he announced that "to develop citizenship and community [was] the task of the next generation [of GM]." And then he went to work designing a pension system for all company retirees.

"If life were fair," said one biographer, "we would hail Charles E. Wilson as a hero."

Now, why do I tell this story? Well, I think that, in it, there are lessons for both today's journalists and today's business leaders. Namely, that today's business leaders *should* be like Engine Charlie, and that today's journalists *should* have a better understanding of the legal role of corporations in our society.

That's why I want to spend some time today correcting a basic misconception that many people have about the nature of corporations in our society.

From Milton Friedman to the Quarterly Earnings Report

So let me begin the basic, what I call false, premise in this area from a legal standpoint. And that is that corporate leaders are required to run their companies in a way that solely maximizes profits for shareholders. Required if not by law, then by their boards. If not by their boards, then by the force of history to maximize profit above all else.

And make no mistake—this belief does have a lot of history behind it.

Milton Friedman, the famous economist, certainly believed it too. In 1970, he famously stated that a corporation has "one and only one social responsibility"—"to increase its profits."

"Few trends," Friedman wrote, "could so thoroughly undermine the very foundations of our free society as the acceptance by corporate officials of a social responsibility other than to make as much money for their stockholders as possible."

Now, few today would put it so bluntly—or absolutely—as Friedman did. But that cabined, self-interested—even selfish—notion of a corporation's purpose still exists.

Rome, Wrigley, and the Business Judgment Rule

So let me state—for the record—that this solely economic view of the business purpose of corporations is wrong legally and wrong historically.

Let me talk a little bit about each.

First, the history.

When the first corporations were established 2,000 years ago in Rome, the Empire licensed them, specifically, to further public purposes. Roman corporations kept the peace. They distributed grain to the needy. They lent money to families for weddings and funerals. They collected taxes.

In Rome, the corporation was a stakeholder in, even a benefactor of, the larger community.

Roman emperors were very insecure. It was the public purpose of these business societies that made the emperor comfortable, that these citizens could come together and do the public good.

And this tradition continued through the centuries: stretching through the Middle Ages into the Renaissance, and even across the Atlantic to the founding of America.

Even in the twentieth century, corporations—recognizing the need for well-focused and well-educated workers—built company towns and colleges across the nation. Corporations and communities have not been legal adversaries for most of history, like they seemingly are today in too many instances. Quite the opposite. Think about it. One really cannot exist without the cooperation of the other.

Indeed, to the corporation, society gives a powerful set of tools: limited liability, perpetual existence, the right to govern itself by bylaws of its own choosing. It also provides the corporation with natural resources, a healthy workforce, and a population of consumers.

And in return, the society depends upon the corporation. It depends upon companies for wealth creation and jobs and hopefully high-quality goods and services.

So no, corporations and communities are not adversaries. They are, rather, interdependent from a clear historical point of view.

Second, the law.

That independence, really, is a principle enshrined in the law too. Let's consider this legal example. In 1919, Henry Ford announced he wanted to use his company to lift the lives of the working class. It was his ambition, he said, "to employ still more men, to spread the benefits of this industrial system to the greatest possible number, to help them build up their lives and their homes."

To do this, Henry chose not to reward his shareholders with the company's profits—but to pour those profits "back in the business." His shareholders were less than enthusiastic about this plan. Two of his largest shareholders, in fact, the Dodge brothers, men who also knew something about cars, were angry enough to take him to court.

And that's exactly what they did.

Eighty-six years ago, Michigan's Supreme Court heard the case of *Dodge v. Ford Motor Company*. The court's ruling wasn't a total victory for Henry Ford (it ordered him to increase the company's dividend). But it did give him the broad authority to exercise his business judgment—and to act to the broader interest of the corporation. That meant he could address the needs of his company's other constituencies—constituencies like employees, customers, consumers, the community, and even the environment.

Directors' "power over [profits]," the court declared, "is absolute so long as they act in the exercise of honest judgment." Put another way, management, the court said, did not have to act solely in the short-term interest of shareholders, and it could reflect the interest of other important stakeholders in the company.

This was a huge victory, as I said, but still a partial one. A corporation's legal right to act in the broader interest of corporate stakeholders wasn't fully solidified until a string of corporate law cases came along later in twentieth century.

Among those cases, perhaps the best example is the one that occurred in the mid-1960s, when stockholders of the Chicago Cubs brought a suit against Philip Wrigley, the Cubs' principal owner.

A little background: Up until this point, Cubs games had been poorly attended. The team had run operating losses year after year. And hosting night games, the stockholders believed, could fix the organization's balance sheet.

But there was a problem. Philip Wrigley refused to install lights at Wrigley Field—a field named after his father. Baseball, he maintained, was a "daytime sport"—and "night games," he thought, "would have a deteriorating effect on the surrounding neighborhood."

Now, most of us can agree that Wrigley's personal view of baseball was outdated even at the time.

But he was, nonetheless, making a point about balancing the interests of the surrounding community with the interests of the shareholders at the time.

And the court seized on that point. Second-guessing company management and directors, it ruled, was "beyond [the court's] jurisdiction and ability."

The case is a great example of what is known as "the business judgment rule," a legal principle you should take note of if you haven't already. The business judgment rule shields, and thereby promotes, directors and managers who advance their corporation's long-term prospects by serving the interests of broader corporate constituents and stakeholders.

All of this is to say corporate leaders aren't legally required to maximize profits solely for shareholders in the short term. In fact, some leaders understand this. They are running their businesses successfully by taking a longer term, more sustainable approach to financial performance while at the same time addressing the needs of broader corporate constituents like employees, customers, communities, and even the environment. This is not only good business in the eyes of these leaders; it also helps assure that their companies maintain a strong social license to operate from society.

Shortsighted Companies

Some critics of corporations may be right—corporations may not be people. They may not have souls. But they are run by people who do have souls—and who do have brains.

And some business leaders and others in the financial world still seem to not understand the legal role of corporations in today's society: to focus on the long-term and sustainable financial well-being of the company and its shareholders, as well as for its broader constituents—employees, customers, consumers, and communities.

But many in the financial world are still holding fast to Milton Friedman's outdated notion that business should be focused on solely maximizing profit for shareholders and focused on that alone. Indeed, the view may still be pervasive, widely held and followed by many.

And that, to be blunt, is not a good thing.

A number of experts, including former SEC Chair William Donaldson, have spoken about this worrying trend. They have noted that now, more than ever, companies and some CEOs feel intense pressure to run their companies to solely beat quarterly earnings expectations.

"Making the numbers," so to speak, has become so entrenched in the corporate conversation, it appears to be the barometer for good corporate management. And CEOs are often judged—and judged harshly—if they can't meet short-term expectations.

This kind of myopia is dangerous; toxic short-term thinking ignited the financial crisis of 2008.

And ultimately, it's self-destructive too.

Eighty years ago, a law professor named E.M. Dodd wrote an article titled "For Whom Are Corporate Managers Trustees?" In it, he argued that "public opinion . . . ultimately makes law." And if the public is unhappy enough with the financial system, it will develop a new one to replace it.

Dodd's idea may seem radical. But recent Gallup polls show that well over 60 percent of the public disapprove of the size, power, and influence of major corporations.

CEOs as Statesmen

Indeed, what I think the business community needs from a legal stand-point right now is *not* a faster quarter-to-quarter rat race.

What the business community needs is to take a breath to take a longer-term and broader view of its constituents. Like Engine Charlie.

There is a need for businessmen and women to become business states-men and stateswomen. Leaders with the vision to set aside the obsession with quarterly expectations—and to adopt a more sustainable approach to capitalism.

This, in fact, is one of the goals of the Committee for Economic Development, of which I'm a member. I also co-chair the Subcommittee on Corporate Governance.

The CED's mission is to show corporate leaders they don't have to choose between rewarding their shareholders and improving the long-term health of their company and society. They can do both at the same time. CED's paper on statesmanship is posted on its website, www.ced.org.

I mentioned PepsiCo's "Performance with Purpose" earlier.

This strategy, as I mentioned, includes investments in R&D to improve the nutrition of our existing products and to help us develop completely new products as well, so that we give our consumers more choices. Witness our dramatically reduced sugar product Pepsi Next, as well as new products such as Tropicana Farms, Trop 50, Quaker Real Medleys breakfast product, and Sabra Hummus and Pretzel Bites. In fact, our CEO will be cutting the ribbon on a new yogurt plant.

Performance with Purpose also requires us to be responsive to the communities in which we work and sell, to reduce our impact on the environment, and to improve our talent pipeline.

These actions do not mean we are sacrificing financial performance.

After all, this isn't philanthropy: This is simply good business.

Thanks in large part to this new agenda, we have delivered an annualized total shareholder return of 6.9 percent, exceeding the Dow Jones Industrial Average by 150 bps (5.4 percent) and the S&P by 170 bps (5.2 percent).

And what this proves is that shareholders benefit when executives take the holistic view of what is required to ensure success, not just on a quarter-to-quarter basis, but on a longer term, more sustainable basis.

So let me conclude by saying corporations may be powerful entities. But journalists have great power too.

By coming here, by attending a program like this, by expanding your education, I think you're doing the public a great service.

And, yes, by "the public," I'm including corporate types like me too. And I think you will make certain that there will be no more businessmen and women who will suffer the fate of Engine Charlie.

So thank you, all. And I look forward to your questions.

REMARKS ON "DIVERSITY AND THE LEGAL PROFESSION" BEFORE THE BOSTON LAWYERS GROUP

June 8, 2005

I had been asked by Benaree ("Benny") Pratt Wiley, a member of PepsiCo's then African American Advisory Board, to speak on diversity before a group of lawyers in Boston. In preparing for this speech, I thought long and hard about the subject. I wanted to be completely honest. I acknowledged in my speech how I had been the beneficiary of diversity efforts by individual executives at Monsanto and PepsiCo when I was hired. Even then, I did not feel I was less qualified than others, and I emphasized in my speech that a diverse attorney should never mean a less qualified attorney.

Good afternoon. It's good to be back in Boston and renew acquaintances with some good friends and outstanding lawyers. I want to commend the Boston Lawyers Group for this event and its work. There is no doubt, in my opinion, that diversity is extremely important to the legal profession. But unfortunately, it's also something the profession continues to struggle with, notwithstanding some notable achievements in this area over the past several years.

To me, there is no great mystery as to how we can achieve greater diversity in the legal profession. But I do recognize there are difficulties and obstacles that must be overcome. So let me share with you my experience and observations regarding diversity in the profession that may, in some small way, help take what mystery there is out of how we might reach our desired results.

I've been practicing law 31 years. For a minority lawyer my age, you really cannot think about diversity without thinking about your own experiences. I grew up in Hannibal, Missouri—a town of about 18,000 people on the banks of the Mississippi River about a hundred miles north of St. Louis. My father was a railroad laborer and my mother a cook. Neither of them graduated from high school. Yet they were very good parents. In fact, I really did not know I was disadvantaged until I went off to college and studied sociology and economics.

My first legal job out of the University of Michigan Law School was at the Monsanto Company in St. Louis, Missouri. Now, I was not hired as a part of any formal diversity effort—but there is no doubt in my mind that the General Counsel of Monsanto made an informal diversity decision when he hired me as the first African American lawyer in the Monsanto law department. So I don't espouse or talk about diversity because this is the fashionable thing to do. I appreciate and try to advance diversity because it has had real meaning and importance in my professional life.

Sometimes we hear the sort of quiet question: Do we really need to have diversity efforts in the legal profession today? Well, let me answer that type of question this way. From 1986 to 2001, while in private practice, I represented clients in a variety of cases and investigations before every litigating division of the Department of Justice (civil, criminal, antitrust, tax, environmental) and before several United States Attorneys' Offices. And it was only in about three cases did I see a lawyer of color on the other side representing the United States. To me, that is quite astounding.

That is why, as Deputy Attorney General, I helped launch the Department of Justice's attorney diversity program. This program was not started just because it was the right thing to do. The Justice Department's diversity program represents a practical, common-sense recognition that an organization like DOJ will be stronger and more effective if its attorney workforce represents a full spectrum of backgrounds, including those defined by race and ethnicity.

Now, it goes without saying, but I'm going to say it: The Justice Department's diversity efforts did not involve hiring or promotional preferences. They were unnecessary and would have been demeaning to the many highly qualified minority attorneys in the Department.

And I think this point needs to be made absolutely clear. There are many highly qualified, diverse attorneys. You needn't settle on an attorney who is not ready for prime time. There are many highly qualified minority attorneys who are successful and represent the best of our profession.

I joined PepsiCo in October last year and consider myself fortunate to be a part of a great company that has a strong commitment to diversity and inclusion. This commitment to diversity certainly was an important factor that attracted me to the company.

I think the main thing that sets PepsiCo apart from other companies and organizations is that diversity and inclusion are about the future growth of the company. At PepsiCo, diversity and inclusion together are a fundamental strategic business priority.

Let's talk about what we at PepsiCo are doing. We've done some things right and we've done some things that haven't worked. But the main point that PepsiCo's CEO Steve Reinemund likes to make is that when it comes to diversity, you've got to direct your efforts on multiple fronts—to employees, to leaders, to suppliers, to trade partners, and to outside advisers.

For PepsiCo, the business rationale for diversity is clear: Minority populations are growing faster than the population overall. In the U.S., racially and ethnically diverse groups are expected to be the majority of the population in our lifetime. Steve believes that any company that can conquer the diversity challenge first will clearly have a competitive advantage.

So for us at PepsiCo, diversity is not about playing defense to meet consumer pressure. Diversity is about figuring out how to attract the best and brightest talent in the *entire population* that will allow us to do the best job possible for our shareholders.

Last year was one of the best years PepsiCo ever had. And Steve believes that at least one point of PepsiCo's top line growth came about as a result of our diversity efforts. For example: Mountain Dew was reinvigorated, broadening its appeal to urban youth; Frito-Lay introduced a new flavor extension in Doritos and Lay's called Guacamole that was targeted for the ethnic community by an ethnically led team of R&D and marketing employees; and Gatorade saw growth from a new line of Xtreme! products targeted to ethnic youth.

We at PepsiCo have made substantial progress over the past three years with our diversity efforts. Representation of women and minorities at every level, and in every function, has increased by at least a percentage point each year. But to be clear on this point, we still have a ways to go.

But there are several things we've tried that have, we believe, helped us move the diversity bar. They are:

- Making our diversity goals very clear and measurable.
- Requiring that 50 percent of our new hires be diverse.
- Ensuring promotion rates among all ethnic groups and women are at parity with white men.
- Ensuring retention rates among all ethnic groups and women are at least as good as white males.

- Tying a substantial portion of senior management bonuses—my pay—to achieving diversity goals.
- Developing training programs involving doing business in a diverse culture.
- Getting outside help. We have created two advisory boards—one African American and the other Latino Hispanic that have given management invaluable guidance in this area. Bennie Wiley is a member of our African American Advisory Board, which is chaired by Earl Graves, the publisher of *Black Enterprise*.

Now, let me talk about the law department.

From a law department perspective, we have been successful in hiring and retaining diverse attorneys. Fifty-eight percent of our domestic attorneys are people of color and women—12 percent women of color (including two Latinas), 9 percent men of color, 37 percent white women. We have also been successful in retaining women- and minority-owned law firms as certified by the National Minority Supplier Development Council and the Women's Business Enterprise National Council.

As I noted earlier, we are on a journey with our diversity efforts both at PepsiCo and in the profession as a whole. One of the places I would like to see us go is that diverse attorneys become fully engaged in the myriad of important and complex issues facing a large corporation like PepsiCo.

Today, I see too few attorneys of color on the front line handling key cases and deals for large corporations. This is unfortunate, not just for the attorneys who are missing these opportunities, but also for the clients who may be missing valuable perspectives that most likely could come from diverse attorneys.

PepsiCo and my predecessor, Dave Andrews, signed "A Call to Action" along with a number of other General Counsel. This is truly a worthy effort. These General Counsel reaffirmed their commitment to diversity in the legal profession and also pledged to make decisions regarding which law firms represented their companies based, in significant part, on the diversity performance of the law firms. These General Counsel understand that the interests of their clients would be best served by having attorneys represent them who reflect the diversity of their clients' employees, customers, and communities.

I want to make the increased use of diverse attorneys on key matters happen at PepsiCo. I recognize this is not as easy as it sounds because it will involve working carefully with our outside law firms. So I have asked two lawyers on our staff, one who is very senior, to review our efforts and give me recommendations on how we can be more objective in dealing with law firms in this area and how we can measure what they are doing on behalf of PepsiCo.

Clear objectives and appropriate measurements are, I believe, the keys to meeting the diversity challenge.

This is not a heavy-handed approach. To the contrary, it is a legitimate approach to make certain that my client receives the very best and most effective legal representation it can, based on my 31 years at the bar.

I believe we're on the right track at PepsiCo on the diversity front. But like the legal profession as a whole, we at PepsiCo cannot afford to stand still and let success pass us by.

As that great American philosopher Will Rogers once said, "Even if you're on the right track, if you do nothing and stand still, you're eventually going to be hit and run over by a train."

I certainly don't want that to happen at PepsiCo. And I also don't want that to happen to the legal profession, which means so much to our country's way of life.

This is important work, and we thank you for what you're doing.

UNIVERSITY OF MICHIGAN LAW SCHOOL COMMENCEMENT SPEECH

May 9, 2009

I have given several commencement speeches, but this one was special. It was my law school alma mater. I'm still particularly satisfied that I could publicly acknowledge Michigan Law School Professor Joseph Vining for the impact he had on my life and career. During the speech, I also read a note Professor Vining had written me about our respective careers and the "circle of life."

It is truly an honor to be asked by my alma mater to share this very special occasion with you.

And greetings to the faculty and staff of our great law school. I know all of you have worked hard to make this day possible.

And greetings and congratulations to the Class of 2009. You have accomplished a great deal and have reason to be proud today. But I do ask that you take a moment to recall all the people who helped you to get to this day—probably most important, your parents and your families. That their efforts are bound up in your own reminds me of a wonderful story I heard Alex Haley—the author of *Roots*—tell several years ago.

Haley and a friend were walking down a long and winding path that was adjacent to a beautiful, rather tall wall that was constructed of a polished, slick stone. As they were making their way down the path, Haley noticed a large turtle sitting atop of the wall. Thinking to himself how impossible it would be for a turtle to climb this tall, slick wall, Haley asked his friend, "How did this turtle get on top of this wall?" The friend thought about the query for a moment and then said, "I don't know, but you can bet on one thing—he did not get there by himself."

Thirty-five years ago, I sat where you sit today, albeit, I think, at the University-wide commencement. But I cannot remember for the life of me who the commencement speaker was, so I have no illusion that what I say today will achieve the permanence of the Gettysburg Address. Perhaps I can only attempt to emulate its brevity.

But using my discretion as your speaker, I would like to take the opportunity to share with you a few brief observations, based on my life experiences, that may prove useful to you as you move on behind the law school. These observations, three of them, on (1) public service, (2) money, and (3) professionalism, are not profound. They are simple. But perhaps you will remember them. I'll then conclude with some personal observations on my career defining the Michigan Law School experience.

Let me begin with public service, which has been such an important part of my legal career. I was in New York City a few years ago representing President Bush at the dedication of the Thurgood Marshall Courthouse. In preparing my remarks for the occasion, I ran across a description of the ideal lawyer that was written by Supreme Court Justice Robert Jackson in 1942. Let me share it with you. Justice Jackson described the ideal lawyer as a lawyer who loved his or her profession and who had a sense of dedication to the administration of justice. To this ideal lawyer, the law was like a religion, and its practice was more than a means of support: It was a mission. This, of course, completely describes Justice Marshall and his dedication to public service. It also describes the dilemma of the modern lawyer.

Today, there are many in the profession, including myself, who are concerned about the practice of law becoming simply another white-collar industry where the non-economic aspects of the profession, which were once considered responsibilities, are ignored. Many of us are also concerned about the seeming reluctance of many lawyers, especially younger lawyers, even in today's economic downturn, to enter public service. Not so with Justice Marshall.

Shortly after he began his law practice in Baltimore, Justice Marshall's teacher and mentor, Charles Houston, cautioned him not to neglect the development of his own practice for the work he was doing for the NAACP on the side. Fortunately for the nation, Justice Marshall did not listen to his teacher's advice and told Houston in 1935, "Personally, I would not give up these cases here in Maryland for anything in the world. But at the same time, there is no opportunity to really hustle for business."

Justice Marshall's career was never about how much money he could make as a lawyer. Instead, his career was one of commitment to the public profession of law—a great example for all of us.

Now a call to public service may be easy for a lawyer like myself who has long ago retired his student loans. But I believe public service is important to a lawyer for reasons that may really be considered selfish. Whether your public service be full time or part time, volunteer work or pro bono cases—it will be important to you as a lawyer and give meaning and satisfaction to your professional life.

My second observation is somewhat related to the first, but more pointed. Never, ever take a job just for the money. I have taken three significant pay cuts in my legal career. In fact, some of you may question my judgment for being so financially unfocused.

However, with the clarity of hindsight, I can tell you that the times I have been most satisfied professionally have been times when I was doing something I wanted to do solely because I felt it was the right thing for me to do at the time and not because the job or position paid the most money.

I have come to realize the obvious. Life is, in fact, a one-time deal. You do not get to go around twice here on earth—and the times you will remember are those (1) when you did something that made a difference, (2) when you risked much for an even greater reward, and (3) when you reached toward the everyday to engage yourself in the broader world.

You will learn to put money in perspective and not always put it first. I believe if you take care of your clients, nourish your development as a lawyer, and value your reputation in the profession, the money will come.

Now to my third observation.

Remember above all, like Justice Jackson observed, that the law is a profession, not a business.

A professional lawyer, by definition, is a person retained to render independent judgment. Giving independent judgment is more important than job security. Independent judgment is the most important thing we lawyers, as professionals, have to offer. Think about this: Without it, we are mere hired guns who trade off the integrity of our profession.

And now, I want to warn you: At some point in your career, and even earlier than you think, you will be invited to abandon your principles to satisfy a client. Don't do it. It's not worth it. Don't be afraid to lose a client—or even fire a client—if it means upholding your independent judgment or what you believe to be right and appropriate.

More than a century ago, Elihu Reed, a renowned corporate lawyer who practiced in New York City, and was a Senator, Cabinet Secretary during the Administration of President Theodore Roosevelt, and Nobel Prize winner, observed that "about half the practice of a decent lawyer consists of telling his clients that they are damned fools and should stop."

Now let me get back to the beginning of my talk and remind you again to not forget those who will have made it possible for you to get where you will be in your professional lives. Stay in touch with your professors and other senior lawyers who will make a difference in your professional lives: partners, judges, and even adversaries.

But today, I want to focus on staying in touch with your professors. I value my continuing relationship with one of my law school professors. It has enriched my life personally and professionally. I have continued to learn from him.

That professor is Joe Vining. As you know, Professor Vining is retiring this year, and I had the honor of attending his retirement dinner two weeks ago at the Lawyers Club. The dinner was a fitting tribute to a terrific academic career and a timely reminder of what you just completed at this great law school. When your minds—some of the best law students in the nation—have met the minds of your professors—some of the top legal scholars in the world—the impact on your lives and careers can be, and often is, great and lasting.

Now as I try to deal with the recent turmoil in our financial markets and the negative impact it has had on the global economy, and I recall the many discussions and exchanges of correspondence over the years with Professor Vining on the role of corporations in society, it is clear to me— and to anyone else who has read Professor Vining's work in this area—that the focus on short-term profit maximization for the benefit of shareholders, while accepted and even driven by Wall Street over the past several years, is a concept that is wrong legally and historically.

Most great public companies strive to be responsible, and this is why I've undertaken research that will review the legal and historical basis of responsible corporate behavior. I was asked to undertake this research by PepsiCo's CEO, and my principal client, Indra Nooyi.

It seems to me that the responsible corporation understands that its best interests, and thus the best interests of its stockholders, lie not only in *extending* its horizons beyond the next quarterly earnings report, but also in *broadening* them to include more than just short-term shareholder returns.

Historically and legally, corporations and society have been interdependent. Society—through state law and a variety of state and federal regulations—allows the corporation to exist and grants it extraordinary privileges like limited liability. Corporations, in turn, create jobs and wealth. They also innovate and invest in their communities. A responsible corporation must understand the interdependence.

To be successful, a responsible corporation must not only perform financially for the benefit of its shareholders; it also has an obligation in the long-term interest of its shareholders to work for the betterment of the society that allows it the privilege to exist and that provides it natural resources and an educated and skilled workforce. I look forward to publishing the results of my research within the next several weeks.

Now, permit me to be a bit personal and read to you something Professor Vining wrote me after I was confirmed as Deputy Attorney General: "Did I tell you, my first job was located in the Office of Deputy Attorney General? The deputy was Nick Katzenbach. Jim Vorenberg was his special assistant for Johnson's 'War on Crime,' and I was Jim Vorenberg's assistant. I spent a great deal of time in what will be your office, and it fills me with a sense of full term that you now should be sitting in an office where I began."

This coming to full term is the nature of things. And, as you move out and begin your professional lives, that sense of full term will come to you as you distinguish yourselves in the profession, your communities, and our nation.

I wish you luck and Godspeed in the process.

Thank you.

"THE RULE OF LAW AND TERRORISM: THE CRITICAL IMPLICATIONS OF A NEW NATIONAL DEBATE" AT THE BROOKINGS INSTITUTION

November 2, 2003

This was my first major speech after I left the Deputy Attorney General position. I had just joined the Brookings Institution as a senior fellow. At the time, there was a great deal of debate about the Patriot Act and how the government was dealing with the threat of terrorism.

Having just left government, I knew that the prospect of terrorist attacks was real. Because some provisions of the Patriot Act were set to sunset in 2005, I proposed in my speech a bipartisan commission to review these provisions away from the shrill and uninformed arguments that were being hurled around at the time. The commission I proposed never came into being, but the key provisions of the Patriot Act were not sunsetted.

————

It was a distinct honor and privilege to serve the Department of Justice for almost two years. By the way, my two years must have been dog years because it feels like I was at Justice for at least six years.

But my experience in the Department was, in many ways, very satisfying. I served during some truly historic times as the Department had to play a critical role in dealing with the terrorist attacks of 9/11 and take lead in helping to restore our financial markets following the spate of corporate scandals that started with the Enron bankruptcy. As a former prosecutor and white-collar defense lawyer, the corporate fraud work was near and dear to my heart. I believe the Department's vigorous criminal enforcement in the corporate and financial areas has played a critical role in our market economy and perhaps helped stave off a wave of potentially unnecessary and unhelpful regulation.

But it was the work on the terrorism front that I found special and want to talk to you about tonight. The reason I want to talk to this distinguished audience about terrorism is that I have recently heard some people, whose judgment and balance I respect very much, question the government's antiterrorism efforts and question the relatively new authorities given the government under the Patriot Act.

Now let me share with you something I said on this subject before I left government. I told the Ninth Circuit Judicial Conference this year that the government's authorities under which it deals with terrorism are not, and should not be, unbridled. There should be appropriate checks and balances in government power. The struggle against terrorism should not change the essential character of this great nation. We should never waiver from the principle that we are a country dedicated to the rule of law.

Shortly after the terrorist attacks of 9/11, I met with retired Justice Bach of the Supreme Court of Israel. It was a very profound experience. Justice Bach left me with a copy of a 1999 decision of the Israeli Supreme Court dealing with the interrogation practices of the General Security Service—also known as "Shin Bet"—in using so-called "moderate physical pressure" in the interrogation of terrorism suspects. The court noted in deciding to prohibit this practice: "A democratic freedom-loving society does not accept that investigations use any means for the purpose of uncovering the truth—at times, the price of truth is so high that a democratic society is not prepared to pay it."

The Israeli Supreme Court's conclusion in the case applies equally to our country: "This is the destiny of democracy, as not all means are acceptable to it, and not all practices employed by its enemies are open before it. Although a democracy must often fight with one hand tied behind its back, it nonetheless has the upper hand. Preserving the rule of law and recognition of an individual's liberty constitutes an important component in its understanding of security. At the end of the day, they strengthen its spirit and [add to] its strength and allow it to overcome its difficulties."

Wise and eloquent words. I referred to them often as we at the Department tried to do what we had to do to keep us safe.

This is all a good prelude to why I want to talk to you about terrorism. As a leader in the Department of Justice, I came to realize that the country's success in fighting the threat of terrorism would increasingly depend on public confidence that the government can ensure the fair and impartial administration of justice for all Americans while carrying out its essential national security and public safety efforts. This is why the concerns I mentioned deserve our attention.

But the level of discussion and debate about the government's antiterrorism efforts is at the extremes. Some view the government's techniques and authorities as unnecessarily authoritarian, while others view those who have concerns as uninformed and willing to unnecessarily sacrifice the country's safety. Much of the debate is shrill and ill-informed on both sides.

This is truly unfortunate, and certainly does not foster the needed public confidence. By necessity, I believe, some of the government's efforts have been aggressive. In dealing with terrorism, the Department's focus could no longer be on just investigation and prosecution. The Department also had to be concerned about prevention and disruption. There has been an increased use of material witness warrants in terrorism cases. There have been the voluntary interviews of certain aliens. The President has designated three persons who are U.S. citizens as enemy combatants.

And there is another antiterrorism measure I would like to single out because of how it fits into the public debate about the government's anti-terrorism efforts. The Department has increased the availability of searches and electronic surveillance under the Foreign Intelligence Surveillance Act. In doing so, the Department issued new directives that have fostered cooperation among national security and law enforcement personnel. To me, this means that the Department undertook necessary measures that will allow intelligence and law enforcement officials to "connect the dots" in terrorism investigations.

The Department's authority to undertake these important efforts was derived under Section 218 of the Patriot Act, and that particular provision will "sunset" or cease to be in effect on December 31, 2005. In fact, 16 provisions of the Patriot Act will sunset in 2005.

Now, I obviously strongly believe that this provision is important to our success in dealing with terrorism. But what I believe is not the point. The point is that it is vitally important that the country have a reasoned, dispassionate, and informed debate about the legal tools and measures necessary in dealing with terrorism. This is the only way we can achieve the public confidence that I believe is necessary if our efforts are to be successful. And we certainly cannot afford to allow the provisions of the Patriot Act, like Section 218, to sunset without the kind of reasoned and careful national discussion I am talking about. Too much is at stake.

I have a modest proposal. This discussion or review of the government's antiterrorism authorities, I believe, should be done outside the partisan wrangling of Congress and outside the unhelpful influence of interest groups.

We should consider establishing either a congressional or Presidential bipartisan commission to review and report on the sunsetting of provisions of the Patriot Act. Such a commission should consist of respected and balanced constitutional scholars and legal practitioners.

I know commissions have, in the past, been misused. For example, they have been used to shield Congress or the executive branch from having to make difficult decisions. But, perhaps, in this instance, a review commission, with an appropriately distinguished membership, will allow us to take one small but very important step toward a reasoned, dispassionate, and informed national discussion about antiterrorism efforts.

I have had a firsthand positive experience with such a commission. In 2000, I participated in what was called the Judicial Review Commission on Foreign Asset Control. It was a bipartisan congressional commission. The primary mandate of the commission was to review the constitutionality of the Foreign Narcotics Kingpin Designation Act's preclusion of judicial review of decisions by the government. After assembling a staff, the commission engaged in informed fact finding, held public hearings, and produced a report to Congress. The commission's work, I believe, also formed a basis for legislative modification of the controversial preclusion of the judicial review provision of the Kingpin Act. The commission's work received broad support from Democrats and Republicans, many career government officials, industry, and even the American Civil Liberties Union.

If after a reasoned and informed debate it becomes clear that public confidence in the government's antiterrorism efforts would be substantially eroded if one more provision of the Patriot Act were not sunsetted, then fine. We as a country should then move on and do our best to ensure public safety.

Too much is at stake to proceed any other way in a country that is threatened by the horrors of terrorism, but whose citizens—all of them—cherish the rule of law. Al-Qaeda, for example, continues to pose a threat to our country, even though we have had some success against it. More than one-third of al-Qaeda leadership identified before the Afghanistan war has been killed or captured. But George Tenet has testified before Congress that the CIA continues to receive information that al-Qaeda is dedicated to striking the U.S. homeland again.

But terrorism is a very serious matter even without an attack on the U.S. homeland. Last year, more than 600 people were killed in acts of terror—200 people were killed in al-Qaeda–related attacks alone. Nineteen were U.S. citizens.

So because we do continue to face the prospect of mass murder of civilians on our soil by terrorists, we should not be complacent. We Americans have an absolute right to be safe on our own soil and free of terrorist attacks. The greatest danger we face as a nation in dealing with terrorism is that we take the very serious threats we face for granted, continue to be ill-informed, and do not try to secure public confidence in our antiterrorism authorities that I believe are necessary to protect our homeland. I know that some of my efforts at Brookings will be devoted to trying to find ways to make our discussion and debate regarding our antiterrorism authorities and measures more informed and reasoned.

Now, I'll try to answer any questions you may have. But remember that in doing so, I'll be guided by what a great lawyer, Emory Buckner, once said. Buckner served as U.S. Attorney for the Southern District of New York from 1925 to 1927. He said the two most useful things a lawyer can say is "I don't know" when he or she does not know the answer, and "I admit" when a mistake is made or a persuasive fact is presented against a position you have taken.

Thank you.

THE HONORABLE LARRY THOMPSON ADDRESS TO FBI SPECIAL AGENTS IN CHARGE CONFERENCE

November 18, 2021

I was very pleased to be speaking before the FBI special agents in charge at the invitation of Director Chris Wray. I've known Chris for a very long time. We worked together at the King & Spalding law firm in Atlanta and when I was Deputy Attorney General. Chris asked me to speak on mentorship. Preparing for the speech caused me to focus on my own career and reflect on what was important. Two important points emerged. First, who were my mentors and why were they important? Second, and perhaps most important, at the end of your career, what is really important? What are your most important achievements?

I: To the Special Agents in Change—Thank You

Thank you for that very kind introduction. I'm honored to be here. And I'm grateful for this privilege.

I don't only mean the privilege of joining you in person—though, given the events of the past 18 months, I won't complain.

I'm talking about something far more special: the privilege I have enjoyed a few times in my career—the privilege of spending time with special agents in charge.

Many moons ago, when I served as Deputy Attorney General, your predecessors briefed me on a variety of complex criminal matters, from fraud and corruption to terrorism and white-collar crime. We were together during the dark hours of September 11, 2001, when special agents in charge helped us find light amidst tremendous trauma and uncertainty. And at Main Justice, I had the pleasure of meeting with special agents in charge countless times.

Even before then, when I was U.S. Attorney in Atlanta, I remember fondly my daily conversations with Special Agents in Charge John Glover and Weldon Kennedy.

I have always held you and your work in the highest regard.

And I have always been struck by this group's dedication to public service—by your professionalism and sacrifice. So let me say two words we can never say enough: Thank you. This country is safer, and stronger, because of you and your service.

II. It Takes a Village . . . and Incredible Mentors

A number of years ago, when I was a young lawyer, I met the legendary writer Alex Haley, the author of *Roots* and a number of other influential books. And I remember he shared a life lesson that has stuck with me for decades.

Haley and a friend were walking down a long and winding path that was adjacent to a tall, beautiful wall constructed with a polished, slick stone. As they were making their way down the path, Haley noticed a large turtle sitting atop the wall. And he thought to himself, "This is very strange, for a turtle to climb all the way up this slippery wall." So Haley turned to his friend and asked, "How do you suppose the turtle got up there?"

The friend thought for a moment and then said, "I don't know, but you can bet on one thing—he did not get there by himself."

So much of what happens in our lives, happens because of other people. Because other people put us in position to succeed.

None of us gets where we are by ourselves.

After nearly a half century in the law, I can say with a reasonable degree of certainty: I've been able to lead a fulfilling life—and, if I may, a meaningful career—because of those who supported me along the way. Parents, friends, teachers, bosses, colleagues. In a word: mentors.

I know how important mentorship is to Director Wray. I know how important mentorship is to the FBI. And I know how important mentorship is to all of us in this room today. From the parents who support our dreams from the beginning, to the friends who believe in us, even when we don't believe in ourselves.

It's the teachers who pulled us aside for the first time and said, "Hey, you've got potential." The bosses and colleagues who took us under their wing and made our success their success.

Or the time we get to pay it all forward, and mentor someone else.

Throughout my career, I've had the great fortune of experiencing all the above. And it's helped me become not only a better lawyer, but a better person and colleague. And so I'd like to share a few stories about mentorship—and to also share a few lessons I learned along the way.

III. My Many Mentors: Professor Vining, Justice Thomas, and Judge Bell
Professor Vining: A Lifelong Relationship

Let me take you back to my law school days at the University of Michigan. (Go Blue! No offense, Buckeye fans. You all know what I'll be doing one week from Saturday.) I had just finished my first year, and I wasn't feeling too hot. I did not have stellar grades. Maybe just okay grades. I got a C+ on an exam for the first time in my life. And while my friends were on the law review, I wasn't.

For those of you who don't know, your first-year law school grades are typically the most important for your job search. So I really felt like I had dug myself into a ditch. That all changed my second year, when I took a class with a professor by the name of Joe Vining. Professor Vining was a corporate law professor—but he was really more of a legal philosopher. I took a seminar with him called Legal Norms and Corporate Policy and was immediately hooked.

At a time when the multinational corporation reigned freely over society, Professor Vining was asking the important questions: What's the purpose of a corporation? Does it really owe its sole allegiance to shareholders? Why do we hold a corporation criminally responsible for the acts of its agents?

I was fascinated by the subject matter. And Professor Vining and I quickly formed a close bond. It was a formative relationship during a rather difficult time. One day, Professor Vining called me into his office to discuss a paper I had written. He told me that he gave me an A+. And he said, "Larry, you're one of the best students I've ever had." To a confused, insecure law student from the small town of Hannibal, Missouri, that compliment, that reassurance of my potential, meant the world.

I certainly didn't think I was one of the best students at Michigan. The objective evidence that I saw didn't seem to suggest it. But Professor Vining saw something in me—and, in turn, helped me see it in myself.

For the past 47 years, corporate criminal liability and corporate purpose have been a central part of my legal work. And it is, in large part, because of him. And I think the lesson is take notice of those with great potential. They may not have the best grades, or the best track record. But when you find someone special, let them know. Don't be afraid to take them under your wing. It can make their day. It can change their career. And it can even start a lifelong friendship.

Justice Thomas: Mentorship Takes Many Forms

Of course, I recognize not every person has a lifelong mentor. And mentorship takes many forms. Sometimes, it just requires a simple conversation—or a new perspective—to make all the difference in someone's life.

Another story: After graduating from law school, I accepted a job with Monsanto, the agrochemical company now known as Bayer.

As I've admitted many times before, I took the job for the wrong reasons. Monsanto offered me the most money. As an aside, that was the last time in my career I took a job because it offered the most money.

I learned a lot at Monsanto, but I had regrets. The work just wasn't where my heart was. I realized I wanted to be a litigator—and that meant joining a law firm. At the time, I happened to be working on a case with a firm called King & Spalding. I mentioned to someone in the firm that I would soon be leaving Monsanto to join a firm in St. Louis, and that person asked if I'd consider joining King & Spalding in Atlanta. It was one of the first major decisions I faced as a young lawyer.

Eager for advice, I turned to another young lawyer I had befriended at Monsanto—who happened to be from Georgia. We ate lunch every week at a Chinese restaurant close to the office, and I casually mentioned that King & Spalding had asked me to join them.

Without missing a beat, he said, "You need to take that offer."

I heeded his advice, and it turned out to be one of the best decisions I made in my career.

Because that young lawyer was right. Although challenging, Atlanta was the perfect place for me to begin my career in the legal world. In fact, I haven't looked back since: Save for stints in Washington and Connecticut, Atlanta, Georgia, is where I've called home on and off for the past 44 years. By the way, if you're curious about that young lawyer who advised me, he has since moved on to bigger and better things. His name is Justice Clarence Thomas.

My point is: Mentorship comes in many dimensions. It's just as much a quick lunch conversation as it is a recurring phone call, catching up with an old classmate or seeking counsel on a life-changing decision. What matters most is that you're there for people when they need you. Because that feeling of support can make all the difference in one's career, and in one's life.

Judge Griffin Bell: Mentors, and Leaders, Set a Powerful Example

Mentors and leaders set a powerful example. My first year at King & Spalding felt a lot like my first year of law school. It wasn't easy. I was only the third Black associate hired in the history of the firm. I was making less money than my job at Monsanto. I was one of only a few Republicans at a heavily Democratic firm. And I was even asked to take the bar exam for a second time because Georgia denied reciprocity from Missouri.

Still, one partner at King & Spalding believed in me early on: Judge Griffin Bell, who was the Attorney General in the Carter Administration. Judge Bell was an outstanding lawyer. He was wise, analytical, and deeply passionate about the law. He's the mentor who taught me that a lawyer's job isn't to vanquish your adversary, but to solve problems for your clients. He's the mentor who encouraged me to apply for the position of United States Attorney for the Northern District of Georgia, which began my career in public service. And he's the mentor who taught me that an organization's commitment to its values—and, by extension, its culture—starts at the top.

The year was 1987, and Judge Bell and I had started a new "Special Matters" practice at King & Spalding. We were retained to represent a large company, and it was one of our first big Special Matters clients. As part of this engagement, Judge Bell and I were invited to what's called a "joint defense meeting," where all the lawyers representing the company's executives, employees, and the company itself were meeting to strategize. It's a lawful agreement in which, upon demonstrating common interest, counsel can share information about their client with other lawyers.

Early on, I was clear the meeting was headed in the wrong direction.

One lawyer would say, "My client is going to testify before the grand jury, and here's what she is prepared to say." Another lawyer would say, "Well, it would be better if she would say something else." And then another lawyer would say, "You need to fine-tune exactly what she's going to say."

Now, if that sounds illegal to you . . . it was. Judge Bell immediately recognized the conversation as witness tampering. I could tell he was very uncomfortable, and his face had turned bright red. So he cut off the conversation. "We need to stop this," Judge Bell announced to the room. "This is not right. A joint defense agreement does not allow for witness tampering." The other lawyers ignored him. And before I could say another word, Judge Bell began packing up his briefcase. He turned to me and said, "Larry, come on. Let's go back to Atlanta." We got up and exited the room.

Remember: This was, at the time, the largest white-collar criminal case King & Spalding had. And Judge Bell was about to walk away from it. A few seconds later, the company's General Counsel ran after us and pledged the witness tampering discussions would stop. Thankfully, they did. Still, I remember that day vividly. As a young partner at the firm, it was a transformative experience, and an important lesson.

Of course, Judge Bell demonstrated good judgment and professional courage—traits of any good lawyer. But it was also a reminder that those at the top set a powerful example for everyone else. That day, I knew that if I ever felt uncomfortable with anything improper, unethical, or illegal, I could walk away with the support of Judge Bell and my firm.

What does this mean for you? For your careers? Well, as special agents in charge, you bear a unique responsibility for the FBI's culture. So I encourage you to do what I know you're taught to do. Create a culture in which those you supervise feel empowered to speak up if they see something wrong. Where they understand the high ethical standards of one another, and the consequences of falling short. And where everyone places trust in each other: in their ability to do their jobs, and to fulfill the mission of the bureau. It's on you to embody the FBI's values every single day—especially in the difficult moments. And I promise, it will have a lasting impact on those around you.

Again, I'm just reinforcing what I know you're already taught to do. But never forget that culture matters to every organization—and a positive culture starts with leaders like you.

IV. From Mentee to Mentor: Meeting Director Wray

One more story: After a few years, I left the U.S. Attorney's Office in Atlanta and returned to King & Spalding as a partner. Beyond serving clients, I was now a part-time recruiter, in charge of ensuring our firm attracted the best and brightest minds fresh out of law school or judicial clerkships.

One year, a particularly strong candidate came to my attention.

This fellow checked all the boxes. Executive editor of the *Yale Law Journal*. A clerkship with the prestigious Fourth Circuit Court of Appeals. Sterling recommendations from colleagues and professors. Needless to say, he was a star and we *had* to have him.

But I heard through the grapevine that we weren't the only law firm that felt this way. Wall Street firms were hungry for new associates, and another very prestigious law firm had offered him the works. Still, I wanted him at King & Spalding. I thought he could make a real difference at our firm, and in Atlanta. So I decided to do what Justice Thomas did with me: meet with him and make my case.

I acknowledged that at the time he'd probably make more money at that Wall Street firm. "But if you come to Atlanta," I remember telling him, "you'll do meaningful work. You'll be a leader in your community. And you'll have the opportunity to grow our firm."

I must have done something right that day, because that young man would soon join King & Spalding as its newest associate. And what began was a relationship I continue to cherish to this day. In case you're curious, that mentee has also gone on to bigger and better things. He became an assistant United States Attorney for the Northern District of Georgia. He became one of my closest advisers when I was at the Department of Justice, serving this nation as principal associate Deputy Attorney General. He became a senior partner at King & Spalding. He subsequently left King & Spalding for public service, taking a huge pay cut. He also happens to be your Director. This nation is in a better place because of you, Chris. Thank you.

By the way, I tell this story not to toot my own horn. Director Wray was destined for greatness, with or without my help.

I share this story because it taught me a lesson: Mentorship isn't a one-way street. In the most meaningful mentor relationships, the mentor learns just as much from the mentee, as the other way around.

I recall one evening, in the aftermath of 9/11, Director Wray and I were discussing military tribunals. At one point, I had remarked that I wanted to make absolutely certain these bad guys—these terrorists—were brought to justice. But Director Wray was quick to call out my mistake. He looked at me and said, "Sir, there's a process here. We can't be focused only on the outcome."

Picture this: It was one of the most tumultuous periods in American history. The pressure was tremendous. And Director Wray was sitting at a table with a lawyer more than 20 years his senior, who happened to be the Deputy Attorney General of the United States. But Director Wray wasn't afraid to speak up. He understood what distinguishes the United States—the DOJ and the FBI—from others. We do the right things—but we also do things the right way.

In retrospect, I realize Chris's leadership in that moment aligns closely with my view of mentorship. It's easy to think of mentorship as an outcome-based relationship. After all, we want our mentees to succeed: with better paychecks, better jobs, and better opportunities. But that's not really what mentorship is about. At its core, it's a symbiotic relationship—each side depends on and benefits from the other. And it's a journey made all the more meaningful because it's shared. Not just with the folks who helped us get to the top, but with those who helped us pick ourselves up and dust ourselves off when we were down.

V. Now, More Than Ever, Mentorship Matters at the FBI

When I think of organizations that embody this principle—of being there for each other, in moments of triumph and in moments of adversity—I think of the extraordinary workforce at the FBI. I have often remarked that the FBI has the most difficult job in the world. To be successful, it has to pitch a no-hitter . . . all 162 games. Because it just takes one single—or heaven forbid, a home run—for the bad guys to win. And as the evidence makes clear, those batting averages are only getting better.

Every day, there are forces seeking to undermine the mission of the FBI—and the public's trust in the bureau—not only beyond our borders, but from within them. As President Bush noted on the twentieth anniversary of September 11, a "foul spirit" inspires violent extremists abroad and at home. Indeed, the threat of terrorism continues to grow, compounded by the alarming rise of lone offenders—and the exponential growth of social media.

Because of greed on Wall Street and elsewhere, white-collar crime poses a serious threat to our financial institutions—as corporate fraud and insider trading become more frequent.

And adversaries around the world, and within our republic itself, remain focused on attacking the heart of our democracy, starting with very sophisticated election interference. We all know the FBI has the resources, technology, and resolve to tackle each of these challenges.

But what has always been this bureau's greatest strength, and what has always been behind each of its greatest accomplishments has never been the brilliance of a single individual, or the addition of a fancy new strategy. It's always been the team.

Like Michigan's great Coach Schembechler said: "The team. The team. The team." Selfless, committed public servants who remain steadfast in their trust for one another and the mission of the bureau. As the threats against this country intensify, *and they will*, it's critical you rely on one another: have each other's backs, work together to build a better agency and better agents. Don't isolate yourselves, and don't try to be a superman or superwoman.

A favorite story makes the case. Muhammad Ali, the heavyweight champion, had just knocked out his opponent. He was feeling pretty good—especially on the plane ride home, where he couldn't help but celebrate his victory with fellow passengers. As the plane was taxiing down the runway, a flight attendant calmly approached Muhammad Ali and asked him to fasten his seat belt.

He refused. The flight attendant then made her rounds through the plane a second time, and firmly asked Muhammad Ali, once again, to fasten his seat belt. He became indignant. "Fasten my seat belt," he said. "Do you know who I am? I am Muhammad Ali. I am the heavyweight champion of the world. I'm Superman, and Superman don't need no seat belt."

The flight attendant then responded, "Oh, you're Superman. Well, let me tell you something. Superman don't need no plane either. Fasten your seat belt!"

Don't make Muhammad Ali's mistake. Lean on each other. Learn from each other. Mentor each other. Because now, more than ever, your colleagues at the FBI need your support. And we citizens need a strong and effective FBI. There are young agents around you, with dreams of one day holding your position. Take the time to answer their questions. There are other special agents navigating difficult times—perhaps on a case, or in their personal lives. Be there for them. Lend an ear and a hand.

And even as your colleagues come and go, in pursuit of other dreams or new adventures, don't forget about them. Make the effort to stay in touch. Because those are the things that make the bureau special. Even today, I look forward to catching up with agents in Atlanta with whom I worked on big cases.

VI. Closing

A few months ago, I was being interviewed by my law firm's public relations firm. They asked me a simple, yet difficult question: "What is your most important achievement as a lawyer?"

As I thought about my answer, I realized: It wasn't a case I won. It wasn't some award I received. It wasn't some big deal I closed. My proudest achievement is—and will always be—working with, learning from, and befriending good and smart people.

People like Professor Vining, Judge Bell, and Justice Thomas. People like Director Wray.

One last story. When I was confirmed as Deputy Attorney General some 20 years ago, Professor Vining sent me a notice.

He shared with me that his very first job was located in the Office of Deputy Attorney General. He said, and I'm quoting here: "I spent a good deal of time in what will be your office, and it fills me with a sense of full term that you now should be sitting in an office where I began."

I've come to believe this coming to full term is the nature of things. And it's more gratifying when we share our lives with people we hold dear. It's why the moment that Director Wray was confirmed to lead the FBI remains one of the proudest of my career.

Years from now, when you have the luxury of seeing how it all comes full term, you'll think of the plots you thwarted, the promotions you earned, and the intelligence you discovered.

But what you will truly remember and what will texture your career with the most satisfaction are the relationships you forged along the way. How lucky you are to do that with the exceptional men and women of the FBI.

I wish you good luck and Godspeed with all of your future endeavors. Thank you for your service.

DARROW K. SOLL LECTURE AT THE UNIVERSITY OF ARIZONA JAMES E. ROGERS COLLEGE OF LAW

September 28, 2016

This was based on my pro bono representation of Sholom Rubashkin. Mr. Rubashkin had received a 27-year prison sentence even though he was a first-time offender and the crime for which he was convicted was a nonviolent one. A clear miscarriage of justice. My two colleagues on the case, Gary Apfel, an attorney, and Rabbi Zvi Boyarsky introduced me to a number of lawyers and lawmakers interested in sentencing and prison reform.

A Father, an Inventor, and an Orthodox Jewish Businessman Walk into a Courtroom . . .

Thank you, Dean Miller. It's an honor to be giving an address in Darrow Soll's name. Though he achieved a measure of fame by defending Mike Tyson, Darrow Soll was a fighter in every sense of the word. He served his country as a U.S. Army Ranger with the 82nd Airborne, and battled prosecutors as a criminal defense attorney. We should all draw inspiration from his fighting spirit.

Dean Miller, thanks for providing such tremendous leadership in the area of sentencing reform. Some of you may not know that 20 years ago, Dean Miller founded the *Federal Sentencing Reporter*, the only academic journal in the U.S. focused on sentencing law, policy, and reform. When it comes to the world of criminal justice policy, there is a lot of misinformation out there. This makes the work of the *Federal Sentencing Reporter* incredibly important.

I know it's customary to begin presentations like this with some humor, and what I'm about to say sounds like a joke: "A father, an inventor, and an Orthodox Jewish businessman walk into a courtroom . . ."

The problem is this isn't a joke, and there's no punchline. Each of their stories opens a window into a federal criminal justice system gone crazy. A system that over-incarcerates, doles out cruel and unjust punishments, spends far too much, and doesn't deliver on its promise of securing public safety.

First, the father: Weldon Angelos was a 24-year-old father of two living in Salt Lake City. In November 2003, he was arrested for selling marijuana to an informant. He had not acted violently and had, at worst, a minor criminal past. What do you think his sentence was? Two years? Five years? Ten? No. Because even though he never brandished or mentioned one, he had a gun. And being in possession of a gun during the drug deal resulted in Mr. Angelos receiving a 55-year sentence. Fifty-five years for a low-level, nonviolent drug charge. Judge Paul Cassell, who presided over the case, noted in his opinion that Mr. Angelos's mandatory sentence was higher than the sentencing guidelines for a three-time aircraft hijacker and higher than the sentence for the rapist of three ten-year-old children. Judge Cassell later resigned, citing the Angelos case as a primary reason for leaving the bench. Weldon's children, six-year-old Anthony, four-year-old Jesse, and newborn Meranda, who was born after the arrest, were left to be raised without a father.

Next the inventor. Krister Evertson was building a clean energy fuel cell in Idaho when he returned home to Wasilla, Alaska, to care for his 80-year-old mother, and to raise cash for his invention. But his life changed forever on May 27, 2004. That's when, as he put it, his "American dream turned into a nightmare." That night, driving near his mother's home, he was run off the road by armored federal agents.

When he came to a stop, they approached his car brandishing automatic weapons. Why? Well, it takes some explaining. Krister used sodium for his invention. He had some left over, so he sold it on eBay. Now, sodium usually has to be shipped by ground because it can be hazardous. So Krister checked "ground transportation" on the UPS bill and sent it on its way. What he didn't know was that in Alaska, UPS actually ships its "ground" packages by air. And when shipping by air, sodium needs a safety label. And that's the moment Krister Evertson became a federal criminal.

A jury eventually acquitted him of that charge, but the feds weren't finished with him. On the day of his initial arrest, Krister Evertson told them that he had more chemicals in storage back in Idaho. That's when the EPA jumped in. They found his storage lot, declared everything inside as toxic waste, and proceeded to dispose of it, destroying his life's work. Federal prosecutors then filed new charges, saying that he had improperly abandoned hazardous waste.

It's important to stop here and notice that Krister's material was not hazardous, and he had not abandoned it. But the EPA said it was hazardous, so the prosecutor didn't need to prove that it was. And his arrest on the earlier charge automatically qualified as his abandonment of the material, so the prosecutors didn't need to prove intent. All in all, after more than three years, a jury sent Krister Evertson to prison. Elliot Ness probably spent less effort getting Al Capone.

And then there's Sholom Rubashkin, an Orthodox Jewish businessman. In 2008, he was arrested for violating immigration law at the kosher meat processing plant he ran. Instead of pursuing the immigration angle, prosecutors decided to try Mr. Rubashkin on 86 counts of financial fraud. The charges alleged that he had inflated the value of collateral on a loan application, that he had falsified invoices, and that he had channeled some customer payments beneath the business's cash needs instead of into a "sweep account."

He was convicted, and even though he had no prior criminal history, and his crime had no victims of fraud, he got a longer sentence than Dennis Kozlowski of Tyco or Jeffrey Skilling of Enron, 27 years in total. The sentence was so harsh that six former attorneys general and 17 former high-ranking officials from the Justice Department signed a letter declaring that they could not fathom how sentencing rules would call for anything close to a life sentence. Seventy-five law professors and former federal prosecutors signed a letter urging Attorney General Holder to investigate prosecutorial misconduct. Surely, this couldn't have been the most important priority in financial fraud prosecutions following 2008. I now am one of several attorneys who are representing Mr. Rubashkin pro bono.

Compare what happened in this case to the wrongdoing admitted to by the large U.S. banks and the billions of dollars in penalties paid. Yet not one bank executive has spent a single day in jail.

So a father, an inventor, and an Orthodox Jewish businessman walk into a courtroom. And what do they have in common? Each is a victim of a federal justice system that has become a federal injustice system.

Now we're hearing a lot these days about reforming the justice system. Michelle Alexander's book on mass incarceration, *The New Jim Crow*, is a bestseller and has been cited by Justice Sotomayor. Secretary Clinton declared in July that "it's time to end mass incarceration." And, as Jay-Z correctly noted in a recent web video, "We imprison more people than any other country in the world [including] China, Russia, Iran, and Cuba." Yes, although I don't agree with a lot of what Jay-Z says, or really even listen to him, this makes sense.

And at the federal level, the statistics paint a stark picture. Between 1940 and 1980, the federal prison population was stable at around 24,000 prisoners. Today, that population has exploded to nearly 200,000.

So this afternoon I want to talk to you about this very shameful and wasteful aspect of our federal criminal justice system. I'll try to explain how we got to where we are and what we can do about it, and how you can help.

The Problem: We Are Putting Too Many People in Jail

Let me start by asking a question: What is the purpose of our federal justice system?

I served as the Deputy Attorney General during the first term of President George W. Bush. My philosophy as a federal prosecutor has always been that the federal government's purpose is to identify, pursue, and prosecute the most significant and highest levels of criminal conduct in society. Complex fraud. Terrorism plots. Organized, multi-state, and even international criminal organizations. The states are supposed to do the rest. But now, at the federal level, we are incarcerating far too many people. Why is this?

Why is it that the number of people sentenced to federal prison has nearly tripled in the past three decades, to 83,000 per year? Why is it that the total federal prison population has grown by a factor of eight, to nearly 200,000—twice the growth rate for the state prison population? Are we more crime-prone? Are we more violent?

No, the truth is, two conscious policy decisions created this reality.

First, we started over-sentencing. From the late 1970s to the late 1980s, the crack epidemic spread through America's cities. It brought tremendous levels of violence to our communities. The homicide rate per 100,000 deaths peaked in 1980 at 10.2 and returned to similar levels throughout the decade and into the early 1990s.

So the federal government responded by increasing its focus on drug crimes. Congress passed a number of laws to limit judicial discretion, laws that created or enhanced mandatory minimum sentences for drug offenses and violent crimes. The Comprehensive Crime Control Act of 1984 increased the mandatory minimum for carrying a weapon during the commission of a crime to at least five years, not to be served concurrently with another sentence.

Many of you are probably too young to remember this, but in 1986, a very promising basketball player named Len Bias was drafted by the Celtics. Less than 48 hours later, while celebrating with some friends, he died of a cocaine overdose. In the wake of his death, President Reagan pushed the Anti-Drug Abuse Act through Congress. The act established the basic framework for drug-related mandatory minimums, which fell anywhere between five years and life imprisonment. The result of these and similar laws was more prisoners serving longer prison sentences. And that's how Weldon Angelos ended up with a 55-year sentence for a minor drug charge.

Second, we started over-criminalizing. We have made it easier for federal prosecutors to put people behind bars by giving them more crimes to prosecute. Does anybody know how many federal crimes there were in 1980? The answer is about 3,000. And how many do you think there are today? About 4,500. And in addition to that 4,500, we've got some 30,000 criminal regulations as well. So we've got more types of crimes. Many of the new crimes do not even have a *mens rea* requirement for conviction and thus violate a fundamental tenet of Anglo-American jurisprudence.

We've also got more people prosecuting those crimes. And when I say more, I don't mean more by a half. I don't mean double or triple. We've got more by a factor of five! Since 1980, the number of federal prosecutors has increased five times from 1,500 to 7,500. So you've got more prosecutors with more crimes to prosecute. And that's exactly what they have done.

As a result of all this, we now have a public policy and fiscal disaster. Now, the level of seriousness in the cases prosecuted by the federal government has decreased. In 2009, just 11 percent of drug offenders sentenced in federal courts were high-level suppliers or importers. Nearly 60 percent were street dealers or below. Low-level offenders, drug and otherwise, who are easy to get, have become the focus. And that's how Krister Evertson ended up on the side of a road, being stared down by a SWAT team.

When the violent crime rate started to decline, people applauded the policy decisions to over-sentence and over-criminalize. They credited the growing prison populations. But as intelligent, critically minded law students, you know better. If this were a law school exam question, you would have identified the flaw in that argument pretty quickly. Correlation does not equal causation.

Let's say someone argues that the growing prison population has caused the decrease in violent crime. Many do. How do you test the validity of this argument? You might try to find evidence that contradicted it. Well, it turns out that one study by the Sentencing Project found that the states with the highest rises in prison populations had the lowest drops in crime rates. And the states with smaller rises in prison population had higher drops in crime rates. You might also try to find a jurisdiction that managed to decrease crime without increasing prison sentences. Well, it turns out that Canada, Britain, and Australia have all decreased crime without incarcerating more people. All of this points to a pretty weak argument that incarcerating more and more people is the only way to reduce crime.

And this increased prison population costs a lot of money. I have two more numbers for you. Can anyone take a guess what the budget of the Bureau of Prisons was in 1980? $330 million. Anyone want to guess what it is now? $6.9 billion. That's a nearly twenty-fold increase. This is simply crazy! The Bureau of Prisons now accounts for well over 25 percent of the Justice Department's total budget. It may even be higher.

Today, it costs $30,620 per year to incarcerate each federal prisoner. John Malcolm of the conservative Heritage Foundation has noted, "I see each prison cell as very valuable real estate that ought to be occupied by individuals who pose the greatest threat to public safety."

So what we are doing now costs a lot. And it's not making us any safer. For most of the twentieth century, our corrections system was marked by a "rehabilitative ideal," rooted in the belief that many, admittedly not all, prison inmates could be reformed and rejoin the rest of us as productive members of society. That was the foundation upon which our corrections system was built. But in the 1970s, that began to shift. The rise in violent crime led the criminal justice system to focus more on simply punitive measures. But a major problem with that punitive focus is that it doesn't seem to be working. Recidivism is dangerously high in our country.

Earlier this year, the United States Sentencing Commission found that nearly 50 percent of federal prisoners were rearrested within eight years of their release. One-quarter were reincarcerated within the same period. If we do nothing and if sentencing reform does not happen, 95 percent of federal prisoners will still be released from prison someday, and we don't seem to be doing much to make sure they don't go back. And you can understand why. With so many resources going into locking more and more people up, we don't have the resources to truly try to rehabilitate the ones who need it. The result is that we are releasing some prisoners who are a real and immediate threat to public safety.

So we've got too many people in prison. We've got a system that's not differentiating between high- and low-level criminals, or between violent and nonviolent offenders. We're not doing a very good job of limiting recidivism either. So we're left with a system that costs a lot of money, and not only does it not improve our safety, it actually diminishes it. Spending almost $7 billion each year on a big government program that fails this much is a classic example of waste and abuse.

The Solution: Sentencing and Corrections Reform

So what can we do about this mess? Well, I've got another statement that may sound like a joke for you. What do the Koch Brothers and Democratic Senator Cory Booker have in common? They're both advocates of sentencing reforms. And they're not the only ones. From President Obama to Speaker Paul Ryan, from John Conyers to Rand Paul, there is remarkable support for sensible, common-sense reforms to our criminal justice system.

Now this Congress doesn't necessarily have the strongest record of bipartisan achievement. Harry Truman famously called the 80th Congress the "do-nothing Congress." But the do-nothing Congress passed over 900 bills into law. The current Congress isn't even at 300.

But even this sclerotic Congress might be able to get something done on sentencing and corrections reform. There is bipartisan support for several sensible bills. There are House and Senate reform bills that seek to make needed improvements to both the front and back ends of our federal criminal justice system.

The Sentencing Reform Act authored by House Judiciary Chairman Bob Goodlatte and Ranking Member John Conyers retroactively reduces mandatory minimums for certain drug offenses and reduces the three-strike mandatory life sentence to 25 years. It gives judges the discretion to, shockingly, use their judgment and determine the right sentences in appropriate situations.

These reform measures actually give federal prosecutors new tools to target violent criminals with enhanced penalties—for example, those offenders with prior serious violent felony convictions.

The Second Chance Reauthorization Act of 2015 authored by Republican Congressman Jim Sensenbrenner and Democratic Congressman Danny Davis provides for public and private funding to improve the outcome of criminals re-entering the workforce, including academic and vocational education.

In 1994, Jim Sensenbrenner advocated for mandatory minimums and harsh punitive punishments, saying, "Once you commit an act of mayhem, you ought to be taken out of society." It's pretty remarkable that the same congressman is a leading advocate for reform, admitting, "We cannot allow our criminal justice system to remain on its current trajectory."

These back-end correction reforms put a new focus on rehabilitation and establish risk and needs assessment as the cornerstone of a new recidivism reduction effort. It is much needed. Through standardized and scientifically validated risk assessments, higher-risk prisoners will have to demonstrate substantial risk reduction progress down into lower-risk categories to become eligible to utilize their earned time credits.

These are just two of several bills that would have an important impact on our sentencing and corrections problems. We also have bills that increase the standard for prosecutors to show intent, and another that would eliminate some of the criminal penalties for trivial conduct. If passed, these reforms could mean that people like Weldon Angelos and Sholom Rubashkin get fairer sentences. It could also mean that millions of productive citizens like Krister Evertson don't need to fear the threat of a criminal prosecution for a regulatory transgression.

Now some critics say that advocates like me are putting the public in danger. Senator Perdue of Georgia has called the reform measure a "criminal leniency" bill. Steve Cook, the President of the National Association of Assistant U.S. Attorneys, has said that we don't even need reform because "the system isn't broken."

Critics like these often point to the case of Wendell Callahan, a crack dealer who was released early because of changes in sentencing guidelines. In January of this year, he was charged with murdering an ex-girlfriend and two of her daughters.

This is truly a tragic case, and we all mourn this loss of life. But a few things need to be made clear. First, under reform proposals, Callahan would have faced an enhanced mandatory minimum because of his prior felony-level assault in connection with a nonfatal shooting. He would have received a longer sentence than what he actually got. He would have been prohibited from any retroactive relief offenders because of his prior crime associated with violence.

Truthfully, the case of Wendell Callahan is a clear example of why we need reform. He is a dangerous criminal who was released without rehabilitation and risk assessment. We spend so much money incarcerating so many nonviolent people that we don't have a lot left over to provide rehabilitation to the most violent cases. And that's how this kind of tragedy occurs.

The point is that these sentencing and corrections reform bills bring our federal justice system closer to its intent—to prioritize and prosecute the highest-level, highest-risk, and most dangerous offenders.

We Know What Successful Reform Looks Like

We know what successful reform looks like. Contemplating this type of justice reform doesn't need to be abstract. We don't need to visualize the future in the clouds. We can look to two states: Texas, and my home state, the great state of Georgia, to visualize what successful justice reform looks like.

In 2007, Texas began reforms designed to utilize alternatives to incarceration and lower the prison population, while also increasing public safety. Texas focused on sentence length, prison programming, and probation. Texas invested $240 million up front but managed to close three prisons and save $2 to $3 billion. The state's population is now more than 20 percent lower, and crime is at its lowest level since 1968.

In 2012, Georgia began reforms to increase alternatives to incarceration. It prioritized prisons for housing high-risk offenders and focused on reducing recidivism. Since that time, violent crime has decreased by 8 percent.

It is possible to reduce imprisonment and reduce crime at the same time. Texas, Georgia, and other states show that sentencing and corrections reform work.

Your Role

And this brings me to all of you. As law students, future lawyers and leaders, you have a unique opportunity, and a responsibility, to address challenges like this one.

One of my legal heroes is Justice Robert Jackson, one of our nation's greatest legal minds. He served as Solicitor General, Attorney General, and eventually on the Supreme Court. He dissented in the Korematsu case, which held the internment of Japanese Americans to be constitutional. He also voted in favor of *Brown v. Topeka Board of Education*. At a time when the language and policy of intolerance has returned to our political scene, the words and work of Jackson seem even more important and relevant.

Justice Jackson once said, "It is not the function of government to keep the citizen from falling into error. It is the function of the citizen to keep the government from falling into error."

When you look at our federal prison population, the costs that our justice system imposes on society, on the ability of everyone to lead productive lives, and on our public safety, there is no doubt that our government has fallen into error.

I have devoted a great deal of my career dealing with the federal criminal justice system. It pains me to see this system become costly, bloated, and an unjust one that fails to do its best or secure public safety. Common sense demands change.

Only together can we achieve the reforms necessary to build a just federal justice system. As I have noted, the coalition supporting sentencing and corrections reform is broad. It includes Democrats and Republicans, conservatives and liberals, faith-based organizations and secular civil rights associations, businesses and nonprofit organizations.

As students, and as citizens, there is much you can do. You can call your Congressman and Senator. You can educate others, share what I've just shared with you with those who might disagree: your friends, your neighbors, your grumpy uncle who sends all of those emails. You can actively mobilize and recruit others in the cause through social media. You can commit to fighting for common sense and fairness today, tomorrow, and for the rest of your careers.

For me, this a righteous cause. I hope you make it your cause too. Please join me and help us fix this tragically broken system.

Thank you.

APPENDIX 15

"AFGHANISTAN AND THE RULE OF LAW" AT THE U.S. INSTITUTE OF PEACE

February 4, 2003

I include this speech simply because of its irony. I immediately thought of this speech a few months ago during the writing of this book while watching the chaos of the U.S. withdrawal from Afghanistan on television. I talked at length about the rule of law and the return of peace and prosperity to Afghanistan. It's a stark reminder that everything doesn't always work out as we plan.

I am pleased and honored to have the opportunity to address you this afternoon. I want to begin by extending the warmest of welcomes to you and to acknowledge the great distance you have traveled to confer with us this week. Your efforts to do so are greatly appreciated.

You have begun a grand and momentous project. Your goal is nothing less than the establishment of the rule of law in your country. On behalf of the United States government, and each and every member of the law enforcement and justice sectors of this country, we honor your commitment to that goal. And we pledge our unwavering support to help you achieve it. The journey toward your goal will not be an easy one. As you know, it will be filled with many obstacles and many dangers. But I am confident that, by working together as partners, we can overcome those challenges and achieve your great aims.

Whatever difficulties you face, whatever setbacks you encounter, you can take strength from the knowledge that you are working toward a new era in Afghanistan's history: an era when violence will no longer decide the affairs of your countrymen, when justice will reign, and when peace and prosperity will return to your nation.

Although your work will be hard, its reward will be great. You have an opportunity that has presented itself only rarely in the long course of human history: the chance to rebuild and remake a system of justice. And, most importantly, you have friends around the world ready to help you in this work. The irony of the tragic events of September 11, 2001, is that in that dark moment of America's history, there dawned a new day of unprecedented international cooperation. As a result, Afghanistan will not be left alone to face the ravages of international terrorism, drug trafficking, and other transnational offenses. You will have friends and partners willing and able to assist you in the fight against crime and injustice.

The noted anthropologist Margaret Mead was quoted as saying, "Never doubt that a small group of thoughtful, committed people can change the world. Indeed, it is the only thing that ever has." You are that group of thoughtful, committed people. But you are not alone. You have an ally in the United States.

Let's talk about teamwork. As you embark on the journey ahead, I offer you this bit of advice. Take with you three things. The first of those things is the concept of teamwork. Pick your teams and let each member of the team do his or her job.

Take, for example, the judiciary. Establishing a functioning judiciary will increase public confidence in Afghan institutions. The judiciary will need its own budget, un-tied to the executive branch or any political parties or interests. It will need its own secure quarters, tenure for its judges, mechanisms for the maintenance of institutional integrity and legitimacy, and a reputation for fairness and equality for all who come before it.

I am a former prosecutor and can tell you the prosecutor's office must play its role as well. It cannot simply serve as a rubber stamp for a police investigation. It must be strong enough to evaluate a case brought to it by the police. If a suspect has been beaten and abused, the prosecutor's office must stand up to the police and be prepared to indict those officers responsible for abuses of their authority. Prosecutors must be empowered to work with the police to ensure investigations that are far-reaching, fair, and worthy of the judicial resources that will be spent to adjudicate the case.

The defense bar should be strong enough to meet the prosecutor as an equal. Defense attorneys should have early access to their clients, resources to investigate their clients' defense, and reasonable notice of all, proceeding to be able to prepare a vigorous defense.

Finally, the police must be as competent at crime prevention as they are at criminal apprehension. The police should be known and trusted in the community and be professional in its methods. Indeed, the entire justice system should be above reproach: unswayed by bribes, undeterred by criticism, unshaken by intimidation. Choose your teams and equip them to do their jobs expertly.

Let's move to inclusion. The second thing that you should take with you on your journey is a spirit of inclusion. More than 200 years ago, when the founders of this country drafted the U.S. Constitution, one of the biggest challenges they faced was getting the individual states to accept the notion of shared government authority. The states were autonomous entities, and proudly so. They did not want to be dominated by a national authority. The drafters of the Constitution devised a plan in which certain specified powers would be vested in the national government, with the remaining powers reserved to the states. Through a series of persuasive articles in newspapers and in pamphlets handed out to citizens across the nation—what we would call a "media blitz" these days—the supporters of the Constitution were able to convince the states to go along with the new plan. The result is the federal system of government we have today. It is a system in which the interests of the states, through their representatives in Congress and through their role in electing the President, are included in the decision-making of the national government.

It is also a system in which the states themselves retain the greatest degree of autonomy that is compatible with a vigorous and effective national government.

Inclusion is not only a structural matter between the federal government and the states. It is also a matter between our people and the institutions of their nation. The spirit of inclusion that makes this country strong is perhaps best exemplified by the picture of the astronauts of the Space Shuttle Columbia as they walked toward the launchpad many days ago, smiling and full of excitement. It is an image that is now seared in the collective memory of our nation. Those lost heroes were among our best and brightest. They were men and women from different cultural backgrounds, from different races, from different countries, yet all united in their personal excellence and their unwavering desire to explore the heavens. They reached the stars. And although they met a tragic and untimely end, the lesson of their lives is clear: Great journeys and great goals are possible when all people are given an equal opportunity to achieve and to serve the public good.

Through inclusion of women and other traditionally disenfranchised groups, Afghanistan will realize new strength. Let's be clear: The United States itself has had to struggle to reach the goal of inclusion. But we recognize it as one of our fundamental strengths. No longer can there be groups of people sitting on the sidelines. The new Afghan justice sector, which will operate in a manner that promotes full respect for international human rights, will be the product of a long-term international sustained effort that every Afghan must contribute to and call his own.

This week will be one in which you can discuss framing the laws and the justice sector institutions to recognize and include all the Afghan people. You will have assistance from the United States and other international entities and governments as you face the challenge of inclusion.

Now let's finally talk about stamina. Finally, the third thing you must have on your journey is stamina. Your goal to establish the rule of law in Afghanistan will only come about through much hard work. The road before you is long, and at times, you will feel like you are making one step forward and two steps back. There is no way to avoid the weariness and frustrations that lie ahead. But again, remember that the United States is on this journey with you. You will not be traveling alone.

Let me remind you of a story of an old man and a river. The old man had embarked upon a long journey to his life's goal, when he came upon a raging river crossing his path. He waded into the river and was tugged by the speed of the rushing waters. Slowly and determinedly, he put one foot before the other until finally, soaking wet, he reached the opposite riverbank. For days thereafter, he gathered up wood, stones, and vines and began constructing a bridge over the rushing waters. One day a woman who lived near the river asked him, "Old man, why are you building that bridge? Since you have already made it safely across, why have you not continued on your journey?" The man lifted his gray head and answered, "Tomorrow, there may be others who follow me for whom the river might be an obstacle. It is for them that I am building this bridge." You too are the builders of a great bridge—a bridge to justice, for all the people of Afghanistan.

I would like to thank the United States Institute of Peace for their vision in organizing this program. Without further ado, I wish you success in the week ahead and an enjoyable time spent in our nation's capital. Good luck and Godspeed.

NOTES

1 "VW 2017 group sales rose to around 10.7 million cars, beating Toyota: Bild am Sonntag," *Reuters*, January 6, 2018, https://www.reuters.com/article/us-volkswagen-vehicleregistrations /vw-2017-group-sales-rose-to-around-10-7-million-cars-beating-toyota-bild-am-sonntag -idUSKBN1EV0R7; Office of Public Affairs, "Volkswagen AG Agrees to Plead Guilty and Pay $4.3 Billion in Criminal and Civil Penalties; Six Volkswagen Executives and Employees are Indicted in Connection with Conspiracy to Cheat U.S. Emissions Tests," press release, January 11, 2017, https://www.justice.gov/opa/pr/volkswagen-ag-agrees-plead-guilty-and -pay-43-billion-criminal-and-civil-penalties-six.

2 Theodore Roosevelt, "Citizenship in a Republic" (speech, Paris, France, April 23, 1910), The Theodore Roosevelt Center, https://www.theodorerooseveltcenter.org/Learn-About-TR /TR-Encyclopedia/Culture-and-Society/Man-in-the-Arena.aspx.

3 Philip C. Jessup, *Elihu Root* (New York: Dodd, Mead & Company, 1938), 133.

4 *Terminiello v. City of Chicago*, 337 U.S. 1, 37 (1949) (Jackson, J., dissenting).

5 Posse Comitatus Act, 18 U.S.C. § 1385 (1878).

6 "Palmer Raids," FBI, accessed September 11, 2023, https://www.fbi.gov/history/famous -cases/palmer-raids.

7 David P. Hadley, "America's 'Big Brother': A Century of U.S. Domestic Surveillance," Ohio State University, October 2013, https://origins.osu.edu/article/americas-big-brother-century -us-domestic-surveillance?language_content_entity=en.

8 Senate Select Committee to Study Governmental Operations with Respect to Intelligence Activities, *Intelligence Activities and the Rights of Americans*, 94 Cong., 2d sess., 1976.

9 Senate Select Committee to Study Governmental Operations with Respect to Intelligence Activities, *Supplementary Detailed Staff Reports of Intelligence Activities and the Rights of Americans*, 94 Cong., 2d sess., 1976, 79–185.

10 Foreign Intelligence Surveillance Act of 1978 (FISA), Pub. L. 511, U.S. Statutes at Large 92, 1783.

11 Office of the Deputy Attorney General, Jamie S. Gorelick, "Instructions on Separation of Certain Foreign Counterintelligence and Criminal Investigations," unpublished memorandum, March 4, 1995, https://www.hsdl.org/c/abstract/?docid=446540.

12 U.S. National Commission on Terrorist Attacks upon the United States, *9/11 Commission Report: The Official Report of the 9/11 Commission and Related Publications*, by Thomas H. Kean and Lee Hamilton, Washington, DC: GPO, 2004, https://govinfo.library.unt.edu /911/report/911Report.pdf.

13 Office of the Deputy Attorney General, Larry D. Thompson, "Intelligence Sharing," unpublished memorandum, August 6, 2001, https://www.justice.gov/sites/default/files/dag/ legacy/2008/12/04/dag-memo-08062001.pdf.

14 *Hearings of the National Commission on Terrorist Attacks Upon the United States, Day 6, Before the National Commission on Terrorist Attacks Upon the United States*, 108 Cong., 2003 (statement of Larry D. Thompson, Deputy Attorney General of the United States), https ://govinfo.library.unt.edu/911/hearings/hearing6/witness_thompson.htm.

15 Uniting and Strengthening America by Providing Appropriate Tools Required To Intercept and Obstruct Terrorism Act (USA PATRIOT Act), Pub. L. No. 107–56, 115 Stat. 272 (2001).

16 He wrote, "Thompson has a sparkling reputation as a man of integrity, and I have no reason to doubt his sincerity." Kurt Eichenwald, *500 Days: Secrets and Lies in the Terror Wars* (New York: Touchstone, 2012), 529.

17 Larry D. Thompson, "9/11 Commission Findings: Sufficiency of Time, Attention, and Legal Authority," Brookings, August 11, 2004, https://www.brookings.edu/testimonies/911 -commission-findings-sufficiency-of-time-attention-and-legal-authority.

18 Associated Press, "Al-Arian, Three Others to Face Jury," *Gainesville Sun*, May 15, 2005, https ://www.gainesville.com/story/news/2005/05/15/al-arian-three-others-to-face-jury /31692968007/.

19 *Hearings of the National Commission on Terrorist Attacks Upon the United States, Day 6, Before the National Commission on Terrorist Attacks Upon the United States*, 108 Cong., 2003 (statement of Larry D. Thompson, Deputy Attorney General of the United States), https ://govinfo.library.unt.edu/911/hearings/hearing6/witness_thompson.htm.

20 *Arar v. Ashcroft*, 585 F.3d 559 (2d Cir. 2009).

21 A Bivens claim is a cause of action for damages against individual federal government officials engaged in illegal searches. See *Bivens v. Six Unknown Named Agents of Federal Bureau of Narcotics*, 403 U.S. 388 (1971), which holds that the Fourth Amendment implies this private right of action.

22 "At the same time, our authorities are not, and should not be, unbridled. I often marvel at those who criticize our actions as overly aggressive when they ignore altogether that almost all of these very actions are subject to judicial review. As a matter of law, the Department's decisions are routinely reviewed by the Judiciary." Larry D. Thompson, "Remarks at the Ninth Circuit Judicial Conference" (speech, Kaua'i, Hawaii, June 25, 2003), Department of Justice, https://www.justice.gov/archive/dag/speeches/2003/062503hawaii9thcircuit.htm.

23　*Berger v. United States*, 295 U.S. 78, 88 (1935).

24　HCJ 5100/94, *Public Committee Against Torture in Israel v. The State of Israel,* IsrSC 53(4) 817 (1999), https://versa.cardozo.yu.edu/sites/default/files/upload/opinions/Public%20 Committee%20Against%20Torture%20in%20Israel%20v.%20Government%20of%20 Israel%281%29_0.pdf.

25　Bill George and Jay W. Lorsch, "How to Outsmart Activist Investors," *Harvard Business Review* 92, no. 5 (May 2014): 88–95, https://hbr.org/2014/05/how-to-outsmart-activist-investors.

26　Siddharth Cavale, "Nelson Peltz Revives Campaign to Split Up PepsiCo," *Reuters*, February 20, 2014, https://www.reuters.com/article/us-peltz-pepsico-idUSBREA1J0B720140220.

27　Holly J. Gregory, "Everything Old is New Again—Reconsidering the Social Purpose of the Corporation," *Harvard Law School Forum on Corporate Governance*, March 12, 2019, https ://corpgov.law.harvard.edu/2019/03/12/everything-old-is-new-again-reconsidering-the -social-purpose-of-the-corporation/; Larry D. Thompson, "The Responsible Corporation: Its Historical Roots and Continuing Promise," *Notre Dame Journal of Law, Ethics & Public Policy* 29, no. 1 (2015): 199–230, https://scholarship.law.nd.edu/ndjlepp/vol29/iss1/6/.

28　Thompson, "The Responsible Corporation: Its Historical Roots and Continuing Promise," 210.

29　*Dodge v. Ford Motor Company*, 170 N.W. 668 (Mich. 1919).

30　Adolph A. Berle, Jr., "Corporate Powers as Powers in Trust," *Harvard Law Review* 44, no. 7 (May 1931): 1049–1074, https://doi.org/10.2307/1331341.

31　E. Merrick Dodd, Jr., "For Whom Are Corporate Managers Trustees?," *Harvard Law Review* 45, no. 7 (May 1932): 1145–1163.

32　Adolph A. Berle, Jr., *The 20th Century Capitalist Revolution* (New York: Harcourt, Brace and Company, 1954), 169.

33　Milton Friedman, "The Social Responsibility of Business Is to Increase Its Profits," *New York Times Magazine*, September 13, 1970, 32–33, 122–26.

34　George and Lorsch, "How to Outsmart Activist Investors."

35　George and Lorsch, "How to Outsmart Activist Investors."

36　Milton Friedman, *Capitalism and Freedom* (Chicago: University of Chicago Press, 2002), 133; Friedman, "The Social Responsibility of Business Is to Increase Its Profits."

37　Friedman, "The Social Responsibility of Business Is to Increase Its Profits."

38　Friedman, "The Social Responsibility of Business Is to Increase Its Profits."

39　"Statement on the Purpose of a Corporation," Business Roundtable, accessed September 14, 2023, https://opportunity.businessroundtable.org/ourcommitment.

40　Council of Institutional Investors, "Council of Institutional Investors Responds to Business Roundtable Statement on Corporate Purpose," press release, August 19, 2019, https://www .cii.org/aug19_brt_response.

41　"The Role of the SEC," U.S. Securities and Exchange Commission, accessed September 14, 2023, https://www.investor.gov/introduction-investing/investing-basics/role-sec.

42　"B Corp Certification is a designation that a business is meeting high standards of verified performance, accountability, and transparency on factors from employee benefits and charitable giving to supply chain practices and input materials." "About B Corp Certification," B Lab, https://www.bcorporation.net/en-us/certification.

43 The Aspen Institute has been a leader in focusing attention on the ills of short-term business planning. The Aspen Institute, "Overcoming Short-termism: A Call for a More Responsible Approach to Investment and Business Management," press release, September 9, 2009, https://www.aspeninstitute.org/wp-content/uploads/files/content/docs/pubs/overcome _short_state0909_0.pdf.

44 "How to Use the GRI Standards," Global Reporting Initiative, accessed September 25, 2023, https://www.globalreporting.org/how-to-use-the-gri-standards/; "Non-financial reporting," National Action Plans on Business and Human Rights, accessed September 25, 2023, https://globalnaps.org/issue/non-financial-reporting.

45 "About GRI," Global Reporting Initiative, accessed September 25, 2023, https://www.global reporting.org/about-gri; Dow Jones Indexes, STOXX Ltd., & SAM Group, "Dow Jones Sustainability World Indexes Guide," version 9.1, January, 2008, http://www.sustentabilidad .uai.edu.ar/pdf/negocios/djsi/djsi_world_guidebook_91.pdf; Thompson, "The Responsible Corporation."

46 "SEC Response to Climate and ESG Risks and Opportunities," U.S. Securities and Exchange Commission, accessed September 25, 2023, https://www.sec.gov/sec-response -climate-and-esg-risks-and-opportunities; "[T]he SEC issued three rule proposals that would each help facilitate comparable ESG disclosures and focus on ensuring statements made to investors are not false or misleading: 1. Enhanced climate risk disclosures by issuers. 2. Enhanced ESG disclosures by registered funds and investment advisers. 3. Modernized rules governing ESG-related fund names." U.S. Securities and Exchange Commission Commissioner Jaime Lizárraga, "Meeting Investor Demand for High Quality ESG Data" (speech, London, UK, October 17, 2022), U.S. Securities and Exchange Commission, https ://www.sec.gov/news/speech/lizarraga-speech-meeting-investor-demand-high-quality-esg -data; Materiality "provides the conceptual basis for the disclosure of certain information used by investors in making voting and investment decisions." Janine Guillot and Jeffrey Hales, "Materiality: The Word That Launched a Thousand Debates," Harvard Law School Forum on Corporate Governance, May 14, 2021, https://corpgov.law.harvard.edu/2021/05 /14/materiality-the-word-that-launched-a-thousand-debates.

47 Thompson, "The Responsible Corporation."

48 Indra K. Nooyi & Vijay Govindarajan, "Becoming a Better Corporate Citizen: How PepsiCo Moved Toward a Healthier Future," *Harvard Business Review* 98, no. 2 (March– April 2020): 94–103, https://hbr.org/2020/03/becoming-a-better-corporate-citizen.

49 In a capitalist system, an individual "neither intends to promote the public interest, nor knows how much he is promoting it . . . . [H]e intends only his own security; and by directing that industry in such a manner as its produce may be of the greatest value, he intends only his own gain, and he is in this, as in many other cases, led by an invisible hand to promote an end which was no part of his intention. Nor is it always the worse for society that it was no part of it. By pursuing his own interest he frequently promotes that of the society more effectually than when he really intends to promote it. I have never known much

good done by those who affected to trade for the public good." Adam Smith, *The Wealth of Nations* (New York: Penguin Classics, 1999), 32.

50 Thompson, "The Responsible Corporation."

51 Thompson, "The Responsible Corporation," 230.

52 Thompson, "The Responsible Corporation."

53 Andrew Countryman, "SEC Charges HealthSouth Rigged Profits by $1.4 Billion," *Chicago Tribune*, March 20, 2003, https://www.chicagotribune.com/news/ct-xpm-2003-03-20 -0303200271-story.html.

54 *New York Central & Hudson River Railroad Co. v. United States*, 212 U.S. 481 (1909).

55 John Carlin, "Top Justice Department Official on Stepping Up Corporate Enforcement," The CLS Blue Sky Blog, October 26, 2021, https://clsbluesky.law.columbia.edu/2021 /10/26/top-justice-department-official-on-stepping-up-corporate-enforcement/.

56 *New York Central & Hudson River Railroad Co. v. United States*, 212 U.S. 495 (1909).

57 Larry D. Thompson, "'Zero Tolerance' For Corporate Fraud," *The Wall Street Journal*, July 21, 2003, https://www.wsj.com/articles/SB105875316053507300.

58 *Arthur Andersen LLP v. United States*, 544 U.S. 696 (2005).

59 Jesse Eisinger, *The Chickenshit Club: Why the Justice Department Fails to Prosecute Executives* (New York: Simon & Schuster, 2017), 38.

60 Eisinger, *Chickenshit Club*, 37.

61 After the permanent injunction in the Waste Management case, Andersen tried to persuade the DOJ to enter into a deferred prosecution agreement, but this attempt failed for several reasons: "the lawyers could not agree on all of the details, Andersen feared that state regulators and accountancy boards would revoke its state licenses, and Andersen's partnership structure made it difficult to reach a decision within the allotted time." The DOJ turned the proposal down. See Kathleen F. Brickey, "Andersen's Fall from Grace," *Washington University Law Review* 81, no. 4 (2003): 917, 924–26.

62 "Arthur Andersen Corporate Criminal Liability and the Rise of Deferred and Non Prosecution Agreements," *Corporate Crime Reporter*, April 26, 2016, https://www.corporate crimereporter.com/news/200/rthur-andersen-corporate-criminal-liability-and-the-rise-of -deferred-and-non-prosecution-agreements/.

63 Cassell Bryan-Low, "WorldCom Auditors Took Shortcuts," *The Wall Street Journal*, July 23, 2003, https://www.wsj.com/articles/SB105890742357617700.

64 It included "senior Department of Justice officials, the heads of the Departments of Treasury and Labor, and the heads of the Securities and Exchange Commission, Commodity Futures Trading Commission, Federal Energy Regulatory Commission, Federal Communications Commission and United States Postal Inspection Service . . . [and eventually] the Department of Housing and Urban Development's Office of Federal Housing Enterprise Oversight." Office of the Press Secretary, "President's Corporate Fraud Task Force Compiles Strong Record," White House press release, July 22, 2003, https://georgewbush-whitehouse .archives.gov/news/releases/2003/07/20030722.html.

65   Office of the Press Secretary, "President's Corporate Fraud Task Force."

66   Larry D. Thompson, "Remarks at the Ninth Circuit Judicial Conference."

67   *Upjohn Co. v. United States*, 449 U.S. 383 (1981).

68   Office of the Deputy Attorney General, Larry D. Thompson, "Principles of Federal Prosecution of Business Organizations," unpublished memorandum, January 20, 2003, https://webharvest.gov/peth04/20041109002842/http://justice.gov/dag/cftf/business _organizations.pdf.

69   Lynnley Browning, "U.S. Tactic on KPMG Questioned," *The New York Times*, June 28, 2006, https://www.nytimes.com/2006/06/28/business/28kpmg.html?referringSource=articleShare.

70   *Upjohn*, 449 U.S. 394.

71   Richard A. Epstein, "The Deferred Prosecution Racket," *The Wall Street Journal*, November 28, 2006, https://www.wsj.com/articles/SB116468395737834160.

72   Epstein, "The Deferred Prosecution Racket."

73   John L. O'Sullivan, "Introduction," *United States Magazine and Democratic Review* 1, no. 1 (1837): 6.

74   Dodd-Frank Wall Street Reform and Consumer Protection Act, H.R. 4173, 111 Cong., 2010.

75   Dodd-Frank Wall Street Reform and Consumer Protection Act.

76   Larry D. Thompson, "Address at University of Michigan Ross School of Business" (speech, Ann Arbor, Michigan, January 31, 2003), Department of Justice, https://www.justice.gov /archive/dag/speeches/2003/013103umichigancapitalism.htm. See Appendix for full text.

77   David M. Uhlmann, "Deferred Prosecution and Non-Prosecution Agreements and the Erosion of Corporate Criminal Liability," *Maryland Law Review* 72, no. 4 (2013): 1295.

78   Jennifer Taub, *Big Dirty Money: The Shocking Injustice and Unseen Cost of White Collar Crime* (New York: Viking, 2020), 37.

79   Chris Dolmetsch, Patricia Hurtado, Clare Roth, and David Voreacos, "Trump Oversees All-Time Low in White Collar Crime Enforcement," *Bloomberg*, August 10, 2020, https://www .bloomberg.com/news/articles/2020-08-10/trump-oversees-all-time-low-in-white-collar -crime-enforcement.

80   Jed S. Rakoff, "The Financial Crisis: Why Have No High-Level Executives Been Prosecuted?," *New York Review of Books*, January 9, 2014, https://www.nybooks.com /articles/2014/01/09/financial-crisis-why-no-executive-prosecutions/?lp_txn_id=1432148.

81   Rakoff, "The Financial Crisis."

82   Zachary Crockett, "The Botched Coca-Cola Heist of 2006," *Hustle*, April 28, 2018, https ://thehustle.co/coca-cola-stolen-recipe; Andrew Clark, "The Real Sting: How Plot to Betray Coke Fell Flat After Pepsi Called in FBI," *The Guardian*, July 7, 2006, https://www.the guardian.com/media/2006/jul/07/marketingandpr.drink; "Pepsi Alerted Coca-Cola to Stolen-Coke-Secrets Offer," *Fox News*, January 13, 2015, https://www.foxnews.com/story /pepsi-alerted-coca-cola-to-stolen-coke-secrets-offer.

83   Associated Press, "Ex-Secretary Gets 8-Year Term in Coca-Cola Secrets Case," *The New York Times*, May 24, 2007, https://www.nytimes.com/2007/05/24/business/24coke.html.

84   United States Sentencing Commission, *The Federal Sentencing Guidelines Manual* (Washington, DC: The Commission, 1991).

85   Lynn S. Paine, "Managing for Organizational Integrity," *Harvard Business Review* 72, no. 2 (March–April 1994): 106–118, https://hbr.org/1994/03/managing-for-organizational -integrity.

86   Paine, "Managing for Organizational Integrity." Paine discusses "[the] number of organizational factors [that] contributed to the problematic sales practices" at Sears.

87   Paine, "Managing for Organizational Integrity."

88   Paine, "Managing for Organizational Integrity."

89   Rule 11 Plea Agreement, *United States v. Volkswagen AG*, No. 16-CR-20394, E.D. Mich. (Jan. 11, 2017), https://www.justice.gov/opa/press-release/file/924436/download; Third Partial Consent Decree, *In re: Volkswagen "Clean Diesel" Marketing, Sales Practices, and Products Liability Litigation*, MDL No. 2672 CRB (JSC), N.D. Cal. (Jan. 11, 2017), https ://www.justice.gov/opa/press-release/file/924426/download.

90   Jack Ewing, "Volkswagen Has Kept Promises to Reform, U.S. Overseer Says," *The New York Times*, September 14, 2020, https://www.nytimes.com/2020/09/14/business/volkswagen -emissions-regulations-reform.html.

91   Department of Justice, "Volkswagen AG Agrees to Plead Guilty and Pay $4.3 Billion in Criminal and Civil Penalties," press release, January 11, 2017, https://www.justice.gov/opa /pr/volkswagen-ag-agrees-plead-guilty-and-pay-43-billion-criminal-and-civil-penalties-six.

92   "VW 2017 group sales rose to around 10.7 million cars, beating Toyota: Bild am Sonntag," *Reuters*, January 6, 2018, https://www.reuters.com/article/us-volkswagen-vehicleregistrations /vw-2017-group-sales-rose-to-around-10-7-million-cars-beating-toyota-bild-am-sonntag -idUSKBN1EV0R7.

93   Ewing, "Volkswagen Has Kept Promises."

94   Ewing, "Volkswagen Has Kept Promises."

95   Christoph Rauwald, "VW CEO Herbert Diess Urges Corporate Culture Change Amid Sweeping Revamp," *Transport Topics*, May 4, 2018, https://www.ttnews.com/articles/vw-ceo -herbert-diess-urges-corporate-culture-change-amid-sweeping-revamp.

96   Rule 11 Plea Agreement, *United States v. Volkswagen AG*, No. 16-CR-20394. ("[T]he Monitor will evaluate . . . the Company's implementation and enforcement of its compliance and ethics program for the purpose of preventing future criminal fraud and environmental violations by the Company and its affiliates, including, but not limited to, violations related to the conduct giving rise to the Third Superseding Information filed in this matter, and will take such reasonable steps as, in his or her view, may be necessary to fulfill the foregoing mandate.")

97   "Dr. Herbert Diess Speech at the Annual General Meeting on May 3, 2018," Volkswagen Group, May 3, 2018, accessed September 28, 2023, https://www.volkswagen-newsroom .com/en/press-releases/dr-herbert-diess-speech-at-the-annual-general-meeting-on-may-3 -2018-188.

98 Randee Dawn, "Cracker Jack is Replacing Toy Prizes Inside with Digital Codes," *Today*, April 22, 2016, https://www.today.com/food/cracker-jack-replacing-toy-prizes-inside-digital -codes-t87811.

99 Jennifer Pellet, "Chevron's Moyo: Boards May Be Ill-Prepared For the Future," *Corporate Board Member*, accessed September 28, 2023, https://boardmember.com/chevrons -dambisa-moyo-boards-may-be-ill-prepared-for-the-future/.

100 *United States v. Wardlow*, 977 F. Supp. 1481 (N.D. Ga. 1997).

101 Kevin Sack, "Officials Acquitted in Bribe Case," *The New York Times*, December 16, 1997, https://www.nytimes.com/1997/12/16/us/officials-acquitted-in-bribe-case.html.

102 Larry D. Thompson, "2003 Federalist Society Address" (speech, Washington, DC, November 14, 2003), Brookings, https://www.brookings.edu/wp-content/uploads/2016/06 /thompson_20031114.pdf.

103 *Regents of the University of California v. Bakke*, 438 U.S. 265 (1978); *Gratz v. Bollinger*, 539 U.S. 244 (2003).

104 *Grutter v. Bollinger*, 539 U.S. 306, 343 (2003).

105 Larry D. Thompson, "Remarks of the Deputy Attorney General for the Diversity Event" (speech, Washington, DC, February 5, 2003), Department of Justice, https://www.justice.gov /archive/dag/speeches/2003/02503diversityeventdojgreathall.htm. See Appendix for full text.

106 Thompson, "Remarks of the Deputy Attorney General for the Diversity Event."

107 Thompson, "Remarks of the Deputy Attorney General for the Diversity Event."

108 Dame Vivian Hunt, Dennis Layton, and Sara Prince, "Why Diversity Matters," McKinsey & Company, January 1, 2015, https://www.mckinsey.com/business-functions/organization /our-insights/why-diversity-matters.

109 Sundiatu Dixon-Fyle, Kevin Dolan, Dame Vivian Hunt, and Sara Prince, "Diversity Wins: How Inclusion Matters," McKinsey & Company, May 19, 2020, https://www.mckinsey .com/featured-insights/diversity-and-inclusion/diversity-wins-how-inclusion-matters.

110 Dixon-Fyle, Dolan, Hunt, and Prince, "Diversity Wins."

111 "Our History: A Legacy of Leadership," PepsiCo, accessed October 2, 2023, https://www .pepsico.com/our-impact/diversity-equity-and-inclusion/our-history. "The Larry D. Thompson Legacy of Leadership Fellowship Program promotes diversity in the legal profession and supports the development of professionals from diverse backgrounds. In honor of PepsiCo's former General Counsel (and former U.S. Deputy Attorney General) Larry D. Thompson, the 10-week program gives first-year law students the opportunity to work closely with in-house legal teams at PepsiCo and Frito-Lay, where they learn about our full operating environment and in-house career paths."

112 Natalia Marulanda, "PepsiCo's Investment in Underrepresented Law Students," Bloomberg Law, July 6, 2021, https://news.bloomberglaw.com/us-law-week/pepsicos-investment-in -underrepresented-law-students.

113 The recent U.S. Supreme Court decision, *Students For Fair Admissions v. Harvard*, 600 U.S. 181 (2023), applies to higher education, so as long as there is no racial or gender

discrimination in employment decisions, private sector diversity efforts will continue to be important and make good business sense.

114 Jessica Flores, "An 8-year-old Was Fatally Shot in Atlanta Near Wendy's Restaurant Where Rayshard Brooks Was Killed, Police Say," *USA Today*, July 5, 2020, https://www.usatoday .com/story/news/nation/2020/07/05/secoriea-turner-8-year-old-fatally-shot-near-wendys -atlanta/5381445002/; Shaddi Abusaid, "NEW DETAILS: Gang investigation leads to 2nd arrest in Secoriea Turner's killing," *Atlanta Journal-Constitution*, Aug. 4, 2021, https://www .ajc.com/news/breaking-2nd-arrest-made-in-secoriea-turners-killing/M6P3ULN67NGWD F67F5PY222GFA/.

115 Richard Fausset, "Charges to Be Dropped Against Officers in Fatal Shooting of Rayshard Brooks," *The New York Times*, August 23, 2022, https://www.nytimes.com/2022/08/23/us /rayshard-brooks-officers-no-charges.html; Atlanta Police Department, "APD Statement on Officer Garrett Rolfe and Officer Devin Brosnan," press release, August 23, 2022, https ://www.atlantapd.org/Home/Components/News/News/3047/17/.

116 Kevin Sack, "Man in the News; Ashcroft's No. 2: A Black Conservative Lauded by Liberals; Larry Dean Thompson," *The New York Times*, February 15, 2001, https://www.nytimes.com /2001/02/15/us/man-ashcroft-s-no-2-black-conservative-lauded-liberals-larry-dean -thompson.html.

117 Larry D. Thompson, "Dealing with Black on Black Crime," in *Critical Issues: A Conservative Agenda for Black Americans*, ed. Joseph Perkins (Washington DC: Heritage Foundation,1987).

118 Joseph R. Biden, "Crime Bill Speech" (speech, Washington, DC, November 18, 1993), Daily Kos, https://www.dailykos.com/stories/2020/6/19/1954559/-Biden-s-Crime-Bill -Speech-from-1993-full-transcript.

119 Jason L. Riley, "Crime Is Up and Democrats Are Scrambling," *The Wall Street Journal*, October 5, 2021, https://www.wsj.com/articles/crime-homicide-murder-law-enforcement- defund-police-blm-atlanta-seattle-new-york-city-eric-adams-kasim-reed-bruce-harrel l-11633464705?st=pbgv9sforv336ja&reflink=article_email_share.

120 Riley, "Crime Is Up."

121 Zaid Jilani, review of *Woke Racism: How a New Religion Has Betrayed Black America*, by John McWhorter, *The New York Times*, October 26, 2021, Sunday Book Review, https://www .nytimes.com/2021/10/26/books/review/john-mcwhorter-woke-racism.html?referringSource =articleShare.

122 Thompson, "Dealing with Black on Black Crime."

123 Jilani, review of *Woke Racism*.

124 Fang (@lhfang), X, June 6, 2020, 2:31 p.m., https://x.com/lhfang/status/126933624738 7877377?s=20.

125 *Confirmation Hearing on the Nominations of Larry D. Thompson to Be Deputy Attorney General and Theodore B. Olson to Be Solicitor General of the United States*, 107 Cong. 18, 2001 (opening statement of Larry D. Thompson, Nominee to be Deputy Attorney General). See Appendix for full text.

126 Larry Thompson, "The Last, Best Hope for Bipartisanship and Common Sense in Congress" (speech, Tucson, AZ, University of Arizona, September 28, 2016). See Appendix for full text.

127 Riley, "Crime Is Up."

128 Abbie VanSickle, "On First Day of New Term, Supreme Court Hears Debate Over First Step Act," *The New York Times*, October 2, 2023, https://www.nytimes.com/2023/10/02/us /politics/supreme-court-first-step-act.html.

129 Thompson, "Dealing with Black on Black Crime."

130 Office of the Deputy Attorney General, Lisa Monaco, "Comprehensive Strategy for Reducing Violent Crime," unpublished memorandum, May 26, 2021, https://www.justice .gov/d9/pages/attachments/2021/05/26/comprehensive_strategy_for_reducing_violent _crime_memo.pdf.

131 Office of Public Affairs, "Attorney General Merrick B. Garland Announces New Effort to Reduce Violent Crime," press release, May 26, 2021, https://www.justice.gov/opa/pr /attorney-general-merrick-b-garland-announces-new-effort-reduce-violent-crime.

132 Keith Richards, *Life* (New York: Little, Brown & Company, 2010).

133 Jan Crawford Greenburg, *Supreme Conflict: The Inside Story of the Struggle for Control of the United States Supreme Court* (New York: Penguin Press, 2007), 259.

134 Marcus Tullius Cicero, *How to Grow Old* (Princeton: Princeton University Press, 2016), 51.

135 Cicero, *How to Grow Old*, 107.

136 Reviewed Work, *Catalogue of One Hundred Drawings by Michael Angelo* [sic], *Composing the Tenth Exhibition of the Lawrence Gallery, at 112 St. Martin's Lane. London. July, 1836*, *North American Review* 44, no. 94 (January 1837): 4, https://www.jstor.org/stable/25103867.

137 Cicero, *How to Grow Old*, 147.

138 Larry D. Thompson, "Commencement Address" (speech, Ann Arbor, MI, May 11, 2009, University of Michigan Law School). See Appendix for full text.

139 Larry and Brenda Thompson, *Tradition Redefined (The Larry and Brenda Thompson Collection of African American Art)* (College Park: David C. Driskell Center at The University of Maryland, 2009).

140 Thompson, *Tradition Redefined.*, 19.

141 Dele Jegede, *Encyclopedia of African American Artists* (Westport, CT: Greenwood Press), 138–142.

142 Marcy Oster, "Rubashkin Appeals Conviction, Sentence to Supreme Court," *Jewish Telegraphic Agency*, April 3, 2012, https://www.jta.org/2012/04/03/united-states/rubashkin -appeals-conviction-sentence-to-supreme-court.

143 *United States v. Rubashkin*, 655 F. 849 (8th Circ. 2011).

144 *United States v. Rubashkin*, 655 F. 849 (8th Circ. 2011).

145 Mitch Smith, "President Commutes Sentence of Iowa Meatpacking Executive," *The New York Times*, December 20, 2017, https://www.nytimes.com/2017/12/20/us/president-trump -iowa-commutation.html.

146 See Acknowledgments section of this book.

147 Dinitia Smith, "A Utopia Awakens and Shakes Itself; Chautauqua, Once a Cultural Haven for Religion Teachers, Survives," *The New York Times*, August 17, 1998, https://www.nytimes.com/1998/08/17/arts/utopia-awakens-shakes-itself-chautauqua-once-cultural-haven-for-religion.html.

148 Lee Hawkins, "Civics Education in Schools Gains Steam," *The Wall Street Journal*, August 11, 2021, https://www.wsj.com/articles/civics-education-in-schools-gains-steam-11628697631.

INDEX

ABOUT THE AUTHOR

LARRY D. THOMPSON is the former U.S. Deputy Attorney General
(2001–2003), the second highest ranking position in the U.S. Department
of Justice. He has also served as Executive Vice President, Government
Affairs, General Counsel and Corporate Secretary at PepsiCo, and as the
John A. Sibley Chair of Corporate and Business Law at the University of
Georgia School of Law.

In 2002, during Thompson's tenure as Deputy Attorney General,
Attorney General John Ashcroft named him to lead the Department of
Justice's National Security Coordination Council. Also in 2002, President
George W. Bush named Thompson to head the government-wide Corpo-
rate Fraud Task Force. In 2017, he was appointed by the U.S. Department
of Justice as the Independent Corporate Compliance Monitor and Audi-
tor for Volkswagen AG. Thompson holds a BA from Culver-Stockton
College, a MA from Michigan State University, and a law degree from the
University of Michigan. He lives in Georgia.